D0988775

World Directors in Dialogue

Conversations on Cinema

Bert Cardullo

THE SCARECROW PRESS, INC.
Lanham • Toronto • Plymouth, UK
2011

Published by Scarecrow Press, Inc.
A wholly owned subsidary of The Rowman & Littlefield Publishing Group, Inc.
4501 Forbes Boulevard, Suite 200, Lanham, Maryland 20706
http://www.scarecrowpress.com

Estover Road, Plymouth PL6 7PY, United Kingdom

British Library Cataloguing in Publication Information Available

Library of Congress Cataloging-in-Publication Data

World directors in dialogue : conversations on cinema / Bert Cardullo.
   p. cm.
  Includes bibliographical references and index.
  ISBN 978-0-8108-7778-8 (pbk. : alk. paper) — ISBN 978-0-8108-7779-5 (ebook)
  1. Motion picture producers and directors—Interviews. 2. Motion pictures—
Production and direction. I. Cardullo, Bert.
PN1998.2.W6665 2011
791.4302'30922—dc22   2010041847

∞™ The paper used in this publication meets the minimum requirements of
American National Standard for Information Sciences—Permanence of Paper
for Printed Library Materials, ANSI/NISO Z39.48-1992.

Printed in the United States of America

Contents

~

Preface

I don't consider myself a professional interviewer, so I'm not writing this preface in order to give "how-to" advice to anyone. All of my interviews with film directors have been done because I *wanted* to do them; I didn't do them for money, certainly, and a number of them lay unpublished—indeed, untranscribed—for a couple of decades. I think the filmmakers in question appreciated my amateur status and may have trusted me all the more because of it. This is especially true of the late François Truffaut, who—as a former journalist himself—seemed charmed by the fact that I had traveled all the way to Paris, at my own expense, just to have a three- or four-hour conversation with him that *might*, or might not, appear in print.

When I call myself an amateur, of course I don't mean "unprofessional." I thoroughly prepare myself for every interview by seeing all of a director's films at least once (DVDs have made this a lot less difficult than it used to be!) and reading everything about him and his work I can lay my hands on. I also prepare lists of "good questions," even though I don't always stick to the list. The trick in an interview is to "read" your subject and figure out how to get the most (by which I mean the best) out of him—and that sometimes means asking a provocative and even inflammatory question that's not on your list. As when, during the first interview I ever conducted (not included here), I asked Vittorio De Sica the following loaded question, and for the second time at that. I include his verbal response, but I wish I could also show you his exasperated, nearly comic *physical* response, which, thirty-five years later, is still vividly etched in my memory:

BC: *Now what about the suggestion made by Italian newspapers at the time that* Miracle in Milan *tended to excite political animosities?*

VDS: Oh, here we go again! Look, mister, I have no interest in politics. I am a member of no party; I am not a propagandist of any ideology. *Miracle in Milan* was inspired by nothing but a Christian feeling of human solidarity. That's all!

My ears are still ringing with Signor De Sica's words, and my mind's eye continues to envision his wrath at the audacity of a twenty-five-year-old novice to ask such a question. Nonetheless, I was happy to endure that wrath just for the chance to meet and talk to the man. And that, perhaps, is the real "art of the interview": how to make contact with your subject, establish your credibility, and set a meeting time and place. The rest, by comparison, is simple. The easiest way to make contact, in my experience, is to use a go-between who knows the director at the same time as he will vouch for you. But a surprising number of European directors, for one group—unlike their uppity American counterparts—are in the telephone book; and if they're not, their national film institutes will readily give you at least a mailing address—the director's home address, that is, not the location of his agent's office. I'm not shy, and I'm not afraid to be told "no," so I just humbly ask for my interviews myself if someone better placed cannot or will not ask for me.

Once you get the interview, naturally, you have to get to the place, and that's usually the filmmaker's place: his house, his hotel, his office, his set, his country. The price of airfare can sometimes be an obstacle, but so can the authorities. When Abbas Kiarostami, for example, agreed to meet, he told me to come to Tehran. Since I was living in Istanbul at the time, I thought that going there, from Turkey, wouldn't be a problem. It wasn't, until the Iranian customs agents waved my American passport in my face, even as I was waving to Abbas behind a large, thick, forbidding wall of glass at Imam Khomeini International Airport. Officialdom sent me back to Istanbul without my interview—which I had begged in vain to be permitted to conduct inside the terminal, in a hotel room. But Abbas later diplomatically resolved the crisis by flying to the Istanbul Film Festival, where I conducted my interview with him in peace.

That interview, like all my others, I tried to make as aesthetically inclusive as I could, as opposed to as academically exhaustive as possible—and I believe my subjects responded to my knowledge of their craft as well as my analysis of their art. That is, my questions focus on practical matters related to filmmaking (which, lest we forget, is variously known as a technology, an industry, a business, an entertainment, and an art) as much as they do on historical, aesthetic, and critical-theoretical issues raised by the films themselves. Among those practical matters, furthermore, I give as much attention to acting, design, and cinematography as to directing, writing, and editing (with some attention paid to finance and audience reception, as well). Needless to say, this is because film is the most "total" of the arts, containing or embracing all the others: literature, painting, sculpture, architecture, photography, music, theater, and dance. Hence any interview of a film artist should itself aspire to be as aesthetically comprehensive as possible.

The easiest directors to interview—easiest in the sense that they have the most information and insight to offer—are those who themselves are the most "aesthetically comprehensive." I speak of auteurs, moviemakers who write, or collaborate in the writing of, every script they direct, in addition to initiating all their projects on their own as opposed to accepting films "on assignment." Moreover, these directors are sometimes complete auteurs in that they perform almost every function that goes into the making of a film, including editing and musical scoring. Why is such authorship important? For the obvious reason that it puts a film on the same level as any other work of art (not so negligible a reason when you consider the relative youth of the cinema as an art form): as primarily the product of one person's vision, supervision, and execution. And that's precisely the kind of person who can give you an in-depth interview about the total art of filmmaking, from script to screen—not a blinkered showbiz chat about what it's like to be rich, famous, and powerful.

Auteurism, properly understood, privileges the well-wrought script, the carefully chosen word, as the place where every narrative film of quality must begin. That so many narrative films do not so begin—that they limit auteurism to signature visual style or stylistic flourish—is the reason why so many of them finally fall short of cinematic wholeness, let alone distinction. And the fact that so many interviews with directors don't end, as well as begin, with the word, is the reason why so many of *them* fall short of completeness, not to speak of excellence. I refer to the editing of interviews, which is a long, painstaking process that entails not only the transcription of a director's words, but also the revising of them (with his approval) for coherence, accuracy, and continuity. Like a good movie, a good interview has got to *move*; and to do that, it has to have not just pointed dialogue, but smooth transitions and strong juxtapositions, too.

Alas, only the interviewer can provide these "connectives" if they are not already there in the conversation. At most, this sometimes means rearranging parts of an interview; at least, it means providing transitional or oppositional elements in the very framing of your questions. I realize that some people value spontaneity and immediacy over this kind of ex-post-facto tampering, but with spontaneity and immediacy often come randomness, repetition, and irrelevancy. For this reason, the art of the interview, like the art of film, is finally in the editing. This is all the more true when you have interviewed a subject who speaks no English and has spoken to you through an interpreter. It's also the case when you have conversed with directors who speak half in English and half in their native language, which you yourself then have to translate at a later date.

The conversations with Eric Rohmer and the Dardenne brothers were conducted, as much as possible, in English; where each director had to use French, I myself translated with the interviewees' permission; the opposite was the case for the conversations with François Truffaut and Jacques Tati, which were conducted almost wholly in French. The same goes, mutatis mutandis, for the interviews with Luchino Visconti and Ermanno Olmi: mostly in Italian, which I was able to translate on my own with the assistance of my mother, a native speaker. Satyajit Ray and, of course, Mike Leigh and Ken Loach all spoke only in English; and Akira Kurosawa, Zhang Yimou, and Abbas Kiarostami, for their part, had their own translator-interpreters present during our meetings.

World Directors in Dialogue is organized, as much as possible, along national or geographic lines, and I have tried to be inclusive in my selections. You'll find Italy, France, Belgium, England, Japan, India, Iran, and China represented here. I would have liked to include a number of other countries and their best directors, and I tried. But Gutiérrez Alea of Cuba, for example, regrettably passed away several weeks before our scheduled meeting in April of 1996; Ousmane Sembene of Senegal cancelled on me three times (he himself passed away in 2007); and Agnès Varda simply refused all requests for an interview. Still, I managed to conduct twelve interviews with some of the men who figured (and figure) most in the making of the movies; in any case, restrictions on length would have prevented me from including all the filmmakers I would have wanted. These directors and I don't always agree during our conversations, but, why must we? Where I am bold enough to differ, say, with Mike Leigh, I hope that our disagreement is a productive or "teaching" one. Where I am cheeky enough to challenge Vittorio De Sica, I trust that his exasperated response to my question is telling as well as comic.

As for the four groupings themselves, they are, aside from being geographically representative, artistically inclusive as well. Among the Italian directors, for example, you will find Visconti, who began as a neorealist but ultimately ventured well beyond neorealism in such films as *The Leopard* (1963) and *Death in Venice* (1971); and then there is Olmi, who inverts neorealism by depicting the human accommodation, rather than resistance, to adverse social and economic circumstances. Among the French or French-speaking, there are the New Wave-become-Old Guard directors Truffaut and Rohmer; Tati, the greatest movie mime and visual comic since Chaplin and Keaton; and the Dardennes, leaders of a newly revived, socially conscious European cinema. In the grouping labeled "Near East, Far East," you will find Kurosawa and Ray—who could be called men of all genres, period, and places—situated alongside Kiarostami, a master of one genre, period, and place. You will also find here Zhang Yimou, the director who introduced Chinese cinema to the West in the 1980s, as Kiarostami introduced Iranian cinema to the West in the same decade—and even as Kurosawa and Ray did the same for Japanese and Indian film, respectively, during the 1950s. Finally, there are interviews with the British filmmakers Loach and Leigh in the last grouping, both men being advocates of a cinema of social conscience that, in Loach's case, often turns out to be a political or politicized cinema as well.

World Directors in Dialogue is the culmination, finally, of my lifelong love affair with the cinema, even though I somehow managed to marry into the theater. That love affair, from the start, has been premised on my belief, or rather knowledge, that not only is film the most democratic of the arts in addition to being the most "total"—making all faces equal and making "travel," through time as well as space, available to people of every social class at the same low price. Film is also the only narrative art form almost instantaneously available, through subtitling, throughout the world. Its immediate international character is what drew me to it, and therefore it is ultimately what made this book possible.

Let me conclude by declaring that the older I get, the less I want to write about film on my own than hear its creators talk about moviemaking from every angle—including but not limited to meaning. I've learned a lot from doing such interviews; it's more fun than individual, essayistic criticism; and (to judge from book sales!) readers seem more attuned to this type of "communal" analysis. The best part of the interviewing process, however, may be what, for want of a better term, I'm going to call the personal side: the connections I've made over the years with a group of human beings who also happen to be great artists. As an instance of such humanity, I'll leave you with the words of Satyajit Ray in response to my thanking him, at the conclusion of our interview, for his generosity and geniality:

> I am in the phone book, and you can knock on my door. Everybody has access to me, anyone who wants to see me. In fact, the people who come to visit . . .

are often very ordinary folks. Not big stars or anything like that . . . In the end, I think it's rather stupid to raise a wall around oneself. This way of doing things—as we have done today—is much more interesting, rewarding, exciting.

I hope that you, dear reader, will feel the same way after your own encounter with the film directors in this book. My deep thanks to the higher administration at the Izmir University of Economics in Turkey for giving me the financial support and academic leave to complete *World Directors in Dialogue*—a book completed, moreover, in a country itself poised between East and West. Above all, I offer my gratitude to all the filmmakers themselves: for their words, for their wisdom, for their work.

ITALIAN EYE-VIEW

Reality, Romanticism, Eroticism . . . and the Cinema

An Interview with Luchino Visconti

Born in Milan into a noble and wealthy family (one of the richest of northern Italy), Luchino Visconti di Modrone, Count of Lonate Pozzolo (1906–1976), was exposed at an early age to art, music, and theater. During his youth, in fact, he mixed with such luminaries as the conductor Toscanini, the composer Puccini, and the novelist D'Annunzio. In 1936, at the age of thirty, he went to Paris and began his filmmaking career as third assistant director on Jean Renoir's *Une Partie de campagne* (1936), thanks to the intercession of a mutual friend, Coco Chanel. During this period, Visconti, previously a Fascist, switched to Communism. After a short tour of the United States, where he visited Hollywood, he returned to Rome to become part of the group associated with the journal *Cinema*. He also became Renoir's assistant again, this time for *La Tosca* (1939), a production that was interrupted by the war and later completed by the German director Karl Koch.

Together with Roberto Rossellini, Visconti joined the *salotto* of Vittorio Mussolini (the son of Benito, and at the time the national arbitrator for

3

cinema and other arts) during the war years and here presumably met Federico Fellini. With Gianni Puccini, Antonio Pietrangeli, and Giuseppe De Santis, he wrote the screenplay for his first film as director: *Ossessione* (*Obsession*, 1943), sometimes considered the first neorealist movie and an adaptation of the novel *The Postman Always Rings Twice*, by James M. Cain. The Italian Communist Party then commissioned Visconti to produce a series of three films about fishermen, miners, and the peasantry in Sicily, but only *La terra trema* (1948) was made. An exemplar of neorealism, this film was based on the novel *I Malavoglia*, by Giovanni Verga.

Visconti veered away from the neorealist path in the 1950s not only with *Bellissima* (1951) but also with his 1954 film, *Senso*, which was filmed in Technicolor. Based on the novella by Camillo Boito, *Senso* is set in Austrian-occupied Venice in 1866 and in it, as in *Bellissima*, Visconti combines realism and romanticism in an attempt to break away from what he describes in my interview with him as the strictures of neorealism. He returned to neorealism one more time in 1960 with *Rocco and His Brothers*, the story of working-class southern Italians who migrate to Milan in the hope of finding financial stability.

Throughout the 1960s, Visconti's films became more personal. Perhaps his best works from this period are *The Leopard* (1963) and *Death in Venice* (1971). Visconti's lush adaptation of *The Leopard*, based on Giuseppe Tomasi di Lampedusa's 1958 novel, chronicles the decline of the Sicilian aristocracy during the Risorgimento, a subject close to the director's own family history. It starred the American actor Burt Lancaster in the role of Prince Don Fabrizio. It was not until his 1969 film, *The Damned*, that Visconti received a nomination for an Academy Award, for "Best Screenplay," which he nonetheless did not win. The film, one of Visconti's best-known works, is about a German industrialist family that slowly begins to disintegrate during World War II. Visconti's final film was *The Innocent* (1976), which features the recurring theme in his work of infidelity and betrayal in the persons of the lusty, sex-starved mistress of a roadside inn, a Sicilian aristocrat at the time of Italy's unification, and an upper-class Roman wife who is neglected by her husband—himself a philanderer.

Openly homosexual, Visconti featured few explicitly gay characters in his films, although they often contain an undercurrent of homoeroticism. He favored attractive leading men, such as Alain Delon, and his final obsession was the Austrian actor Helmut Berger, whom he directed in *The Damned*, *Ludwig* (1972) and *Conversation Piece* (1974).

The following interview took place in a hotel in Munich, Germany, in early 1972, just before Visconti began filming *Ludwig*.

Bert Cardullo: *If it's acceptable to you, Signor Visconti, I would like chiefly to discuss two earlier films of yours today:* Bellissima *and* Rocco and His Brothers, *each of which, one could say, is an offshoot of postwar neorealism. But before we do that, let's talk a bit about two very different, relatively recent pictures directed by you:* Death in Venice *and* The Damned. *Is it true that you threw a tantrum at the 1971 Cannes Festival because* Death in Venice *did not win first prize, that you threatened never to return to Cannes, and that the only way the jury managed to calm you down was by coming up with a new prize called the "25th Anniversary Award" for your cumulative body of work? Isn't it possible that* Death in Venice *didn't get the top prize because of its somnambulant tempo and its relentless scrutiny of its own opulent décor?*

Luchino Visconti: Where did you hear such nonsense? The prize they gave me at Cannes, in any event, was much more important than the one they gave to Joseph Losey for *The Go-Between*. This was a special prize for all my films, including *Death in Venice*, and it means a lot to me.

BC: *Some critics and audiences feel that the love depicted in* Death in Venice *is homosexual love, and that your film, even more than Thomas Mann's 1912 novella, is simply the study of a repressed homosexual who is suddenly seized by an overwhelming desire for a stunningly handsome adolescent boy.*

LV: The love in my film is *not* homosexual. It is love without eroticism, without sexuality. Love is the most important sentiment; sex is important, too, but it is a consequence of love. The boy in the story represents the sentiment of love. He is the symbol for beauty, and Aschenbach, pursuing the ideal of beauty, is ecstatic once he sees that this ideal does in fact exist. But, of course, it has its fatal aspect as well.

BC: *In Mann's novella, Aschenbach was a writer, but in your movie, he is a composer. Why?*

LV: It was easier for me to give the impression I wanted by making Aschenbach a musician, and I also wanted to use the music of Gustav Mahler. I believe that Thomas Mann was thinking of Mahler when he wrote *Death in Venice*; there is much evidence to support this theory, including testimony from Mann's daughter. Mahler's daughter, for her part, became anxious about her father's reputation when she learned that I was making this film; but, after she had seen the picture, she wrote me and said that her mind had been put completely at ease.

BC: *There aren't many Krupps around these days, but if there were, it's doubtful that their minds would have been set completely at ease by* The Damned, *your bone-chilling portrait of that German industrialist family and its role in the rise of Nazism. One scene stood out for me: the one in which Helmut Berger, as the clan's most enterprising pervert, brutally rapes his otherwise murderous mother, played by Ingrid Thulin.*

LV: Well, there are a number of scenes in the New American Cinema that make the one between Helmut and Ingrid look tame—like a family matter. What happened in Andy Warhol's *Trash* was a little stronger than incest, wouldn't you say?

BC: *Yes, but, as far as I'm concerned, Warhol's title describes the quality of his film as well.* Trash *is beneath serious consideration, but* The Damned *is not. The sea of sadism, incest, and homosexuality that surged through your film was surely an artistic exaggeration, wasn't it?*

LV: There is invention in *The Damned*, to be sure, but the invention is in the direction of reality. That family *was* the Krupp family, and all those S.A. troops were indeed homosexual. The way in which I showed "The Night of the Long Knives"—I refer to the slaughter of the young boys in their beds—was exactly the way it was reported by witnesses. That means that *The Damned* is a sociopolitical document in addition to whatever else it is.

BC: *Did you yourself have any trouble of your own with the Fascists in Italy?*

LV: They arrested me in my house one night. I told them they were crazy, but still they took me from one prison to another. Finally, they were going to shoot me—but thank God the Americans arrived just in time and saved me.

BC: *On the subject of God, are you a practicing Catholic?*

LV: Let's just say that I am a Catholic. I was born a Catholic, I was baptized a Catholic, and I cannot change what I am. Certainly I could not easily become a Protestant. My ideas and habits may be unorthodox, but I am still a Catholic.

BC: *What do you think of the sacrament of matrimony? I ask because marriage and the family, at least the family, will be at the heart of our discussion of* Bellissima *and* Rocco and His Brothers.

LV: I do regret not having children, but I do not regret never having married. People usually get married because they are afraid of being alone. But you can be unmarried and have a beautiful relationship—and not just with one person! The ideal state is to have children and not marriage. I myself think I might have been a very good father—perhaps I do have children somewhere, who knows?

BC: *What's a woman's place, then?*

LV: In the home, with the men who marry them. They should be women: that's enough, if they do it well. Bed, kitchen, mothering: that's their place, just as all of us have our place, our duty, our job. A woman's job is to get man to eat the apple, to compromise him, if you will.

BC: *I guess that you will agree that Maria Callas is an exception to this rule.*

LV: Yes, but I was never interested in luring her into the world of cinema. She should have stayed in opera—where I directed her in productions like *La Somnambula* and *La Traviata*—and not made *Medea* with Pasolini. I don't like this movie; singing is Callas's real talent, not acting. She is not a movie actress.

BC: *Let's move now to a discussion of* Bellissima *[The Most Beautiful, 1951]. Why did you direct this movie, whose subject seems to be so different from the ones that you had treated in your previous films?*

LV: The choice of one subject over another does not depend exclusively on the will of the director. A combination of factors, naturally including the issue of money or finance, determines which films get made in the end. I had to pass, for example, on *Tale of Impoverished Lovers* [filmed by Carlo Lizzani in 1954] and Prosper Mérimée's *The Coach of the Blessed Sacrament* [filmed by Jean Renoir in 1952 as *The Golden Coach*], but then Salvo D'Angelo presented to me the script of *Bellissima*, by Cesare Zavattini. For some time I had desired to make a movie with Anna Magnani, and it was precisely Magnani whom D'Angelo had in mind for the leading role in this picture. So I accepted the project. D'Angelo reinvigorated my interest in making a film with an authentic "personality" like Magnani, a film whose inner or ultimate meaning would derive in part from its star. And he interested me in finding out what the relationship would be between me, as the director, and a "diva" like Magnani. The result, I believe, has been a most felicitous one.

BC: *What did it mean to you, then, to make such a film of "atmosphere" or personality?*

LV: A film centered *around* a personality. It meant a lot, because I don't believe that the use of a star or personality automatically turns a movie into a wholly commercial vehicle. You can have it both ways if you use the actress correctly—you have to use her correctly in this case, since she is at the center of the picture. *Bellissima* is the story, after all, of one woman, or, better, of a crisis in her personal history: a mother who has had to renounce her own secret, petty-bourgeois aspirations but tries to realize them through her daughter. Then the mother becomes convinced that, if an improvement in her life is to occur, it must come from a different direction. And by the end of the film she returns to find her home, and her husband, just as she left them. She also returns with the knowledge that she loved her daughter badly by trying vicariously to achieve her own dreams of movie stardom through a child. This mother knows now, as well, that the world of show business, which she thought was so wonderful, is in fact quite deplorable.

BC: *Did you make changes in Zavattini's original script, or did you use his scenario as it was first presented to you?*

LV: Yes, I made a number of modifications. To begin with, the girl's father in Zavattini's original script was a corporate or office employee; in the finished film he became a simple laborer. Second, while in Zavattini's screenplay the child was totally rejected at her screen test, in my film she gets a chance to work in pictures—so that her mother can become aware that she is only living through her daughter and finally refuse to sign a contract on the girl's behalf. These were my main structural modifications, if you will. But during the filming I made many other small changes as I traveled, in the end, a remarkably different road from the one traversed by Zavattini in his scenario. There was also some rewriting of the dialogue, and that had a lot to do with the improvisatory manner in which Magnani likes to work.

BC: *Did this result in too obvious a contrast between Magnani's acting style and that of the actors playing her child and her husband in the film—both of whom were acting for the very first time?*

LV: No, certainly not. Because Magnani's improvisatory flare has natural instinct behind it, not theatrical artifice. Moreover, she knows how to place herself on the same level as her fellow performers, and she also knows how to carry them along with her—how to raise them up to her level, as it were. I wanted this particular—and extraordinary—aspect of her personality, and I got it. In the other major parts, Gastone Renzelli [the laborer] and Tina Apicella [the child] fulfilled my expectations completely. Especially the child: one of a kind, she is. She demonstrates that having a sophisticated or adult intelligence has nothing to do with acting instinct. After fifteen days on the set, Miss Apicella knew all there was to know about the acting trade—so much so that sometimes she left me and the crew baffled. In one scene, for instance, she had to cry. She was quite calm, even tranquil, up to the moment that I gave the signal for action, upon which she immediately began to cry; and when I yelled "Cut!" she immediately stopped crying. And she did this more than ten times in a row. All this from a child of five-and-a-half!

BC: *What's the best way to get a good performance from actors who are not professionals? Do you use coaxing, or do you rely merely on suggestion?*

LV: Something between coaxing and suggestion. It's a kind of collaboration between me and them. I try to give them as much leeway as possible, but at the same time I let them know what it is I want them to express. This method worked perfectly with Magnani as well. Left completely to her own devices, I have to say, she would never achieve a happy result.

BC: *It seems to me that whether Magnani fully understands or adheres to the script doesn't really matter. She's like a character out of the commedia dell'arte, which, as you know, was essentially an improvisatory art.*

LV: The scenario serves as the base or framework of any film. And it is necessary always to have it in place. But neither the action nor the dialogue can be "set in cement," so to speak. In realistic films, for example, the actors sometimes simply cannot say, or will not say, things in the way a literary person has composed them at a typewriter. For the rest, I take it that the author of a film must be a single individual: the director. But a big part of his job is casting the actors: if he does this well, a good portion of the picture is already made and the remainder can be created on the spot. Such was the case with Magnani and company.

BC: *This way of working appears to be adapted to a single type of film: Bellissima's type. You seem not to be taking into account the fact that this method may be inadequate for other kinds of film. The kind, for example, in which a deeply layered, highly elaborated text is the point of departure, and a text that therefore* *requires actors who are absolute masters of their craft. For their part, the Soviet theorists of the 1920s supported the idea that the actor must have a solid technical base and thorough cultural or intellectual preparation; they also believed that the actor should collaborate on the script itself.*

LV: Well, everyone has his own method or point of view when it comes to making a film. But as far as the actors go, I insist on asserting that if an actor has talent—what I like to call the cinematic instinct—then a good director can get a good performance out of him apart from this actor's "preparation" or "technique." Talent is the one thing absolutely necessary in itself, and it can't be taught; everything else can be supplied.

BC: *Of course, everything else has to be supplied if you're dealing with non-professionals.*

LV: Not necessarily. Vittorio De Sica, it's true, supplied everything for his non-professionals; he even acted out the scenes beforehand and then asked his amateurs to mimic what he had done. But if you can discover an actor somewhere in your non-professional—an acting talent, as I have stated—then a balance can be struck and the actor can give as well as get. That's the kind of non-professional performance which makes the most "sense" to me. We're not dealing with beauty contestants here, after all—just breasts and legs and buttocks. I'm talking about working with people—non-professional actors—of character, of feeling and temperament, who know how to do more than merely move around and show themselves off from this or that vantage point.

BC: *Is there any way to change this?*

LV: Change what? What's there to change? Send Gastone Renzelli and Tina Apicella to acting school?

BC: *Could you say something about neorealism and the Italian cinema?*

LV: The big mistake of neorealism, to my way of thinking, was its unrelenting and sometimes dour concentration on social reality. What neorealism needed, and got in a film like De Sica's *Miracle in Milan* [1951] and even Pietro Germi's *The Road to Hope* [1950], was a "dangerous" mixture of reality and romanticism. I hope that I supplied this in *Bellissima*, as well. After all, these are poor people, the characters in this film, and to enable her family to escape from poverty, the mother turns to the dream-world or fantasy-factory of the popular cinema. Now that's a romantic notion! Yet, at the same time, the mother returns to sobering reality at the conclusion of the picture, and she accepts it—accepts that the illusionary world of show business is a kind of bad drug to which her own impoverished condition is far more acceptable, as long as it is ameliorated by the love of one's family. This is another romantic notion, of course, but it's firmly grounded in social reality. So we are back in the world of neorealism at the end, with a slight yet elevating twist. And thus I tried to have it "both ways" in this film.

BC: *Another, related question: what's the situation in the Italian cinema in general right now? Does it have serious problems?*

LV: I can respond in just a few words: the situation is disastrous. The problem is one of subject matter, of material: it is often on the lowest, most vulgar level. We are in a period of decline. The war of course is long over, and now Italy is a prosperous country, but its prosperity has brought with it rampant commercialism, all-consuming materialism, and smug complacency—a combination that is never good for art, and especially not for an art as "public" as the cinema.

BC: *Let's move to the subject of* Rocco and His Brothers, *a film that has more in common with* Bellissima *than one might think: its "improvement" on neorealism through a "dangerous" mixture of reality and romanticism, as well as the fact that Rocco itself is star-centered: in Alain Delon. Why did you use Delon in the role of Rocco?*

LV: Because Alain Delon *is* Rocco. If I had been obliged to use another actor, I would not have made the film. I wrote the role for him, and Rocco is the main character in the story. After all, the title of the picture is "Rocco *and His Brothers.*"

BC: *What exactly is Rocco's role?*

LV: I really don't want to betray the film by recounting too much of its plot. Nonetheless . . . A mother and her five sons live in the Lucania region of southern Italy, but, in order to find work, they all eventually move north to Milan. Rocco is the first one seized by a desire to escape to the north. He wants to leave, so he just runs away from home, and, inspired by his example, the other brothers quickly follow suit. Though she would rather stay at home in the south, their widowed mother doesn't want to be separated from her sons, so she too goes north along with her boys.

BC: *It's Rocco, then, who serves as a role model for his brothers?*

LV: It's more or less fated to be this way, but that is not immediately evident, nor is such a familial "fate" preconceived on Rocco's part. In Milan, the family settles in a slum. At first everyone looks for work, but no one finds it. Very quickly, the situation there deteriorates and the domestic atmosphere becomes polluted.

BC: *Even for Rocco?*

LV: Yes and no. Rocco is pure, you see, the only one who can successfully resist this degrading environment and preserve his integrity. He is also the person who suffers the most, for he is conscious of the familial tragedy, of the irresponsibility of certain of his brothers in the face of the vicissitudes of life that are destroying them. Rocco's drama is therefore double because, in ad-

Alain Delon as Rocco Parondi and Annie Girardot as Nadia in Visconti's *Rocco and His Brothers.*

dition to his own suffering, he takes upon himself the misery of every other member of his family.

BC: *What are the stages of this domestic tragedy, the events that trigger it?*

LV: Well, the situation is tragic at the very start. The events that follow are the natural consequence of the social situation in which this family finds itself. That is what I was always at pains to show. And, at the same time, I must insist on the communication gap between Italians of the north and those of the south. We also have our racists, you know, and they are not only of the linguistic kind.

Discouraged because they can't find work—disheartened is perhaps a better word—three of the brothers end up becoming boxers. But, above all else, please do not write that "Luchino Visconti has made a boxing film." This is merely one element in the picture, almost an exterior one or an accessory; simultaneously, boxing is of course intended to be a symbol of physical violence in the face of the figurative violence that Rocco's family encounters.

Confronted by the difficulties of life in the big city, the brothers fall from grace one after the other. The one who falls first, Simone, is Rocco's favorite. (For this role I engaged the actor Renato Salvatori.) Simone arrived in Milan almost in rags, but soon he was outfitting himself in silk shirts; and the audience well understood the source of his newfound income without explicitly being shown that he had become a gigolo. In the end, this character plays a very important part in the drama. For what happens to Simone makes clear that the reasons for, or causes of, a family's survival—or self-destruction—are not the unique location in which it finds itself, as you might expect. Basically, this family, had it remained united, in Milan or anywhere else, would have had a chance to survive intact. Staying together would have been its best strategy for success, if you will.

Another element apart from unemployment divides the family, however, and pits two of the brothers (the others are too young) against one another. In the same ghetto as theirs lives a call girl named Nadia. She is also poor by birth, but her job permits her to live better than those around her. Every day, she lures young men into her bed, and for them she represents luxury of a kind, even mystery. Only Rocco remains insensitive in the beginning to the charms of this urban princess. But such precise delineation is unnecessary here, since all these characters are part of the same reality. I don't need to assign it any poetic quality, for poetry emanates naturally from this environment—from the clash between fish out of water, as it were (Rocco and his displaced family), and the highly toxic water in which they now find themselves (the city of Milan).

Still, in her mysterious way, Nadia herself is a character apart from this environment, and one who intervenes directly—almost constantly—in the tragedy, precipitating its events. This is because she falls in love with Rocco, the family's only hope for salvation. Nadia and Rocco's rapport, which forms gradually, is difficult to fathom. There are so many "shades" to their relationship that I simply could not explain them all in mere words. You have to see the film. But the result of Rocco and Nadia's liaison is obvious: it arouses the jealousy of others. And Rocco suffers as a result, because saving his family is more important to him than Nadia's love.

It is the "fallen" Simone who is the first to fall passionately in love with Nadia, but she scorns him. Naturally, he is jealous of Rocco, who for his part feels guilty, yes guilty, for being loved by a woman whom he himself does not really love, and whose love, he knows, could only placate and even change for the better his favorite brother, Simone. But Rocco also wants Nadia, and this feeling at times shames him. Already trapped in a dizzying downward spiral where his material life is concerned, he now finds himself hounded by moral dilemmas to which he cannot find a solution. And because no material hardship can destroy him, it is his reason that begins to waver. Up to a certain point, though, Rocco is able to remain whole, spiritually as well as physically.

Already harassed and even harmed by a kind of social fatality, however, Rocco is remorselessly reduced to a slow death, to a more or less long decay. And it is Simone himself who will be the clumsy instrument of his demise: driven in the end by extreme jealousy (Nadia has ridiculed him at the same time as she has clearly stated her preference for Rocco), he loses his head and murders this girl who has sown discord among brothers. After Nadia's death Rocco finally becomes bereft of all reason, his "escape" to Milan having removed forever the possibility for him of a normal and healthy life. His mother, for her part, subsequently returns to southern Italy with the youngest of her sons.

BC: *Is Nadia really the cause of Rocco's folly-become-madness?*

LV: To the extent that one can assign causes to madness, yes. These characters are linked: Nadia loves Rocco, who can no longer stand the sight of Simone, who is otherwise his favorite brother and the lover of Nadia. The lines of this story are simple yet unerring, and the very setting of "cold," utilitarian Milan lends itself to such a narrative. I had no intention, however, of treating this film as a melodrama; for me, it is a realistic tragedy.

BC: *Can you tell me if, in the choice and structuring of the subject matter of* Rocco and His Brothers, *you were open to any influences or suggestions from others?*

LV: In everything each of us does—artistic or otherwise—there is something that preceded us and from which "suggestions" might arise, without one's ever noticing, out of a thousand different directions. For *Rocco and His Brothers*, a piece of fiction about which I thought for a long time, the major influence was probably Giovanni Verga's *I Malavoglia* [*The House by the Medlar Tree*, 1881], with which I have been "obsessed" ever since I read it for the first time. (The other novel by Verga that comes to mind in this context is *Master Don Gesualdo* [1899].) Actually, now that I think about it, the core of *Rocco and His Brothers* is more or less the same as that of Verga's novel. In this way, *Rocco* is similar to my earlier film *La terra trema* [*The Earth Trembles*, 1948]—itself a kind of adaptation of *I Malavoglia*. Indeed, *Rocco* could almost be called Part II of *The Earth Trembles*.

To this "obsession" of mine caused by a major work by the Sicilian Verga, I would have to add two other "obsessions." First, I had the desire to make a film about a mother who, believing that she is the "master" of her own sons, wants to exploit their energies for the satisfaction of the everyday needs of the family—and this without taking into account the diversity of their individual characters and the potential of each of her boys, from whom she asks too much and who will, necessarily and forcefully, disappoint her. Second, the problem of housing has always interested me. And in *Rocco*, it allowed me to connect the problems of the miserable south (another element in *Rocco* that can also be found in *The Earth Trembles*) to those of the modern north, in the person of the city of Milan.

Besides these two reasons for wanting to make *Rocco and His Brothers*, there were others: for those, you'd have to take a look at the Bible as well as Thomas Mann's *Joseph and His Brothers* [1933–1943]; you'd have to read Balzac's *Lost Illusions* [1837–1939], where the illusions are necessarily those of a man who must be *disillusioned* in the face of the brutal aggressiveness of capitalist society; and naturally you would have to consider the work of Giovanni Testori, on whose novel *The Secrets of Milan: The Ghisolfa Bridge* [1958] *Rocco* is based. You might also look up Rocco Scotellaro, the poet of Lucania, who wrote five parables about the peasants of his native region. Finally, there is a Dostoyevskyan character whose inner life, in more than one aspect, resembles that of Rocco: Prince Mishkin from *The Idiot* [1869], a representative of illustrious goodness as an end in itself.

But there are even more reasons: in Italy, Elio Vittorini had already sounded the alarm about the differences, the *conflicts*, between North and South in his book *Conversations in Sicily* [1941]. And Antonio Gramsci convinced me, through the acuteness of his historical and political analysis, that Southern Italy is a market for a type colonialist exploitation by the ruling classes of the North, which has always tried to keep the South in a state of economic subjection. I discovered in Gramsci, the founder of the Italian Communist Party, the foundation of a realistic, practical solution to the overarching problem of Italian unity or solidarity: an alliance between the workers of the North and the peasants of the South, so as to break up the power of the agri-industrial capitalist block. All these mental "solicitations"—sometimes imponderable ones, I must admit—gave rise to the story of *Rocco and His Brothers*, as well as to the story of Rosaria, their mother.

Energetic, strong, stubborn, Rosaria is the mother of five sons who are themselves strong, handsome, and healthy, just like the five fingers of a hand. To recapitulate, her husband dead, this woman is drawn to the north by the mirage of the big city, to which she moves to escape her misery. But, ultimately, Milan does not permit two of her five sons such a happy lot. Simone, who looks the strongest but is in reality the most feeble, goes berserk and kills the prostitute Nadia. Rocco, the most sensitive and sensible, the most spiritually complex of Rosaria's brood, achieves a success that, for him—given the fact that he considers himself to blame for the misfortune of his brother Simone—is a form of self-punishment. Rocco becomes famous thanks to boxing, a sport that repels him because, faced with an opponent in the ring, he feels unleashed in himself a fierce hatred against everyone and everything—a hatred, moreover, that he abhors.

Ciro, the most practical, the wisest, the most optimistic and forward-looking of all the brothers, will be the only one to urbanize himself completely and become a member of the greater Milan community, well aware of his new opportunities as well as responsibilities. The youngest boy, Luca, will perhaps remain in the Basilicata region in southern Italy (to which he has returned with his mother), especially if conditions down there finally change for the better. As for the remaining brother, Vincenzo, he will content himself with living a modest but nonetheless secure life together with the wife he has taken. So each of these three, one could say, has been restored to grace.

BC: *What were the stages leading to the creation of your final shooting script for* Rocco and His Brothers?

LV: For the first time, I wrote the story all by myself. Then I collaborated with Suso Cecchi d'Amico and Vasco Pratolini on the "treatment" of that story-idea for the screen. Next, I made my own little private expedition to Milan to get at the heart of this metropolis, as well as to identify the places where my characters could live (particularly districts filled with large, gray, anonymous buildings, such as Ghisolfa and Porta Ticinese). On the basis of this research, I wrote the first draft of the screenplay of *Rocco and His Brothers* with the assistance of Suso Cecchi d'Amico, Festa Campanile, Massimo Franciosa, and Enrico Medioli.

I did, however, make another trip to Milan before getting down to work on this draft, and the second trip allowed me to develop the characters, as well as the premises, in greater detail. For example, in the initial "treatment" of the story, we highlighted the nostalgia of people from the south who move to Milan. But, chatting with a number of such migrants, I realized that they had no desire whatsoever to leave the big city, that they were unwilling to return to their native region because—they said—it's better to subsist in Milan than to suffer and succumb in southern Italy. I also noted another element during my second trip to Milan—the particular way in which Sicilians create a home, or turn a "foreign" place into their own—and we took this into account when writing the actual screenplay.

In the end, we were aiming to make the script more "modern"—more scientifically realistic, if you will—than it had been in the treatment stage. But, of course, we were also concerned with more than the documentary side of realism. For instance, in the first draft of the scenario, Rocco died in a boxing match held on a day when he knew he was in poor physical condition and should not fight; and in the second version, Rocco, not Simone, was arrested for the murder of Nadia. Finally, we came up with the ending that you see in the finished film (Rocco's deranged acceptance of his own repeated pummeling in the ring, a self-punishment no less natural than any other)—an ending absolutely devoid of the melodramatics of the ending in the first draft, and devoid as well of the artifice of the conclusion to the second version.

BC: *Did the definitive, written scenario undergo any changes during filming, or did you just follow the script faithfully once you were on the set?*

LV: Naturally, there were changes during the filming; the script always serves only as a basis or springboard for the shooting to come. I invent as I need to when filming, especially as I take into account location, weather, and light, and perhaps above all as I re-think the dramatic necessities of the narrative—what *has to* happen, that is, as opposed to what might happen. This is the way I work on each of my films.

BC: *Is it true that you had to change the last name of Rocco's family from Pafundi to Parondi? If so, why?*

LV: Yes, it's true. "Pafundi" was the original name of the family in *Rocco and His Brothers*, but this upset one of the many real-life Pafundi families in Lucania. I was even threatened with a lawsuit. So, to avoid wasting time and money on a lengthy legal case, I changed the name in the script—in the dialogue—and I used what were then modern optical techniques to black-out "Pafundi" from the back of the characters' boxing robes, as well as to white-out the name from the posters advertising their matches.

BC: *In* The Earth Trembles, *in* Bellissima, *and in* Rocco and His Brothers, *you were always dealing with, and even focusing upon, mothers. How are the respective mothers in these films—Maruzza Sicilienne, Maddalena Romaine, and Rosaria Lucaine—similar? What do these three female characters have in common?*

LV: These are three "moments" in the development of one character: the mother. The mother in *The Earth Trembles* seemed to be overwhelmed or overpowered by events; Maddalena of *Bellissima*, she was tough as well as tender, and she is related to Rosaria in *Rocco and His Brothers* in the sense that she tries in vain to point the way to her daughter's success. Like Maddalena, Rosaria will also be disappointed, but even more so because of the origin of her disappointment in her own "exteriorizing" of internal feelings, her always overdoing the momentousness of a particular situation, be it a joyful or a painful one. Sound familiar?

BC: *In conclusion, do you agree with the French director René Clair when he says that "a good script must be able to 'narrate itself' in a mere phrase or two"?*

LV: In one word, I would say—a word that puts the imagination in play and inspires the director who will listen to it.

BC: *What's more important to you: your enjoyment in making a film or an audience's enjoyment in watching it?*

LV: Neither. What I want above all from a film is that it make people think.

BC: *Think about what, that's the question. You are a member of an aristocratic family, you once held the title of count, and you are even reported to be a millionaire, but you have been charged with voting—and filming—"left" and living "right."*

LV: Look, Italy is a republic now. I am no longer a count; I am nothing. My family was very rich, yes, but I am not. I work all the time. I do like to live comfortably, but that does not prohibit me from having ideas about social reform. I don't have to wear a burlap bag and live in a stable to entertain such ideas, do I? I feel that the world is becoming a better place, for all people, and that we don't need Maoist extremism to make it an even better place. Society can't go backward, it must go forward.

BC: *Well, art moved forward when the cinema was invented, I think we can agree on that. If the cinema hadn't existed when you came of age, by the way—when it came time for you to choose a profession—what would you have done?*

LV: I would have invented it.

Luchino Visconti Filmography

Ossessione (1943)
La terra trema (1948)
Bellissima (1951)
Senso (1954)
Le notti bianche (*White Nights*, 1957)
Rocco e i suoi fratelli (*Rocco and His Brothers*, 1960)
The Leopard (*Il Gattopardo*, 1963)
Vaghe stelle dell'Orsa (*Sandra of a Thousand Delights*, 1965)
The Stranger (*Lo straniero*, 1967)
The Damned (*La caduta degli dei*, 1969)
Death in Venice (*Morte a Venezia*, 1971)
Ludwig (1972)
Conversation Piece (*Gruppo di famiglia in un interno*, 1974)
L'Innocente (*The Innocent*, 1976)

Bibliography

Bacon, Henry. *Visconti: Explorations of Beauty and Decay*. New York: Cambridge University Press, 1998.

LeMancini, Elaine. *Luchino Visconti: A Guide to References and Resources*. Boston, Mass.: G. K. Hall, 1986.

Nowell-Smith, Geoffrey. *Luchino Visconti*. 3rd ed. London: British Film Institute, 2003.

Servadio, Gaia. *Luchino Visconti: A Biography*. London: Weidenfeld & Nicolson, 1981.

Stirling, Monica. *A Screen of Time: A Study of Luchino Visconti*. New York: Harcourt Brace Jovanovich, 1979.

Tonetti, Claretta. *Luchino Visconti*. Boston: Twayne Publishers, 1983.

Reflecting Reality—and Mystery

An Interview with Ermanno Olmi

Although thematically he inverts neorealism by studying the human accommodation to difficult external circumstances, Ermanno Olmi (born 1931) is perhaps the best exemplar after neorealism of the neorealist *style*, with its disdain (in theory if not always in practice) for dramatic contrivance and fictive invention. His films offer slices of life—of ordinary people's unspectacular lives—with indefinite or inconclusive endings; they simulate documentary methods in staging and photography, as they are all shot in actual locations and almost all of them feature non-actors; and they aspire not to proposition or evocation but only toward accurate representation. Moreover, in the wake of the economic boom following Italy's postwar recovery, Olmi has consistently focused on elemental work situations positioned between the charm of apprenticeship and the regret-cum-relief of retirement,

Sandro Panseri (left) as Domenico Cantoni in Olmi's *Il posto.*

in which everyday concerns are held up against a long view of the not-too-distant future. Olmi's later works depart from the neorealist style of *Il posto* (*The Job*, 1961) and *I fidanzati* (*The Fiancés*, 1963), his second and third pictures, but even they are characterized by a kind of non-discursiveness in which their heroes are always poised between human solitude and membership in some kind of community, be it that of family, village, or office.

Il posto, for its part, ushered something new into world cinema: a sense of intimacy between director and characters that surpassed anything in the canon of Italian neorealism. In the intervening years, this film has had a profound effect on directors as diverse as Wu Nien-jen, Abbas Kiarostami, and Martin Scorsese (whose *Raging Bull* [1980] contains more than one visual quotation from *Il posto*). And if it has not achieved the same legendary status as three movies released only one year earlier, in 1960—Antonioni's *L'avventura*, Visconti's *Rocco and His Brothers*, and Fellini's *La dolce vita*—this is probably on account of *Il posto*'s soulful intimacy, its refusal to distance itself from its characters or subject in an age where detachment, irony, and objectivity are valued above all else. To wit, even though Olmi has almost always filmed people on the lower end of the economic ladder, leading unexceptional lives, he treats the details of these lives with the care or close attention—but without the embellishment—that a Quattrocento master would have lavished on an episode in the life of Christ. The result is that his great films (*Il posto*, *I fidanzati*, *The Tree of Wooden Clogs* [1978], *The Legend of the Holy Drinker* [1988], and the first half of *Genesis* [1994]) lack the aesthetic, even romanticized, luster that attaches to the aforementioned classics.

Furthermore, these pictures by Olmi also lack the kind of charismatic sweep we have come to associate with grand artistic visions whereby, in the work of an Antonioni, a Visconti, or a Fellini, the artist's sensibility acts as a kind of majestic, all-encompassing umbrella over the characters and the action. Olmi, like the Frenchman Robert Bresson, paints on a smaller canvas, where his passionate humanism can completely infuse his cinematic art. His films thus feel like one-to-one exchanges between real people; indeed, you have the impression that the director is walking hand in hand with each of his characters. The sensation is that these choices of his are not only his but that others have made them too. Perhaps because of his peasant-worker background, Olmi's ambition thus seems to be to look at the world *with* others, not as an aristocratic intellectual.

As befits a master filmmaker, Ermanno Olmi is reluctant to give interviews; he prefers to let his films speak for themselves. Ever a shy, self-effacing man, Olmi was especially sparse with words when awarded the Golden Lion at the 1988 Venice festival for *The Legend of the Holy Drinker* as well as the Golden Palm at the 1978 Cannes festival for *The Tree of Wooden Clogs*. And there hasn't been a published interview with Olmi for quite some time. One reason for the reticence is his embarrassment at having to answer those all too frequent, nagging "how are you?" and "what have you been doing?" questions. For between the Cannes premieres of *The Tree of Wooden Clogs* and *Keep Walking* (1983) lay five years of inactivity, then another four years until *Long Live the Lady!* (1987) won the Silver Lion at Venice. During much of this time, he had been wrestling with a long and sometimes paralyzing illness, from which he has since recovered; still, several years of inactivity continue to separate his feature films.

Before proper introductions could be made between us, Olmi queried why I had bothered to come to interview him at all: "You know *my* answers as well as *your* questions, so what's the sense of it?" Nonetheless, speaking in rounded phrases with a sonorous voice, he began to muse philosophically about his profession, about how he seldom needed to go far from home to film a story that was "part of me," about how the only measure of a film's importance is the common denominator of man—or the need for spiritual values, for mystical tenderness between human beings, in a cold world. *Genesis: The Creation and the Flood*, for example, is "about us," not a homage to a distant deity in some picture book. Like all his masterpieces, this portion of *The Bible* (produced by Lux), his feature-length episode in the series made for Raiuno and Lube-Beta Film, is meant to be a personal encounter, a film carved with a storyteller's imagination from handed-down oral tradition, and one that can enchant the hearts as well as minds of an audience.

In the same room with us sat Loredana Detto, Olmi's wife, taking it all in with the same wistful charm and anchoring attention that captured the heart of the youth Domenico in *Il posto*. The story of a Lombard peasant boy applying for an available office job in a large Milan company, and at the same time falling shyly in love with the young secretary, Magali (Loredana Detto), the core of the film is a reflection on work, on the deadening, overly regimented, oppressive world of the white-collar workforce—a reflection in this case drawn from Olmi's own recollections of himself as an eighteen-year-old looking for and finding employment at the Edisonvolta Company. (*The Tree of Wooden Clogs* is also autobiographical, in the sense that it was drawn from stories about country people told to him by his grandfather.)

The following interview took place in August 2008 at Ermanno Olmi's home in the Lombardy region of northern Italy, northeast of Milan. My plan was to get the director to open up a little more than usual both by getting him off the subject of his individual films themselves—the circumstances surrounding their making, the people in them, the amount of money they made, their critical reception, etc.—and by scrupulously avoiding questions about his personal life. In order to accommodate me, Olmi spoke in high Italian (as opposed to his native Lombardy dialect) as much as possible.

Bert Cardullo: *I'd like to focus today, Signor Olmi, on a general or theoretical discussion of the cinema, of your cinema, as opposed to a specific discussion of your individual films themselves. Is this acceptable to you?*

Ermanno Olmi: Yes, that's fine. It also makes for a nice change of pace.

BC: *Nothing much happens in an Olmi film—that is, if you require the equivalent of a roller-coaster ride with all the requisite thrills and chills. Instead of giving your audience a boldly defined series of actions moving the story along at a furious pace, you share with that audience small moments that gradually build into the powerful understanding—emotional as well as cognitive—of an experience. Using real people instead of actors, you follow your subjects as they live in real time, gently shaping their lives into fiction with your authorial hand. Why do you work in this way?*

EO: Shooting freely with a handheld camera, never selecting anything in advance, I find that everything happens almost spontaneously. It doesn't happen by design, by planning. Why do I work in this way? Because it is important that the operative technical moment be enveloped in the many emotions that are in the air at the moment one lives in the scene. There must always be a participation, a collision with the moment; this is what determines the choice of image. Otherwise, it's like going up to a loved one and first thinking, "When we meet, I'll touch her hand, and then kiss like this, then say these words. . . ."

BC: *Working in such a way, do you get frustrated by the limitations of the frame?*

EO: The frame is not a frustration to me, perhaps also because I work without pre-planned shots. The frame becomes a way of focusing, not a composition in itself, because it corresponds to the things I want to look at in a particular moment. It's good that there is, outside the frame, "a discussion that continues," as it were—something I can imagine and even desire. The same is true in literature, where there are phrases that let you think of an infinity of other words which are even more beautiful because they aren't said.

BC: *In pre-packaged movies of the Hollywood kind—which are born on the drawing table, as they are planned out by the art director and all the technical staff—the camera merely establishes a framing angle selected in advance, and all the things written in the script occur within this fixed frame.*

EO: My own procedure, as you know, is different. At the beginning, I don't think about the camera. I think about the ambience and all the events that are to be presented: place, lighting, people, color. I construct the fiction I need. When I feel that this fiction corresponds to my needs, then I go to the camera and let myself be dragged along by the event without establishing beforehand that "here" I'll do a close-up, a long shot, or a camera movement. With each shot I participate in the event almost instinctively, gathering up what happens and responding accordingly. It's rare that I decide anything in advance. I invent the action at the moment it takes place.

I almost always work with a handheld camera and, having to get direct sound when there is dialogue, I need a very heavy camera since I shoot in 35mm and therefore have to put it on a tripod with wheels. I never do dolly shots or tracks; I never put the camera at a level higher or lower than a horizontal line drawn at eye-level, though sometimes I go out on a balcony or shoot through a window. The camera is on this wheeled tripod, but I move it as if it were part of me, and always at my own height. I always use the camera in this objective way.

BC: *What's the difference between your method of filming and the one used in documentaries?*

EO: The difference from the documentary isn't so much in the techniques of shooting because, for example, as in my films, in a documentary there isn't any elaborate lighting, to name just one technical element. For me, the technique of shooting is almost the same. The difference is that in a documentary I shoot a reality from outside my will; thus my critical participation in the event lies only in choosing with the camera the image that, at that moment, I find most interesting in a documentation of the event. In the case of a fiction film, reality doesn't happen outside my will, but is organized within me, inside my consciousness. Thus, my critical judgment and my suggestion of content lie above all in the organization of the event. As for my approach to the shooting, I do it just as in a documentary, such that I do not deceive the viewer with a suggestion made through certain acrobatics of the camera or through the use of a redundant little touch in the lights or the atmosphere.

In sum, even when the camera is objective in this way, the subjectivity is my own.

BC: *Doesn't this make you feel all alone, as if you are creating a world to the exclusion of everyone else?*

EO: I never feel alone. I'm convinced that participating with me in the action, in this event, are many others. It's not my personal point of view. Certainly it is, in the sense that I decide. However, the sensation I have is that these choices of mine are not only mine but that others have them, too. I really don't feel exclusive, that I exclude anybody. There is a certain type of intellectual who, either out of presumption towards himself or contempt towards others—which is the same thing—has the ambition to be so subjective, to be the only one, to observe life and events from such an isolated perspective. My ambition, instead—perhaps because of my peasant/worker extraction—is to look at the world *with* others, not as an aristocratic intellectual, an elitist, but as someone who mixes with other people as much as possible.

BC: *But there are excellent directors who, unlike you, work with camera operators. As you have been saying, you yourself are behind the camera.*

EO: Well, everyone makes love the way they want to, in the way that they themselves feel. Again, conventional shooting is like going up to a loved one and first thinking, "When we meet, I'll touch her hand, and then kiss her like this, then utter these words. . . ." Certainly we go to this intimate meeting with a whole series of motives, but it is only during the meeting itself that these motives assume their final expressive physiognomy. There is another reason I am behind the camera. Because otherwise it would be like going up to a girl and saying, "I love you but now he's going to kiss you for me."

BC: *Why do you use non-professional actors in your films?*

EO: I use non-professionals for more or less the same reasons I choose a real landscape over one reconstructed in the studio. For *Barry Lyndon*, Stanley Kubrick looked all over Europe to find the countrysides and atmosphere that corresponded to his expressive needs. Onto this countryside, this atmosphere—this choice that he made from the real—he grafted his professional actors. I prefer to continue such a relationship with reality, but not with professional actors. The real tree is continuously creative; the artificial tree isn't. The fake tree responds to the creative needs of a fact (let us call it) already laid out and defined, and stops there. The real tree has continuing virtues: it responds to and reflects light in ever new ways. When you shoot in the studio, you've set up the lighting in advance; the lights are the same from beginning to end. You can shoot the same shot a hundred times and it will be the same. The real tree, on the other hand, is in continual evolution, modifying itself inside the situation, so much so that you become anxious lest you not be able to capture a particular moment when the light is changing. This, too, is very beautiful, because between the first shot and the fourth and the fifth there are variations—the shot is continually palpitating, in a manner of speaking. Thus it goes with actors, as well.

BC: *So you're saying that you can never get this same effect—of "palpitation"—from a professional actor.*

EO: I have always felt in professional actors a bit of cardboard with respect to the great palpitating authenticity of the real character, who was not chosen, as professionals are, for their beautiful looks, or because they characterize a certain type. For instance, in a film about peasants I choose the actors from the peasant world. I don't use a fig to make a pear. These people, these characters, bring to the film a weight, really a constitution of truth, which, provoked by the situations in which the characters find themselves, creates palpitations—those vibrations so right, so real, so believable, and therefore not repeatable. At the twentieth take the professional actor still cries. The *real* actor, the character taken from life, won't do more than four repetitions. It's like capturing a light: either you get it at that moment or you don't get it at all. But it isn't that he exhausts himself; he becomes something else. And my emotion lies also in following these things, at the moment they occur.

BC: *What's the relationship of your non-professional performer to the reality from which he is drawn?*

EO: Since all manifestations of life are life, it's not that there is more life in a man, in one of my non-professionals, than in a frog or a tree. Life is life represented in all forms of expression. It's so extraordinary and mysterious that we cannot know all these forms of life. Truth is the same thing. It's not true, for example, that there is more truth in dialogue between real persons than in a poem or a piece of fiction. This depends on the presuppositions that have generated the words or the dialogue, the truth of one's authentic emotions. False emotions are always discovered for what they are.

Some would say that the raw material of film is the image, but it's not just the image. Today we have the image, sound, rhythm. All that is so simple, and at the same time it is complex, just like the unwinding or playing out of life itself. While sound is one moment here, and the image there, cinema is this extraordinary instrument that allows you to reproduce—but "reproduce" isn't the exact word—to *repropose* some of those moments, some of the fractions of life, to select and compose them into a new mosaic through the editing. This operation consists of choice, image, sound, rhythm, *synthesis*.

In the case of my films, they contain a reality that is entirely taken from the real. Within this reality there is the echo of the documentary, but this is documentation that is critically penetrated and put at the service of the content presented.

BC: *Unlike many commercial directors, then, you see the cinema as a whole art, as an art unto itself.*

EO: Yes, for in a certain sense, it's a contradiction to use cinema as a substitute for literature, for music, for the theater. Even when we want to make a film full of conceptual ideas, it's obvious we must make choices of representation from life—choices embodied in image, sound, and rhythm—to express those ideas. This means that the image, the music, the action aren't by themselves sufficient vehicles to express a concept. They become significant, if at all, all together. And this is why I must express a concept or an idea through the dialogue between the main characters, shots of their faces, shots of how they move, in what situations, in what light, with what rhythm. It's not that one element repeats the other; but, just as in literature I choose this word rather than one that closely resembles it, so too in film I choose precisely that word because only that word can express the particular thing I want. Then I choose this image because it can say something better than anything else, and that sound because . . . You see? It's as if the cinema were a language that, instead of having only words, has words, images, sounds—a language, in short, that is the language of life itself. We speak with gestures, with looks, with the very sound of the word as well as with its meaning. If I say "Good evening" to you in three different ways, the sound is different each time, as is the facial expression and therefore the meaning. This is cinema: nouns, adjectives, parts of sentences that belong to a special syntax and organization.

BC: *How does lighting figure in everything you've said so far, in your approach to the filming of reality?*

EO: Beauty, emotions, must be revealed by indications that most resemble reality, not by artificial ones; and this certainly includes lighting. Why? So that the viewer's approach to the screen isn't protected or even deceived by devices, but that instead he succeeds in discovering by himself certain values, certain atmospheres, certain states of mind, through indications on the screen that are more those of life than those of theatricality, in the sense of spectacle.

When I do use artificial illumination, it's because such illumination is necessary for the effects of the film stock; otherwise, sometimes the light doesn't reach the film. But I also do this at the same time that I respect the natural environment much as possible.

BC: *What about filters?*

EO: I never use special filters to alter or in some way modify the tonalities of the natural atmosphere. For instance, when I shoot a close-up of the female lead in a romantic situation, I don't use filters that normally a script would call for in order to make her seem commercial beautiful or alluring. To give you a technical example from shooting, when I film in a particular place, I don't set up the framing and then, on the basis of that framing, establish the lighting. I first set up the kind of lighting that will allow me to shoot anywhere in that location.

Since I do the camerawork myself—I operate the camera, which is not the same thing as doing the lighting, for that is the job of my cinematographer—

I know exactly what I have shot, so much so that often I don't even have to look at the developed film, the rushes or the "dailies." I just call the developer and if he says the negative is okay, it's fine for me.

BC: *I am assuming you do your own editing.*

EO: Of course. I am one who still works a great deal at the Movieola. For *The Tree of Wooden Clogs*, I was there for a whole year. The editing is the moment when all the emotions I felt when I began to think about the film, to conceive it, to choose the locations, the faces—all these things—the editing is the moment when everything comes together. You could say that during this time, I total my bill, I work out this choice or that synthesis, I sum up the emotion of all my emotions concerning this particular film. It's not administrative work in the sense that I look at the script and say, "Okay, for this scene we need such-and-such a cut. And for that scene a close-up is required." It's a new creative moment, an extraordinary moment. This is because I rarely write systematic, organized screenplays; instead, I scribble lots of notes. When I'm shooting, I arrive on the set with all these notes—little pieces of paper filled with jottings about dialogue, atmosphere, faces—and there, on the set, I begin a new critical-creative phase—not critical-executive—as I think about the shots I want to take. The editing, naturally, is a continuation of this critical-creative process.

BC: *Where, or how, does your writing begin?*

EO: First I write down the suggestion or indication of a subject or a story, then I divide it up into many chapters, many moments, like the movements of a concerto. And everything that comes into my mind regarding one of these chapters—at any moment when I am scouting locations or the like—I write down on pieces of paper and incorporate them into the chapter in question. Then, when it comes time to shoot, I organize the fraction of the story I am shooting in the most specific way possible. But when I'm there, shooting, I am often, let's not say ready to change everything, but to add or to subtract as I see fit. That's why I never have a "completed" script. This is how I like to shoot, how I frame my shots and film the action.

When I'm at the Movieola, I don't look at any of the written stuff again. It's a new event that is occurring at the editing table. So artistic creation, like romantic love, is always in the act of becoming; it's always in motion, with no real stops. For when there are stops, one isn't making love.

BC: *What do you think of the manipulative aspect of filmmaking, of how movies manipulate their audiences—all movies, possibly including your own?*

EO: Everything is manipulated in a sense, everything: not only the cinema but the economy, religion, any of man's activities can be corrupting—or saving. It really depends on the moral basis upon which you do these things, both in producing and in consuming them. Even the automobile can be corrupting or saving. If we use it to dangerously pass others, to give us a sense of power through the engine's horsepower instead of through the horsepower of our own minds and imaginations, then the automobile can be a negative thing. For example, even neorealism degenerated at a certain point because it had become a fad, a fashion, a slick operation, and suddenly it was enough to qualify as a "neorealistic" director if you made a certain type of film, in a certain way—never mind its substance. This also happened to the French New Wave after a while, where if you didn't make the camera jiggle when you were shooting a subject, somehow it didn't seem "real." But it's real if *you* are real in front of what you are shooting, if the things that you are filming have an authenticity of their own. If not, you may as well work in the theater, which has its own aesthetic and reason for being apart from those of the cinema.

So unmasking the illusion is fine, if that's what it takes to keep realism from degenerating into artifice. For, clearly, resemblance to reality is not reality. This is obvious—or it should be.

BC: *You are beginning to sound like a Brechtian in the cinema.*

EO: Yes, but sometimes, even in Brecht's aesthetic, this attempt to "disenchant" the spectator, to remind him that what he is seeing is *theater*, in itself reinforces the magical component of theater. When the grandmother tells her grandson a fairy tale, the story of Little Red Riding Hood with all the emotions inherent in it—the girl, the woods, the wolf—the grandmother's face continually reminds the grandson that between the reality of the fairy tale and himself there is always his grandmother's face. Nonetheless, sometimes the grandmother increases, by her very tone and expression, the fairy tale's power of suggestion, its forcefulness. So this attempt to mediate between the magic of theatricality, or the illusion of reality, and the experience of the spectator—to disenchant or distance—can be reinforcing instead of the opposite.

In my opinion, however, neither takes away from or adds very much to the need man has to experience both the emotion of fear, at a child's level, and the satisfaction of recognition, at an adult level, through the telling of the fairy tale. This is because we all want to share the feeling of not risking ourselves, of not being in direct contact with the frightful event, but instead in the comforting arms of Grandmother, in the armchair at the cinema, or in our living rooms in front of the television set, which protects us and guarantees our safety. We even protect ourselves to the point that sometimes authentic reality—television news or documentary film, for instance—becomes transformed, in the safety of our homes, into its own kind of fairy tale, by means of which we see real events far removed from our consciences and our responsibility. In such a fairy-tale atmosphere, these events do not touch us physically or morally; we participate in them neither in body or soul. What we see "enchants" us, and we want to see it in the context of this enchantment. Indeed, we enjoy the fact that, yes, theater and cinema—especially the cinema—remind us of reality, but they remind us even more of the fairy tale. This is why we can watch with total concentration and excitement as people fight and kill each other on the screen, at the same time as we self-assuredly stir our coffee or eat our popcorn.

BC: *These things are hard to talk about in terms of classifications or designations— fairy tale, reality, disenchantment, empathy, etc.—this is something I have learned.*

EO: Yes, and let's take Brecht again as an instance. What does Brecht try to do? To "disenchant" us so that our critical faculty is always active. Thus he says, "Don't be taken in by this. Be careful, I am acting; watch carefully so that you won't be taken in." I understand this critical distance. The spectator in the cinema or the theater feels fear; he tells himself that what he's seeing is not real so that he can feel defended against it; and then he returns back to his fear. Such critical distancing is like Grandmother's face: it's Grandmother who is telling the story, and this is why her grandson can comfortably feel his fear. Such a theory as Brecht's is important for the viewer, but what happens? Brecht doesn't always achieve—in fact, he rarely does—the result that he intended. Why? Because if you come with your own ability to critically distance yourself from an aesthetic event, to analyze it by yourself, sometimes you can be disturbed by someone who wants to "cue" your distancing or to distance you from what you're seeing even more than you ordinarily would be. If, on the other hand, you don't have any ability, on your own, to critically distance yourself from an aesthetic event—if you are over-emotional, let us say, and feel immediately stirred just by the exterior aspect of characters kissing or horses galloping—you can feel equally disenfranchised by someone who wants to pull you back from what you are seeing.

Or the opposite: an emotional spectator can take the distancing devices so seriously that he becomes nothing *but* distanced from the artistic event, to the point that he has completely, and misguidedly, suppressed his emotional involvement in that event.

Participation in an artistic event, in short, is many-sided and more complex than most theorists make it out to be. One can participate in an emotion, for example, but, at the same time, one can force a series of "postponents" on one's emotions that cannot be seen with the eyes and may not even be acknowledged by the conscious mind. People are different, and so is the camera: the same camera in the hands of ten different people shooting the same picture will, without question, take ten different pictures.

BC: *Could you speak a bit now about your early experiences of the cinema and your contact with American movies?*

EO: I would very much like to do so. When, as a child, I went out the cinema, I always felt good, and I felt especially good when I started seeing the differences between Hollywood cinema—*global* Hollywood cinema, if you will, not just the American variety—and the cinema of Italian neorealism, particularly the first films of Roberto Rossellini. I was between fifteen and seventeen years old at the time, and in those years I passed from the loving arms of my grandmother, who told me wonderfully suggestive fairy tales, to the bitter embrace of my father, who began to introduce me to life's complexities and disappointments. The films of Rossellini mark this turning point for me. I remember leaving a screening of *Paisan*—there were only seven or eight of us in the audience, although the cinemas were always packed when they showed popular American movies like *I'll Be Yours* or *The Man I Love*. I went to see *Paisan* probably because I had already seen all the other movies around. And strangely enough, this picture made me realize that it was time to tear myself away from my mother's bosom. Leaving the movie theater after *Paisan*, I continued to experience the strong emotions I had felt while watching this film, because it was life that I had seen up on the screen—not movie formulas. And the cinema began to fascinate me, the idea of making films from a unique perspective but always in collaboration with others. Film, for me, is a way of being together with other people, both when I make films and when my films are in the company of their audience, the viewers.

I loved Hollywood movies very much at the time, but if today my grandmother came back and wanted to take me on her knee and tell me the story of Little Red Riding Hood, I wouldn't like it, of course. This is what we call becoming an adult viewer.

BC: *I guess television didn't enter into the picture for you in the late 1940s.*

EO: No, not at all: I was too young and the medium was too young. But I do think that if people today would turn off their own television sets, film could still hold great value for them. In fact, if it weren't for the cinema, contemporary society would be very disorganized. The cinema is a kind of comfort, especially when it's a false mirror like that of Snow White's stepmother. We *want* the cinema, that representation of ourselves which somehow says we are all fine and good, even when it presents the negative aspects of life. We are saved, you could say, by this filmic mirror that continually deceives us; we are its ultimate beneficiaries, we as a society, as a people, as individual human beings.

As far as I am concerned, however, I could live without cinema if they took it away from me. But I couldn't live without my wife, my children, my friends—without people, especially those near and dear to me. This may seem like an infantile choice—your family or the flicks! (as you Americans like to call the movies)—but it's worth keeping in mind in an era where much writing about film, and many movies themselves, seem to have less and less to do with human life as most of us experience it from day to day.

BC: *Well, there are a lot of businessmen who would disagree with your choice of family and friends over the cinema.*

EO: Naturally. Since ours is a society—a global or international one at this point—that strains to achieve certain objectives, among which profit towers above all others, it's obvious that the cinema as a mass medium, as a means of popular communication, is strongly and even intensely utilized to such an end: the attainment of profit, which need not be of the exclusively monetary kind. It could be ideological "profit" as well. Whole economies themselves initiate their own strategies for profit, by means of which the masses, within a grand design constructed by just a few, fall into a financial trap. But there comes a time when the economy revolts and turns against not only its protagonists, the industrial giants, but also against the workers themselves. Then there must be some kind of reckoning, some taking into account, if not a revolt itself, and this must involve everyone, including the "organizers of profit." So it is with the cinema. At the beginning, when the audience saw a train on the screen rushing towards them, they hid under their seats; they were afraid, given film's power of visualization. Today, to give only an inkling of what has happened since, you have to stab a man in the stomach nine times to get the same effect. And everyone is paying a very high price, figuratively as well as literally, for this kind of exploitation. But I think that any event—social, political, economic, or artistic—produces certain negative effects that were *meant* to be produced by betraying certain ideas or principles. The only question is how long it will take for a revolt on the part of those who produce as well as those who consume the cinema. I am not an optimist at all cost, but I do believe in the will to survive of life itself, and that when we have come to the end of our cunning and cleverness to trick the good earth, and with it saint cinema, into producing more and more, the both of them will rebel against us. Film art—cinematographic suggestion, if you like—will refuse at a certain point to participate in its own corruption and even prostitution. This is not just a discussion involving the cinema, however, as I have tried to make clear, because the cinema is only one element in the general economic noise that surrounds us.

BC: *It is certainly true today that many an auteur—one who has the talent to make quality films—is strongly influenced by an anxiety for commercial success.*

EO: Yes. For example, if their film doesn't make millions more than another movie released at the same time, lots of directors feel inferior and even disconsolate—so much are they influenced by this logic of exaggerated profit. But the moment will come when we become so pained by the economic and artistic choices we have made that we will go back to looking at ourselves in the mirror, to looking into each other's eyes sincerely, and finding there the reality we have sacrificed to the bitch-goddess of capitalistic success.

Ermanno Olmi Filmography

Il Tempo si è fermato (*Time Stood Still*, 1959)
Il posto (*The Job*, a.k.a. *The Sound of Trumpets*, 1961)
I fidanzati (*The Fiancés*, 1963)
E venne un uomo (*A Man Called John*, 1965)
Un Certo giorno (*One Fine Day*, 1969)
Durante l'estate (*In the Summertime*, 1971)
L'Albero degli zoccoli (*The Tree of Wooden Clogs*, 1978)
Cammina, cammina (*Keep Walking*, 1983)
Lunga vita alla signora (*Long Live the Lady!*, 1987)
La Leggenda del santo bevitore (*The Legend of the Holy Drinker*, 1988)
Lungo il fiume (*Down the River*, 1992)
Il Segreto del bosco vecchio (*The Secret of the Old Woods*, 1993)
Genesi: La creazione e il diluvio (*Genesis: The Creation and the Flood*, 1994)

Il Mestiere delle armi (*The Profession of Arms*, 2001)
Cantando dietro i paraventi (*Singing Behind Screens*, 2003)
Tickets (2005), along with Ken Loach and Abbas Kiarostami
Centochiodi (*One Hundred Nails*, 2007)

Bibliography

Bachmann, Gideon. "Ermanno Olmi: The New Italian Films." *The Nation* 198, no. 22 (25 May 1964), 540–543.

Bertellini, Giorgio. *The Cinema of Italy*. London: Wallflower, 2004.

Bondanella, Peter E. "*Il posto/I fidanzati*." *Cineaste* 29, no. 1 (Winter 2003), 73–74.

———. *Italian Cinema: From Neorealism to the Present*. 3rd ed. New York: Continuum, 2001.

Brook, Clodagh. "Beyond Dialogue: Speech-silence, The Monologue, and Power in the Films of Ermanno Olmi." *Italianist* 28, no. 2 (2008), 268–280.

Brunetta, Gian Piero. *The History of Italian Cinema: A Guide to Italian Film from Its Origins to the Twenty-First Century*. Trans. Jeremy Parzen. Princeton, N.J.: Princeton University Press, 2009.

Cardullo, Bert. "Married to the Job: Ermanno Olmi's *Il posto* and *I fidanzati* Reconsidered." *Cambridge Quarterly* 38, no. 2 (June 2009), 120–129.

Landy, Marcia. *Italian Film*. New York: Cambridge University Press, 2000.

Marcus, Millicent. *After Fellini: National Cinema in the Postmodern Age*. Baltimore: Johns Hopkins University Press, 2002.

———. *Italian Film in the Light of Neorealism*. Princeton, N.J.: Princeton University Press, 1986.

Monaco, James. "The Tree of Wooden Clogs." *Cineaste* 30, no. 1 (Winter 2004), 58–59.

Restivo, Angelo. *The Cinema of Economic Miracles: Visuality and Modernization in the Italian Art Film*. Durham, N.C.: Duke University Press, 2002.

Samuels, Charles Thomas. "Ermanno Olmi." In Charles Thomas Samuels, *Encountering Directors*, 99–115. New York: Da Capo, 1987.

Sorlin, Pierre. *Italian National Cinema, 1896–1996*. London: Routledge, 1996.

Witcombe, R. T. *The New Italian Cinema: Studies in Dance and Despair*. New York: Oxford University Press, 1982.

Wood, Mary P. *Italian Cinema*. New York: Berg, 2005.

FRANCOPHONE
COMMUNICATION

"Comedy Belongs to Everybody"

An Interview with Jacques Tati

Jacques Tati (1908–1982) was the great comedian of French film, probably the greatest movie mime and visual comic since Chaplin and Keaton. Like Robert Bresson, Tati worked slowly, controlling every detail of his films himself from script to cutting; also like Bresson, Tati refused to compromise with either technicians or producers. As a result, though his first film appearance occurred as early as 1932, Tati made only six feature films. Like Chaplin and Keaton, Tati came to films from the music hall. Before taking to the stage, however, he took to sport—tennis, boxing, soccer. And Tati's comedy often combined the athletic field and the music hall. But he was sensitive not only to the comic possibilities of his body but also to the visually comic possibilities of film.

Also like Chaplin and Keaton, Tati played essentially the same character in each of his pictures. That character is inevitably a loner, an outsider, a charming fool whose human incompetence is preferable to the inhuman competence of the life around him. Tati's Monsieur Hulot (even the name recalls Charlot) merely goes about his business, totally unaware that the world around him has gone mad and that his naïve attention to his own affairs turns its orderly madness into comic chaos. Again like Chaplin and Keaton, Tati's Hulot neither looks nor moves like anyone else in the universe. He leans forward at an oblique angle—battered hat atop his head, pipe thrusting from his mouth, umbrella dangling at his side, trouser cuffs hanging two inches above his shoes—an odd human construction of impossible angles, off-center and off-kilter.

In his first feature film, *Jour de fête* (1949), Tati plays a village postman who, struck by the "modern, efficient" methods he sees in a short documentary on the American postal system, decides to streamline his own operations. The satiric theme that runs through all of Tati's work—the coldness, even inefficiency and wastefulness, of modern technology—is already well developed, but, more importantly, so is the visual style. Many of the gags in *Jour de fête* depend on the use of frame-lines and foreground objects to obscure the comic event—not so as to punch home the gag, but to hide and purify it, so to speak, to force the spectator to intuit and sometimes invent the joke for himself.

Tati took four years to make his next film, *Les Vacances de Monsieur Hulot* (1953), which introduced the character he was to play for the rest of his career—an apparently traditional, easygoing, middle-class gentleman who comes to spend a conventional week at a completely conventional middle-class resort. However, Hulot's troubles with bathers on the beach, with his sputtering car, with a violently bucking horse, even with the twang of the hotel's dining-room door, and, finally, with a warehouse full of fireworks, reduce the conventional, routine-driven tourist resort to unconventional hysteria. Tati's comic attack thus exposes the resort—supposedly a place devoted to leisure and fun—as the domain of the dull, the monotonous, the dead. Monsieur Hulot is the force that converts this dead place of play into a genuine funhouse by bombarding it with uncanny objects, sounds, and movements. We in the movie theatre, like those few vacationers who take the time to notice Hulot's spontaneous, disruptive activities, also discover what genuine, active fun really is. The warmth of Hulot's characterization, plus the radiant inventiveness of the sight gags, made *Les Vacances* an international success, yet the film already suggests Tati's dissatisfaction with the traditional idea of the comic star. Hulot is not a comedian in the sense of being the source and focus of the humor; he is, rather, an attitude, a signpost, a perspective that reveals the humor in the world around him.

Mon Oncle (1958), Tati's first film in color, features Monsieur Hulot again—this time as an old-fashioned, simple, mild-mannered uncle of a family of upper-middle-class suburbanites. Here, Hulot's traditional and somewhat archaic lifestyle in an old quarter of Paris is contrasted with the antiseptic and mechanistic environment of his brother-in-law, Arpel, who lives in an ultramodern house in the city's new suburban wasteland and works as an executive in a plastics factory. Hulot's unaffected ways naturally clash with the complicated machinery of his suburban relatives' lives: their fancy gadgets that open the garage doors and kitchen shelves; their bizarrely shaped furniture that is designed for everything but comfort and function; their gravel-lined, flagstone-paved "garden" that is suitable for everything except growing things and enjoying the sun. In this struggle of humanity versus the artifact, the gadgets win the battle (as they always do in physical comedy), but Monsieur Hulot wins the satirical war.

Tati's next film, *Playtime* (1967), took him three years to complete and was shot in color and 70 mm Panavision with five-track stereophonic sound. Here Tati offers a series of quietly humorous vignettes about a group of American tourists who come to see the "real" Paris and end up experiencing a space-age city of steel, glass, chrome, and plastic. Hulot was now merely one figure among many, weaving in and out of the action much like the Mackintosh man in Joyce's *Ulysses*. Widely regarded today as a modernist masterpiece, *Playtime* is a film not of belly laughs but of sustained, intelligent humor, and it clearly represents Tati's finest achievement.

As in *Les Vacances*, the underlying theme of *Playtime* is the creative use of leisure and the genuine fun that can result from active perception rather than the passive acceptance of planned or canned routines. The American tourists of *Playtime* parallel the vacationers in *Les Vacances*, and in *Playtime* they eventually do have fun, despite their overly packaged tour, simply by observing the oddities of Hulot and, even more important, the surprising oddities of the world itself. Like *Les Vacances*, *Playtime* is very much about itself, about our having fun by watching a film closely and by finding its comic inventions for ourselves rather than being fed them by a pre-packaging film director. Indeed, this is a motion picture that liberates and revitalizes the act of looking at the world. Its geometric modern city planned and constructed by Tati himself, *Playtime* invites us to explore its vast spaces without a dictatorial guide. Just as Tati the actor refuses to use his character to guide the audience through the film, so does Tati the director refuse to use close-ups, emphatic camera angles, or montage to guide the audience to the humor in the images. *Playtime* is composed almost entirely of long-shot tableaux that leave the viewer free to pick up the gags that may be occurring in the foreground, the background, or off to the side. The film in this way returns an innocence of vision to the spectator, for no value judgments have been made or hierarchies of interest been established for him.

Playtime was a multimillion-dollar commercial failure, however, and since he had financed it himself, the director was nearly bankrupted. To recoup his losses, Tati made *Traffic* (1970), a minor Hulot film that comments upon the auto mania of modern industrial society. His last work was *Parade* (1974), a sixty-minute children's film made for Swedish television that featured Tati performing pantomimes at a circus show. After this, he developed the scenario for another Hulot film to be called *Confusion* but was unable to find backing for it. Although Jacques Tati had made only six features when he died at the age of seventy-four, in their blend of social satire, wry charm, imaginative physical gags, and ingenious aural as well as visual devices, these movies have not been surpassed by those of any other postwar cinematic comic—French or otherwise. Moreover, they deserve to be ranked with the greatest of silent film comedies.

The following interview took place in Paris in the summer of 1980, at the offices of *Cahiers du cinéma*.

Bert Cardullo: *Do you need to be a comic in order to be funny?*

Jacques Tati: What I tried to do from the beginning—since *Jour de fête* and even the first short that I made with René Clément—is to endow the comic character with more truth. There used to be a school of comic film in which the character entered, as it were, with a label reading: "You will see, I am the little entertainer of the evening, and I can do a whole lot of things: I can juggle, I can dance, I can act very well, I am a very good mime, I perform gags." It was the old circus school, or that of the music hall, which is about the same. What I have tried to do, for my part, is to prove and show that, all things considered, everyone is entertaining. There is no need to be a comic to perform a gag.

Once, for example, I saw a very serious gentleman who was on his way to some administrative board meeting—he really had the kind of hat you need for that kind of event. After locking the door on the driver's side of his car with the key, he remembered that he had forgotten to lock the door on the passenger's side: so he walked around the car to go lock the door from the outside. And, while locking it from the outside, he got his necktie stuck in the door. So he was stuck with the door locked and the key in hand, but he couldn't reach the door with the lock. Of course, it was easy for him to get out of that one—by taking off his necktie! Yet, while putting it on in the morning, he certainly didn't think he would have to take it off under such circumstances.

There is no need to be a great comic character in order to have something comical happen to you. The more formal an event, the more decorum surrounding it, the more comical it becomes. Once I saw on the news Albert Lebrun, the President of the Republic, who came to inaugurate the statue of the King of the Belgians. The audience was bent over double, and I must admit that there is not a single comic in the whole world who would have made people laugh like that guy. I must tell you that story, because it's something really terrific.

That day, it was raining. Lebrun was wearing a frock coat and was holding his top hat in his hand. And then someone brought him a bunch of flowers that was at least four meters high. The look he took at the flowers meant something like: "Now really, this is not possible: how I am going to manage?" Still, he made a first attempt: he handed his top hat to the first guy who was positioned next to him, a captain of the Republican Guard who was standing at attention with his saber. The Republican Guard looked as if he were saying: "But I can't put this on top of my saber for you; that would not be possible." Then, Lebrun made a second attempt (while all this was being filmed, and the people were wriggling with laughter), as he thought to himself: "I must absolutely get rid of this top hat." He looked around in the crowd for someone who could help him. He found another character who was also wearing a frock coat and who also had a top hat. And he gave *him* his top hat, so that the character in question found himself with two top hats. So, then, it became quite something! Lebrun managed to take his flowers and, as they were all setting off to go put the flowers down at the foot of the monument, the character in question—the one who had received the President's top hat—looked inside the hat to see where the President of the Republic had bought it! And nothing had been cut from the documentary film of this event. In fact, the guys had framed it all in a magnificent way!

BC: *Did you ever think about making a film without the character of Hulot?*

JT: Well, I tried to put him on exactly the same level—not in his behavior, because he has another nature—as, say, Monsieur Arpel, to take the example of *Mon Oncle*. Moreover, in *Les Vacances de Monsieur Hulot*, the character of the boy was almost more developed than that of M. Hulot. But, yes, I would have liked to be able to make a film without the character of Hulot—I make no mystery about it—and only with people I see, I observe, I meet in the street. I would have liked to prove to these individuals that, in spite of everything, something always happens to them within a week or a month that can create a comical effect. Comedy belongs to everybody.

In *Mon Oncle*, the maid is a comic character, the Italian merchant too, and so is the neighbor—she does much more than Hulot. One can reproach

Hulot—or at least me—for not developing his comic appeal, but each time he goes a little too far, people don't believe him anymore. I have even been obliged to cut some of his "business." I would like people to feel that the character of Hulot the uncle is not a circus character, to believe that he is really an uncle. People still tell the story of the mailman. For my part, I have moved a little beyond that. The mailman had his story told in *Jour de fête*, and I did not want to make a sequel to *Jour de fête* at all. Today—unless people saw the film and know the character and his profile—I could walk around with the same gait, the same way of wearing my hat, the same umbrella in London, Paris, or Berlin, and no one would think: "Who is that man who wants to play the fool in the street?" I could even perform the same gags, involving different people from those in the film, without any major difficulties. Well, almost!

BC: *Precisely, how does your comic talent differ from, say, Chaplin's?*

JT: I can give you a good example of that. There is no doubt that, when someone like me does or tries to do something comical, one systematically refers to Chaplin. He made fifty-seven or fifty-eight films, among which there were fifty-six successful ones—that's a fairly normal assessment of Chaplin's oeuvre. But people often don't know what they're talking about when they compare him with me; they get the styles confused, and that is very bad.

Take, for instance, a gag in *Les Vacances de Monsieur Hulot*. Monsieur Hulot arrives at the cemetery. He needs a crank to crankstart his car, so he looks for one in his trunk. While looking for the crank, he takes out a tire tube, the tube falls to the ground, the leaves stick to it, the tire tube is transformed into a funeral wreath, and—this wreath—the undertaker thinks that M. Hulot has just brought it.

You are going to say here: "Monsieur Hulot did not find any gag in this material." That's right: he didn't find any. What he did could have been done by any absentminded man who had no comic intention. The comic *invention* comes from the screenwriter or from the situation, but what happened to Monsieur Hulot could happen to a lot of people. There are many Hulots in life, come to think of it. He didn't invent anything!

In Chaplin's case, if he had found the gag good enough to put in his film—which I am not so sure about—he would have made the same entrance as Hulot, but, seeing that the situation was turning into a catastrophe (there is a religious ceremony and his car trouble interrupts it), he would have ended up with a tire tube in his hand after opening the trunk and would have stuck the leaves on the tube by himself. *For the viewers*, he would have transformed the tube into a funeral wreath, and it would have been accepted as such by the undertaker supervising the service. And the viewers would have found this character wonderful because, at the very moment when no one could have come up with anything to get him out of this situation, he invented—on the screen, for the viewers—a gag. And it is this gag that would have caused the laughter and would have made people say, "He was great." You cannot say that about Hulot. He was not great, because it could have happened to you, to anybody: you are looking for something in a car, something falls out of it, you pick it up—that's normal. This is where you feel that there are really two completely different, totally opposed schools, because Hulot never invents anything and Chaplin is always inventing something.

BC: *Indeed, what is typical of the Tramp is his immense facility for adaptation, combined, paradoxically, with his naïveté. Hulot, on the other hand, is passive. Moreover, in the way you present matters, you don't change things—you just make sure people see them.*

JT: Let me tell you something here that I would have liked to put in a film if it had been possible. One day, I saw a man who wanted an oil change; as he was in a hurry, he stayed in his car, saying: "I don't have time, so hurry up; besides, I must read my paper." The attendants then raised him, in his automobile, about two meters high. This man was very fat, sitting there in his car reading his paper. The men started changing the oil underneath him, and then I realized one got the impression that the guy was sitting on a toilet.

Now lots of people would have gone by without seeing him; but for me, this is the kind of detail that is irresistible. I wanted to stop passersby and tell them, "Look," and then I thought to myself: "No, that would of course be very rude, very vulgar, not particularly refined." Nonetheless, seeing a man sitting in a car with, well, you have seen an oil change for yourself—the scene was simply mind-boggling. It is a pity you cannot put that into a film. I am convinced there are very often situations such that there is no need to be a comic in order to experience or undergo them. In *Mon Oncle*, the maid, by contrast, does perform a real number, but if she did that in a house . . .

BC: *Yours is the reversal of the traditional equation in comic films where you have a normal world confronted by a comical character—Chaplin, for instance. Hulot, on the contrary, is the most normal of your characters, and the world is made comical precisely because Hulot is not.*

JT: That's exactly right. You will see why. Imagine Hulot enlisted in the army. A real tough guy comes to talk to the colonel and says: "Look, pal, I would like to know what we are going to do this afternoon; it can't go on like this, because we are bored stiff." The colonel immediately punishes him with eight days in the stockade, lots of chores, or something of the kind. Now the character of Hulot comes to see the colonel, takes off his cap (he does not salute), and says very politely, "Good morning, colonel!" "Stand at attention!" barks the colonel. Hulot stands at attention. "Do you know where I can find a hairbrush?" asks Hulot. The colonel thinks to himself, "I cannot possibly punish this guy with eight days in jail, for he approached me very politely and even bowed." The colonel's rank naturally forbids him from answering, "You can certainly get a hairbrush at the quartermaster's stores." So, this time, it is the colonel who feels embarrassed; it is he who finds himself in a comical situation. He is the one who makes us laugh, because he is the one who is asking himself what attitude he should take. To stall, he can perhaps push his cap slightly to the side, put his hands in his pockets, whistle, kick a pebble, even take something out of his pocket that he does not really need. And it is Hulot who will have put him in this situation. But he will have done so unwittingly. Come to think of it, Hulot is really naïve.

This is why those who prefer this kind of entertainment, who like to laugh in this way, go see a film of mine two, three, even four times. And conversely, I can understand very well why some people want to leave halfway through the film. They say, "I don't understand at all why people find this funny," because, in order to appreciate such humor, you probably have to bring to it what these folks can't: a little self-scrutiny.

BC: *You cannot possibly identify with Hulot; neither can you identify with those whom or that which he ridicules, since the nature of a comic is to laugh at the expense of someone: one would have to laugh at oneself at that very moment. One is put in a situation that is not subsumed under any of the comic categories—a situation, in fact, that is completely new.*

JT: When I saw the audience of *Les Vacances de Monsieur Hulot*, I wished I had put up a sign before the screening with some explanations or pointers: "You're about to go on holiday, you are going to see people you know and others you know less. . . ." The viewer must make a little effort, I think, to enter the comic universe created by Hulot. If he expects tricks or gags from Hulot, he will undoubtedly be disappointed. He thinks to himself: "Why doesn't this character come up with something, why doesn't he defend himself?" For it is his defense that would make this viewer laugh. Chaplin's

Jacques Tati (left) in *Monsieur Hulot's Holiday.*

comic system itself is partly based on deception, which makes the spectators laugh a lot, because in deception there is invention. Look first of all at the two characters' heights, which are completely opposed. Hulot is tall, and he cannot hide—he cannot conceal himself behind a lamppost or anything else—whereas Chaplin could hide behind a small trash can, leave his hat on the can, then sneak behind another small can, while making people believe that he was still in back of the first one, whereupon he would come back to grab his hat. Hulot, by contrast, has the stature of a rather steady or stand-up guy; he behaves exactly like any man from Paris or even from the provinces.

BC: *Especially in* Mon Oncle. *And his absence, from that point of view, is telling. Ultimately, he could almost be completely absent.*

JT: That would be the ideal film. I would like people to see Hulot less and less and to see other people or characters more and more.

BC: *You want to make him intervene from a distance, only through his moral attitude?*

JT: Precisely.

BC: *Instead of Chaplin, one would have to mention someone like Buster Keaton with regard to Hulot.*

JT: Yes, because he does not construct a system or instigate an action: he *undergoes an experience.* Do you remember the gag in *The Navigator?* You know, when he goes to hang the captain's portrait. As the ship is reeling, you can see through the porthole the face of a guy who seems to be checking out what he himself is doing: it is irresistible. I saw that at the Edinburgh Festival. All morning long, they were presenting comic sketches from all the comics since the beginning, starting with Little Tich. You could sense a very clear difference between each artist's technique, on the one hand, and his formula for getting laughs, on the other hand.

The sketch featuring Little Tich was dazzling. His filmed music-hall bit was so simple yet filled with such vigor that it was stunning. Then came Harry Langdon, whose comedy was very refined and very personal; next Chaplin; then Max Linder, who constructed his gags more or less in a way that anticipated Chaplin. At the end, they projected a scene from *Les Vacances de Monsieur Hulot* and one could really sense that Hulot was continuing the comic tradition; he belonged to the same cinematic school, but without concessions. What is important about Hulot is that there are no concessions. Once the gag is finished, matters don't go any further; the formula is not exploited. Lots of people have reproached me for this, incidentally. But to return to my very first example, the man with his necktie, his two car doors, and his key, that is *all* that happened to him. Granted, the situation could have been exploited further: his wife could have come by and caught him in the company of a young woman who had come to help him, etc. Under the pretext that "this is entertainment," one could have gone on and on. But not at all: what is funny is precisely the fact that it stops where it stops.

BC: *Conversely, in Chaplin, there is the combination of extreme economy in the scenic element with a maximum of theatrical exploitation. For example, in* The Circus, *in the scene where he is locked up in the lions' cage, there is a mind-boggling chain of gags carried to its logical extreme. Let's take an example from* Mon Oncle *as a contrast. The gag with the espalier tree begins approximately halfway through the film and strangely reappears toward the end. Could you explain to me what your intentions were there, as well as the mechanism of the gag?*

JT: The nephew, the Arpel son, gets along very well with his uncle. By accident, he breaks a little branch on his family's espalier tree. So when the uncle arrives, his nephew goes to see him and asks him to fix the damage.

The uncle then cuts, which is the only thing to do; but, as he cuts, he realizes that the damage has become even more obvious. And, little by little, he is about to cut off everything. Right at that point, Madame Arpel comes by—let us not forget that we are at a reception—and the guy cannot go on doing his particular number.

Now, in the past, only the spectators used to watch what was happening on the screen; the actors who surrounded the comic never realized, or showed they realized, that they were in the middle of a gag. But I always do the contrary: the actors are on the same level as the viewers and realize at the same time that some gentleman has, say, forgotten to close the door. In Laurel-and-Hardy movies, you could see people tossing custard pies, pots, and pans, yet the others on screen looked as though they were going about their business without noticing in the least that some fellow was walking around with a pot on his head.

So, the arrival of Madame Arpel interrupts the uncle's trimming of the tree. When the reception is over—no one is left, the garden is empty, the Arpels are going to bed—it is time to finish the job. I refer to the short sequence at night—suspense, as it were, around the escalier tree. We guess—at least that's what I think people guess—that Hulot is finishing the work he started. And then there's no mention of it anymore. There are no more reasons to mention it. Moreover, if Madame Arpel does not go out there the following morning, she does not see the tree. When our children break something in my mother's garden, we don't see it five minutes later; most likely we find it the following Sunday. It is only the day after the next that Monsieur Arpel, coming home, sees the trim-job in his headlights—and the job, I admit, is a real catastrophe. This sequence may be very badly constructed for a film, but, in reality, I think it would have happened in such a way.

BC: *This tendency of yours is much more obvious in* Mon Oncle *than in* Les Vacances de Monsieur Hulot. Mon Oncle *thus seems to me to be a greater act of aesthetic daring than* Les Vacances de Monsieur Hulot, *even as Hulot was in comparison to* Jour de fête. *And* Jour de fête *itself was already daring when compared to traditional comic films. The comical nature of the universe surrounding Hulot in* Mon Oncle *makes this an almost "Martian" film—one that does not resemble in the least anything we are used to seeing in the cinema.*

JT: After *Les Vacances de Monsieur Hulot*, I said to myself: "It's a pity I didn't shoot the film in color." I must admit that color often gets in the way of either a dramatic effect or an actor's work. The presence of a very good actor is more visible in black and white, because one does not focus on anything other than his expressions, his gestures, and his voice. Every time we find an actor stunning in a film, most often, even if we don't realize it, the film was shot in black and white.

But for *Les Vacances de Monsieur Hulot*, I regret that I did not use color. The shades of color on the beach in the small striped tents, in the people who get a tan little by little—all that I would have liked to show. Color would have given the film some additional truth, because when you remember some scenes or pictures from your holidays, you remember them in color. You dream in black and white—I do, at any rate—but the images from vacation, those are in color. Whatever the case, color can be an extraordinary asset. So, I said to myself: "I am going to tell the story of *Mon Oncle* in color." The shades of color that you find in a modern neighborhood are completely different from those you find in an old neighborhood. The greens have become very bright, the yellows look almost as if they come from electric lamps. The Americans have worked a lot on color processing, and they use quite a lot of bright colors in their movies. By contrast, in that little old neighborhood where we shot *Mon Oncle*, I had to work with old, velvety colors.

That was my first starting point. Then, I said to myself: "I must make my actors move, not my camera." People have often reproached me in the following way: "Tati does not use technique much!" I am sorry, but I know very well what a traveling shot is. I can also put a camera on a crane and raise it five or six meters high: all I have to do is sit next to the cameraman and say, "Let's go up!" And I know how to use a panoramic shot to follow whatever I want. Now I am not saying that technique cannot serve the dramatic construction of a film that absolutely requires it—where, for example, it is absolutely necessary to crawl with a gentleman in order to see what he sees while he is crawling.

But my story in *Mon Oncle* is completely different: it takes place in two settings and I want to see the characters evolve in those settings. I am certain that, after you have seen the film, you could very well be invited to the Arpels' and know exactly that this button is on your left, that the water starts flowing when the bell rings, that Madame Arpel makes you visit her living room, that the child's bedroom is on one side . . . and I think I have told a story with pictures. In the second version that I made, I shortened the movie's first, short conversation, which was really without interest; it even encumbered the picture, so to speak, preventing you from seeing what needed to be seen. The story is better told with pictures, sound, and music. Indeed, *Mon Oncle* is almost a silent film.

BC: *There are no camera movements at all in* Mon Oncle?

JT: There are some movements, but you do not sense them. I tried to give the impression of relief or perspective through the static shot. I did not even change lenses. If you change lenses, you change everything: your chair no longer looks the same, the difference between objects is altered, and space itself changes. If I photograph you with one lens, for example, and change to another when I come closer, I make the surface of your seatback larger: it is therefore no longer the same chair. In color this is even more obvious, because the shapes change but the salient colors remain the same. What is also important in the use of color is not to put colors in places where people shouldn't be looking. If the main actor wears a dark gray or ivory necktie and a meaningless extra wears a blue one, automatically people will focus on the extra and will consequently miss something that the main character does or says. You must always increase the importance of a character through color. Arpel, who dresses like a pseudo-gypsy, is wearing a pigskin jacket, a real pigskin jacket, at the reception, whereas the neighbor is in red, because she is important and you will have to follow her at this event. In fact, the reception is given in her honor!

BC: *Did you use a shooting script on the set?*

JT: I worked a lot on my story, but, no, I didn't bring a shooting script to the set. I knew the film by heart and I shot it out of memory. In the evening, I started by repeating the story to myself: I saw the pictures come before my mind's eye and I learned them by heart. Then, on the set, I knew exactly what I was going to ask the actors to do and what I was going to do: I didn't need to go looking for the information on a piece of paper. And since I knew the story by heart, I could lose or invest myself in it fully, without holding back. Does that smack of too much artifice?

BC: *No, it smacks of consciousness of the relations among all the elements of cinema. You were at the same time free and restrictive. Nothing was haphazard, yet there was room to improvise.*

JT: But I didn't improvise. I knew everything in advance. I did the editing while I was shooting; I edited the film in my head, out of memory. Really, I assure you, in all my films I did absolutely everything I wanted to do. If you don't like that, or them, I am the only one to blame.

I am extremely worried when I see so many good filmmakers who are obliged to submit to all kinds of constraints. Today, all you have are constraints, everywhere. But I was able to make my film where I wanted, in

Saint-Maur, and I was able to build the house I wanted for Hulot. I think this is important in the end. There aren't that many countries today where a guy in the movie business can say, "Not only did I make a film, but I also made the film that I wanted to make." Bresson is just such a director, and I love what he does. I find it a shame that he doesn't make more films.

BC: *Indeed, you were the only two French filmmakers who did exactly what you wanted to do, and who had enough stubbornness to endure from the moment your film began shooting to the moment it got released. In Bresson's case, of course, he is still doing exactly what he wants to do in the cinema.*

JT: What is really a shame is that only one door is open to young filmmakers: that of commercial cinema. And this is very dangerous. After *Jour de fête*, and more so after *Les Vacances de Monsieur Hulot*, I had some offers to go and make a Franco-Italian co-production. It was to be called *Totò and Tati*. You get the idea! I said to myself: "No! Hulot does not have the obligation to be in *Totò and Tati*." It's not that Totò is bad: in fact he is a very good actor; but the simple fact that the picture was going to be called *Totò and Tati* already tells you more than you want to know. I believe that one's artistic independence is a must, and it is up to the individual to defend it in all cases.

And yet, it is difficult to resist commerce when you realize that by making one such film or by accepting one such role, you will earn a sum of money that will enable you to change your life a bit, have more pleasures, have your house repainted, even change houses. In this modern world, people are, after all, and no matter what, extremely driven by their material needs; money impresses them and, in the end, they will make quite a lot of concessions—not only artistic ones, alas—to achieve a more luxurious lifestyle. As for me, it is not courage that makes me resist; commercial considerations simply leave me cold.

Nonetheless, I have a lot of fun: I take strolls with Madame Tati, we go to little cafés, we make friends with the waiter, he tells us stories, so does the boss, and his wife has different stories from her husband's. We are never bored, never; there is always something to do. I confess that ending up one day in the Arpel house does not appeal to me in the least.

Above all, I love to whistle, and I think that the day I will no longer be able to whistle in the street—this will be a very bad day, indeed. They may look stupid, but I like people who whistle in the street. Sometimes when I get out of the editing room, I whistle. And, you know, I believe that this has great importance. I don't know whether you can feel it in my films—I may not have made the matter clear—but what I condemn in the "new" life is precisely the disappearance of any respect for the individual.

In the past, in a garage, there could be somebody called Monsieur Marcel. Monsieur Marcel had his screwdriver; he was the foreman; and, when you came to see Monsieur Marcel, he listened to the sound of your engine, even as a good doctor listens to your heart. Then, just by using his screwdriver, he made your car burn up two liters of gas less per one hundred kilometers such that you could drive ten kilometers an hour faster. There are so many exceptional guys like Monsieur Marcel among technicians, you can't even imagine! But these days, I have the impression that, with all these mechanics dressed like navy officers, one no longer gets the chance to chat with a Monsieur Marcel: his screwdriver has been put away; now they just change your engine: there's no need to fix it anymore.

Related to this, I miss the old buses with their open-air upper decks. The new buses have lost their personality. In Paris, these platforms were wonderful meeting places. And everyone had his own way of pulling the little chain to request a stop. Some pulled it eccentrically, others made it twirl, still others had discovered the secret way to make the bus stop at once: three little pulls, then one more pull. There were conversations, too, lots of them. Today people get on the bus, and, inside, it may be more practical, but I'm not so sure: the driver is in a glass cage, and one no longer knows whether one should buy a movie or bus ticket from him; he deals with you through a small porthole but he does not answer you, for he cannot. People must wait in line, whereas this process used to go much faster: you just stepped onto some stairs, everyone pushed, you climbed, and, in brief, you got to your place.

These days, I feel sad because I have the impression that people are having less and less fun. They obviously dress better, they clearly wash more, they certainly have more hot water, they surely imbibe cooler drinks; and now their windows are larger, which means that they can get additional sun, but, in the past, they lived on the street more and got all the sun they wanted there.

I had some proof of this because we had to shoot *Mon Oncle* in two different neighborhoods. In the modern neighborhood—the big buildings of Créteil—we couldn't get a hammer, a broom, or a wheelbarrow. There is a Board of Administrators, there is a Superintendent of Buildings, there is another man in charge of all the rooms; ultimately, there are so many forms you have to fill out just to get a wheelbarrow that we gave up. "I have a six-year-old son and a four-year-old daughter," a tenant told me, "and within the first week of my stay there, I received a report, as they say in the army, because the kids walked on the grass." For the kids, you know, they built small playgrounds in cement with some sand here and there. The grass is nice, but if you may not even walk on it, what's the point?

In the small neighborhood of Saint-Maur, by contrast, the three tenants on the ground floor, who were living in only one room (get this!), built us a small makeup area with a partition around it—inside their own room! They even gave us the key. On the same street, there is a lady who buys groceries for her neighbors. I felt that these people knew one another and helped each other out. We could get everything we wanted on the market square of Saint-Maur and on that particular street. It was really incredible!

Well, I have the impression that this kind of generosity has almost disappeared from our world. People don't stop their cars anymore at pedestrian crossings. They drive right through because they're in a hurry. They don't really know where they're going, though; and the Americans have gone to the moon—to the moon! Today, with all this so-called progress, the only pleasure left to a Parisian who wants to leave the capital on a Sunday, after working all week long, is to stay for four hours behind the wheel of his car one way and four hours on the way back, just to go take a breath of fresh air in the country for the three remaining hours.

The situation in the United States is comparable or worse, wouldn't you say? Today, an American, because of his neighbors and because of advertisements, cannot possibly think of keeping his car for more than one year. In 1978, it is impossible for him to drive a 1977 car because the newer automobile has an engine with increased horsepower! In the past, when people bought a new car, it was extremely important; you went to the garage for a test drive and thought about the matter for days! Today, an eight- or nine-year-old American kid just sees that the new car's door handle is slightly different, and he knows that it will change again in 1979; he has no respect anymore, so he puts his feet up on the seat cushions and throws his candy wrappers on the floor. Everything is like that now. And when the kid gets angry, well, he starts shooting! You know that this is a problem in America—the kids in the street scare you to death.

I believe it's important that children once used to shine the hubcaps, that their mother made the seat covers herself, that the whole family participated together in something. Now people don't participate in anything anymore; there is nothing to do, nothing left to work at. Everything changes constantly, including toys. Each time one of them breaks, the parents say, "Well, we'll just buy another one!" I had little children once, too, and therefore all these matters worry me a lot. One day, around tea time, I said to my kids, "Let's go camping and make our own tea!" So we started looking for firewood, we made a fire, and we boiled the water. My children then spent a wonderful afternoon, because they had something to do. But today, no one has time to look after children anymore. I believe that, in the past, my parents had a little more time to spend with us! We lived in Saint-Germain-en-Laye, and my father worked in Paris; it took him an hour to get there, yet I passed many enjoyable hours with him and my mother.

I wanted to express all of that, as it were, in *Mon Oncle*. We are losing it, all this simplicity, and that's what is worrying me. Especially in a country like ours, which used to be great! I wrote a story by the way—no one wanted to film it—about the occupation of Germany by the French. Yes, in 1943, I saw the Germans occupied by the French: since all their soldiers had left for the front and they had previously requisitioned numerous French chefs, engineers, civil servants, and laborers, there were all these Frenchmen in Germany, a kind of French resistance everywhere, which would have been a great subject for a movie. In Berlin, you could find a Frenchman who sold meat across the street from the zoo and made a lot of money—selling it to French people rather than to Germans, whom he told that supplies were scarce.

The Italians forced to work in Germany did something rather similar. This is a good topic, right? It's no use showing the Occupation here: everyone lived under it and it was far from being funny; but there, it was extremely comical. When I said I wanted to make a film about this subject, I was told: "What are you thinking? It's not possible!" I admit that perhaps it was not the thing to do, but this was truly a very funny situation. Picture in your mind's eye a Nazi captain, a warrior carved in oak who is thirsty for a drink, and then, behind the bar, a French guy who has just downed a carafe of wine, but who tells the German that there isn't a bottle left in the house!

What bothers me most today is that Paris itself is being destroyed. This really aggravates me. If we need additional housing, and God knows we do, let's build new cities; there is enough room. But we should not demolish nice old buildings in Paris for the sake of new apartment buildings. Paris will end up looking like Hamburg. And it is uniformity that I dislike. You go to a café on the Champs-Elysées these days and you get the impression that they will soon announce the landing of Flight 412; you don't know anymore if you are in a pharmacy or a grocery store. In the past, everything had flavor. I remember going to a delicatessen once with my grandmother: there was some sawdust on the floor, they cut us thin slices of salami to give us a taste of it, the room smelled deliciously of oak and pepper. Today, when you go to a restaurant it's as if you were eating in a clinic; people sit in windows and when you pass in front of a snack bar, you can see people's socks. Snack bars seem to have been created so that you can stand at attention even when you're eating—your whole life through, as a matter of fact.

No, I don't agree, not at all. Either that or people like me have not been able to adapt; all this change came too fast. It came so fast that lots of people have been left behind. And what are we to do with them now? Before, the Parisian guy riding his bicycle used to whistle. Now, he has a small engine in the rear! You will protest: "It's more practical, because now he doesn't have to pedal anymore." All right, but that small engine means you can't hear him whistle anymore, if in fact he is still whistling. And you can forget about having a savory conversation anywhere, let alone with a stranger on the street.

BC: *Of course, I am also sensitive to these matters. All the same, things change. There is between the modern bus and the bus with the open-air upper deck the same difference as between the horse-drawn trolley and the older bus.*

JT: But no, not at all! Change has been proceeding too rapidly for the last four or five years. You told me a moment ago in a very nice way, which moved me a lot, that Monsieur Bresson and I were the only ones who assumed we had the right to do whatever we wanted in the cinema. Why is that? Perhaps because we were the only ones left who actually were willing to fight for that right.

BC: *To be sure, there are things for which it is worth fighting. But you cannot dispute the fact that, because the population of Paris is growing, one needs to make traffic more fluid and one needs more high-rise apartment buildings. What one can do, however, is have a more acute consciousness of what one loses with the disappearance of buses with open-air upper decks. And your films give us that consciousness.*

JT: Yes, people say, "Tati took more than two years to make a film." I can assure you, though, that I was not wasting my time. I worked every day, every day. I could have gone as fast as the new buses; and, if I had done so, a film would have taken me only three weeks to complete. But I don't think I could have made *Mon Oncle* or any picture of quality in three weeks! Not even in three months.

I was once offered an incredible contract to make, every week, a comic film for American television. This contract was supposed to last for thirty-seven or thirty-eight weeks. With the money they were promising me, I certainly could have bought a lot of things!

BC: *Please excuse me for playing the devil's advocate. But instead of saying, "I certainly could have bought a lot of things," you might have said, "I could have made* Mon Oncle *and any other films I so desired."*

JT: What if I was able to make *Mon Oncle* and other films without the American money?

BC: *You were able to make* Mon Oncle *thanks to the success of* Jour de fête *and* Les Vacances de Monsieur Hulot. *But what if those two films had not been successful?*

JT: Then, I would have raised the necessary money in a different way. Personally, I could not film something that I didn't want to film. I'd rather go back to doing music-hall sketches. But when you have chosen to make your career in the cinema, which is wonderful, you must admit—I live for the movies, after all—you must make your film the way you want to, or else you must get out. For instance, if Fellini needs me for a particular reason (there was once talk of an Italian film of *Don Quixote*), or say that Bresson is looking for a guy like Hulot to play a special part, then, yes, I feel that I would do it. What worries me is your story about the bus that must go faster or must be more streamlined. When I see someone, in Boulogne, who is going to make a 350-million-franc film in thirty-seven days, whatever you may say, I don't believe it. You cannot, in thirty-seven days, tell a very important story. I was extremely inspired by *Une Partie de campagne* by Renoir, I must admit, but I am certain that it was not made in twenty-four hours. You can feel it there more than in any other film: the long time required to do such extraordinarily good work, especially in the creation of the characters.

Now, really, cinema should have continued a little bit as it was. What troubles me is that young filmmakers today may no longer choose their story, may no longer choose their actors, may no longer do whatever they want. These days, filmmaking has become an industry, on the same level as the car industry. In the past, there used to be twenty-six car manufacturers: today, there are only four left. And in America, there are only four big corporations remaining that make films; in France, as well, you will soon have only three movie companies left. Soon people will start telling you: "To make a good film, here is the recipe: you need a good story. In theory, it's better if you choose a best-selling book, because then you can be sure that your story is good. You give it to Monsieur X and Monsieur Y to adapt because they know their business, too. Next, you give it to Monsieur Whatshisname, who has never flubbed a traveling shot in his life and who is therefore a very good cameraman. After that, hire the very best editor, whose name is Monsieur Whatchamacallit and who edits wonderfully well. And then, when the editing is finished, get such-and-such a musician, because every time he plays something, it is a hit." You put all that together and, commercially, the thing will hold water. That is also true for a 403 Peugeot car, however. You get the best cushions, the best gear box, the best engine, you put everything together, and you can be certain that it will work! But the cinema is not, or should not be, a mass-produced automobile.

Some day, I would like to meet a young person who will take me to the movies to see something—be it long, short, or medium-length—with characters who move as I have never seen them move, with sounds that I have never heard, or with a story that I could never have imagined. Even if there is no story at all, even if you have to look for it, or if you can find it immediately but then find out that it's not the real one—but *something*. But no, the silence is total!

Jacques Tati Filmography

Jour de fête (1948)
Les Vacances de M. Hulot (*Monsieur Hulot's Holiday*, 1953)
Mon Oncle (1958)
Playtime (1967)
Traffic (1971)
Parade (1974)

Bibliography

Bellos, David. *Jacques Tati*. London: Harvill, 1999.

Chion, Michel. *The Films of Jacques Tati*. Toronto: Guernica, 1997.

Fischer, Lucy. *Jacques Tati: A Guide to References and Resources*. Boston: G. K. Hall, 1983.

Gilliatt, Penelope. *Jacques Tati*. London: Woburn, 1976.

Harding, James. *Jacques Tati: Frame by Frame*. London: Secker & Warburg, 1984.

Maddock, Brent. *The Films of Jacques Tati*. Metuchen, N.J.: Scarecrow, 1977.

~

An Auteur for All Seasons

An Interview with Eric Rohmer

Eric Rohmer (1920–2010) was a French film director, screenwriter, and film critic. A major figure in the postwar New Wave cinema, he was once an editor of the influential periodical *Cahiers du cinéma*.

Rohmer was the last of the French New Wave directors to become established. He worked as an editor of *Cahiers du cinéma* from 1957 to 1963 while most of his *Cahiers* colleagues—among them Jean-Luc Godard and François Truffaut—were beginning their directing careers and gaining international attention. After directing several shorts, Rohmer made a series of *contes moraux* ("moral tales") that brought him to international attention; among them were *My Night at Maud's* (1968), *Claire's Knee* (1970), and *Chloe in the Afternoon* (1972), each a sensitively observed study of romantic love. His later films included *The Marquise of O . . .* (1976), *Full Moon in Paris* (1984), and *Autumn Tale* (1999). In Rohmer's obituary in the *Daily Telegraph* he was described as "the most durable filmmaker of the French New Wave," outlasting his peers and "still making movies the public wanted to see" late in his career.

The following interview—possibly Rohmer's last—took place in April 2008 in Eric Rohmer's office in a Paris apartment building.

Bert Cardullo: *I'd like to focus our discussion today on your* Six Moral Tales, *M. Rohmer, because they constitute your first, and arguably most important, series, to be followed of course by the* Comedies and Proverbs *and the* Tales of the Four Seasons.

Eric Rohmer: That's fine with me. It was with the *Moral Tales*, you know, that I came to the conclusion that audiences and producers would be more likely to accept my ideas in this form than in any other. Instead of asking myself what subjects were most likely to appeal to audiences, I persuaded myself that the best thing would be to treat the same subject six times over—in the hope that by the sixth time the audience would come over to me. It is better, in fact, to see the *Moral Tales*—and the *Tales of the Four Seasons* or the *Comedies and Proverbs*—as a distinct collection. There is a relationship between all the films in each of these three series, and that is where the real interest lies. The public often tells me that I make films which resemble each other, and it is right, but this is normal on my part because I am a complete auteur—that is, someone who creates the film, who treats the subject, and at the same time I am the man who shapes the image.

BC: *Let's begin with a little background. What happened to the French New Wave, anyway?*

ER: Well, it's not the New Wave anymore, I can tell you that! We're old now. Obviously Truffaut died some time ago, but both Claude Chabrol and Jacques Rivette have made films recently, and Godard—I understand that he is preparing to make another film. If we have the same cinema as when we started out, or if we have evolved, it's not up to me to say. It's true that Godard has probably grown more as a filmmaker, but he has grown away from the public, whereas Chabrol has become a more commercial filmmaker. Still, I think we are all loyal, more or less, to the same principles we had when we first constituted the New Wave. Myself, I have kept the same idea of cinema and I always do my films in my own little way: films that are not too expensive. I like shooting nature, even when I am in a studio, and I give extra importance to the poetry of cinematography. So I am still very much adhering to the theories I expounded in my early film articles.

As for the accusation I sometimes hear that I am not "modernist" or "leftist" enough, I say that I am not afraid of not being modern; you have to go against the grain of the times, I believe. That said, I have always been interested in using new technology. The first article I ever wrote—even before my work for *Cahiers du cinéma*—was for a journal called *Revue du cinéma*, and it was on the use of color over black and white. This was at a time when most people preferred black and white, but I thought, as I do now, that there was room for both. And I said so. I also championed the use of direct-sync sound in this early piece.

BC: *Have you always been interested in the cinema?*

ER: No, I couldn't say that. I became interested in cinema very late, when I was a student. Up until then I despised the cinema; I didn't like it—I just liked reading, painting, and then music a little later. I didn't take any part in theater, I didn't go to it very much. I liked the classical French theater of Racine, Corneille, Molière, but to read it rather than see it. I came to like cinema because I liked silent films, but I didn't discover film through just going to the movies.

BC: *And then you began to write for* Cahiers du cinéma?

ER: No. When I discovered the silent film, I wanted to make films. I tried to make amateur films, but I didn't have any money, I didn't have any equipment; I didn't have anything at all, and so I had difficulties. I joined film societies and got involved in organizing these, and I made friends there and with these friends we had the idea—we were all very young then—of publishing a Film Societies Bulletin; we even wanted to start a critical review. It was at the time when *L'Ecran Français* had just folded and there was no longer any weekly film journal. So we tried to found a very small film journal, for we didn't have much money, and we published five issues of it, one a month for five months. It was called the *Gazette du cinéma* and was in the same format as *Combat* was at that time. And those who wrote for that review besides myself were Jacques Rivette, who published his first article there, and Jean-Luc Godard also published his first article there. I don't think Truffaut wrote for it, but he was one of our friends. As for Chabrol, he didn't write for it, either, though I knew him by then.

After the *Gazette du cinéma*, there was the magazine to which I previously referred, called *Revue du cinéma*, which after the war had gone through various stages; the first series of the *Revue du cinéma* had appeared in the 1930s. It was founded by a critic named Jean Georges Auriol, then it disappeared, and it reappeared after the war, published by Gallimard. It was for this *Revue du cinéma* that André Bazin wrote; the editor was Jacques Doniol-Valcroze. Then Jean Georges Auriol died in an accident and Gallimard stopped publishing it. So Jacques Doniol-Valcroze and André Bazin decided to start another film journal with the help of a distributor in Paris called Léonide de Quéjème, who acted as a silent partner in this venture. So they began to publish *Cahiers du cinéma*—they wanted to keep the title *Revue du cinéma* but as that still belonged to Gallimard they couldn't. And very different kinds of people, lots of them, started off writing for that review. There was a little core of young men who were known as the young Turks because they had rather violent ideas, and these were François Truffaut, Jacques Rivette, Jean-Luc Godard, Claude Chabrol, and yours truly; André Bazin called us "Hitchcocko-Hawksians" because we admired both Alfred Hitchcock and Howard Hawks. I made my début as a critic as a member of this group. On the whole we were very unified because we had very similar tastes.

Then Truffaut wrote a violent article for *Cahiers du cinéma* attacking the French "cinema of quality," people like Autant-Lara, René Clément, and so on. A weekly magazine called *Arts* noticed this piece and asked François Truffaut to become its film critic, or at least to write some film criticism for it. Truffaut was still very young, only twenty-one or twenty-two, when he became the film critic for *Arts*; as there were plenty of films to write about and he couldn't handle them all himself, he called on his friends and most of the *Cahiers* people lent a hand, especially myself. For a time Truffaut and I did all the film reviews for *Arts*. At this time the *Cahiers* people were spreading out to all the magazines: André Bazin, for example, had begun writing for the *Nouvel Observateur*.

BC: *During this time did you still want to make films yourself?*

ER: I hadn't given up the idea—we all tried now and then—but it was very difficult. We all had made some amateur films, using whatever means we could, but in general these films weren't very successful because we didn't have anything—not even a camera. When we asked people to lend us their cameras they wanted to do the camerawork themselves, and sometimes the photography was pretty bad as a result. So we had problems. Then my own story gets entwined with that of the New Wave, at least with the most important part of it because most of the New Wave people were also *Cahiers* people. We didn't call ourselves that—it was the press that decided there was now a New Wave. And it was Chabrol who got us started, for he had succeeded in making a film, *Le beau Serge*, without having done anything before, by setting up his own production company with money of his own. He was very worried because the film almost didn't get released, and if it hadn't, then the entire adventure of the New Wave might have stopped there; but Chabrol succeeded in making the film and even in making another one, *Les Cousins*, because his first film impressed the state committee that gave out subsidies and so he got a subsidy to make another one. Then *Le beau Serge* was finally released and was a big success.

A little after Chabrol came Truffaut's *The Four Hundred Blows*, though this wasn't his first film as he had already made a short in 35mm, *Les Mistons*. Then, or even a little before that, in an almost desperate attempt, for he had practically no money—nothing but the film stock itself—Rivette made *Paris Belongs to Us*, but he too had previously made a short film, *Le Coup du Berger*. I, too, had made some 16mm films, but my first real film was produced by Chabrol's production company in 1959, a year after *Les Cousins*, and that was *Le Signe du Lion*. And at the same time Godard was making *Breathless*, but he turned to a producer outside the *Cahiers* group, Georges de Beauregard, and that's how he met Raoul Coutard. In any event that's how I got started, at the same time as what came to be called the New Wave.

BC: *Then you began your series of* Contes Moraux *with two films in 16mm?*

ER: Yes, the first two are in 16mm. This was because the New Wave had by now established itself, and those whose films had done well were setting out on successful careers, but those whose films hadn't done so well, like myself with *Le Signe du Lion*, were having problems continuing. So I decided to go on filming, no matter what, and instead of looking for a subject that might be attractive to the public or a producer, I decided that I would find a subject that *I* liked and that a producer would refuse. So here you have someone doing exactly what he wants to. And as you can't do that in 35mm, I made the films in 16mm. That way it didn't cost very much, just the price of the film stock; and I found people willing to work for me out of friendship, either as technicians or actors. The first was a very short film, only twenty-five minutes long, the second a bit longer than that; and then I decided to make the third, which was *La Collectionneuse* [1967], and I realized that, as long as you were economical in the amount of film you used, it wouldn't really cost much more to work in 35mm, especially if you used color. Fortunately, I met a friend who could advance me enough to pay for film stock and we used 5,000 meters for a film that ended up being 2,500 meters long—that means almost a 2:1 shooting ratio, which is very economical. And that is how I made what turned out to be the feature-length *La Collectionneuse*, with virtually no money.

BC: *Can you tell me something about the subject matter of these first two films?*

ER: In the first two *Contes Moraux*, I'm telling the story of a young man who meets up with a young woman precisely at the time when he's looking for another woman. You find this idea very clearly in the first film, *The Bakery Girl of Monceau* [1963], which is about a boy who sees a girl in the street and falls in love but doesn't know how to become acquainted with her. He tries to follow her to find out where she lives, but loses track of her. So he makes up his mind to conduct a systematic search for the girl, and, though he usually eats in a restaurant frequented by students, he decides to go without dinner and use the time to look for her in the district where he thinks she lives. When the young man gets hungry while exploring the area, he goes into a bakery shop and buys some cakes to eat, which he continues to do for several days—both visit the bakery shop *and* explore the area. He notices that the assistant in the shop is becoming interested in him, perhaps even falling in love, and, as he is getting a bit bored, he starts flirting with her. He gets caught up in the game he's playing with her and finally makes a date, just to see what will happen. But even as he is going to meet the second girl, he comes across the first girl, the one he'd seen right at the beginning of the story—who happens to live right opposite the baker's but had sprained her ankle and couldn't go out, which is why he hadn't seen her. She had seen him go in there every day, however; and, thinking that he knew where she lived, this first girl just assumed the young man went into the shop so that she would notice him. She doesn't know anything about the other girl in the bakery. It's a very slight story, only an anecdote really.

The second film, *Suzanne's Career* [1963], is a little more complex because it lasts longer. It's the story of a young man who has great admiration for one of his friends, a student; he's younger than this student and rather dominated by him. At the same time the younger fellow holds it against the older one that he sees him a lot with girls he—the student—doesn't like very much. For example, the older guy has a girl that he doesn't like at all; she's not even a student—she has a job in an office—and he finds her and her situation a bit vulgar. The student neglects the girl and wants to get rid of her; and this girl, who is in love with the student, attaches herself to his younger friend and begins to flirt with him, solely because of the latter's friendship with the one she really likes. The younger guy wants to get rid of her, too, but he can't. So *Suzanne's Career* is the story of this boy who reluctantly spends all his time with this girl who's trying to make advances to him, and at the same time his older friend amuses himself by jeering at the girl, by making terrible fun of her—he even takes all her money because she's ready to do anything to keep him. The younger boy is ashamed of all this but he doesn't dare do anything to antagonize the friend he admires so much. And that's the situation: he's ashamed of going along with the game his friend is playing, but he doesn't have the courage to reproach him frankly and say "no."

There's a second woman involved, also, an attractive young girl; and the boy in the film is a little bit in love with her, but she looks on him as just a youngster and isn't interested. There's really nothing but failure in *Suzanne's Career*: the younger guy spends all his time with a girl he doesn't like and the one he would like to go out with is inaccessible, and each time he sees her he doesn't know what to say and is aware that she would refuse him anyway. The characters are all young: the boy, for instance, is eighteen, and his friend is twenty-one.

BC: *Do you ever plan a theatrical release of these two short films?*

ER: No, because they are really very amateur films. If I were ever to show them it would have to be in a very small cinema, and I think the public would just find them too amateurish.

BC: *Do you think this idea of the man who hesitates between two women is the connecting link between all the* Contes Moraux?

ER: He doesn't really hesitate; it just happens that at the very moment that he's made his choice, made up his mind, another woman turns up. But there isn't really any hesitation; all that happens is that his choice is confirmed. In *La Collectionneuse*, for example, the guy just spends a week with the girl and then leaves her. In *My Night at Maud's* [1969], too, it's an adventure for the young man, but he doesn't hesitate between one girl and another; and if *he* had had an affair with Maud, it would have lasted a week and then it would have been over. In *Claire's Knee* [1971], the hero's choice is already made: he's going to get married, and if he has an adventure it's nothing more than that.

BC: *Did you start this series—the* Contes Moraux—*with very precise ideas about the subject matter?*

ER: Yes, I had had the stories in my mind for a long time, and when I started the series I knew what the theme of each *Conte* would be. But I hadn't developed the narratives—in my mind, they were still very vague.

BC: *You've made some of the* Contes *in color and some in black and white. . . .*

Jerome (Jean-Claude Brialy) prepares to touch the knee of Claire (Laurence de Monaghan) in Rohmer's *Claire's Knee.*

ER: Three in black and white, two of them in 16mm and My *Night at Maud's* in 35. *La Collectionneuse* and *Claire's Knee* are in color and the final one, *Chloe in the Afternoon*, was in color, too.

BC: *Why did you choose black and white for* My Night at Maud's?

ER: Because it suited the nature of the subject matter. Color wouldn't have added anything positive to it; on the contrary, it would only have destroyed the atmosphere of the film and introduced distracting elements that had no useful purpose. This is a film that I saw in black and white; I couldn't see any color in it. There is nothing in it that brings colors to mind, and in fact there literally weren't any colors in what I filmed: for example, I filmed a town in which the houses were gray; certainly there were a few colored road signs and the like, but I avoided these—you don't see them because they weren't interesting. There is a stone church and there are no colors in that church. Then there is snow—no color there, either. The people are really dressed in black or in gray; they themselves are not wearing anything colored. The apartment also didn't have any color in it—it was decorated in gray already. I was concerned above all in My *Night at Maud's* with exploiting the contrast between black and white, between light and shadow. It's a film in color in a way, except that, again, the colors are black and white. There's a bedsheet that is white: it's not colorless, it's *white*. In the same way the snow is white, white in a positive way, whereas if I had shot it in color, it wouldn't have been white anymore; it would have been smudged or soiled, and I wanted it purely white.

BC: *So you don't agree with directors like the late Michelangelo Antonioni (among others), who said it's no longer possible to make films in black and white and that all films should be in color?*

ER: I would agree that nowadays the normal thing would be to make films in color, and it might seem a bit archaic to film in black and white. And yet I don't agree really. I think that people have a very strong feeling for black and white; it doesn't just exist in photography, it's there in drawings and engravings, too—painters created pictures in color, but they also worked in black and white for drawings and engravings, in order to create a certain effect. As a result I think that black and white is now accepted by the public, so I think that people are wrong when they say that black and white is impossible nowadays. It's a very curious phenomenon. I think that black and white will always exist, even if it's true that it will be an exception and the use of color will remain standard. It's quite apparent at the moment, however, that filmmakers aren't particularly inspired by color; most films in color have the same banal look about them and might as well be in black and white. Color adds nothing to them. For me, color has to *contribute* something to a film, and if it doesn't do this, I prefer black and white. For, despite everything, it gives a kind of basis, a unity, from which to work, which is more useful to a film than color badly used.

BC: *What would you say color contributes to* La Collectionneuse *and* Claire's Knee?

ER: I didn't use color as a dramatic element in these pictures, as some filmmakers have done. For me it's something inherent in each film as a whole. I think that in *La Collectionneuse* color above all heightens the sense of reality and increases the immediacy of the settings. In this film color acts in an indirect way; it's not direct and there aren't any color effects, as there are, for example, in Bergman's *The Passion of Anna* [1969], only his second film in color, where the color is very deliberately worked out and he gets his effects mainly by the way he uses red. I've never tried for dramatic effects of this kind, but it's true that the sense of time—evening, morning, and so on—can be rendered in a much more precise way through color. Color can also give a stronger sense of warmth, of heat, for when a film is in black and white you get less of a feeling of the "hotter" moments of the day, and there is less of what you might call a tactile feeling about it.

In *Claire's Knee*, I think color works in the same way: the presence of the lake and the mountains here is stronger in color than it would be in black and white. This is a film I couldn't imagine in black and white. The color green seems to me essential in *Claire's Knee*, and I couldn't imagine it without the green in it, either. Also blue, the cool or even cold color. In short, this picture would have no value for me in black and white. It's a very difficult thing to explain—it's more a feeling I have that can't be reasoned out logically.

BC: *What exactly do you mean by the word "moral" in the title of this series of films?*

ER: In French there is a word *moraliste* that I don't think has any equivalent in English. It doesn't really have much connection with the word "moral"; a *moraliste* is someone who is interested in finding out what goes on inside man. He's concerned with states of mind and feelings. For instance, in the eighteenth century Pascal was a *moraliste*, and a *moraliste* is also a particularly French kind of writer like La Bruyère or La Rochefoucauld. You could also call Stendhal a *moraliste* because he describes what people feel and think. So *Contes Moraux* doesn't really mean that there's a moral contained in them, even though there might be one and all the characters in these films act according to certain moral ideas that are fairly clearly worked out. In *My Night at Maud's* these ideas are very precise; for the characters in the other films they are rather more vague, and morality is a very personal matter. But they try to justify everything in their behavior and that fits the word "moral" in its narrowest sense. "Moral," however, can also mean that these characters are people who like to bring their motives, the reasons for their actions, into the open; they try to analyze and are not people who act without thinking about what they are doing. What matters is what they think about their behavior, rather than their behavior itself. The *Contes Moraux* aren't films of action, they aren't films in which physical action takes place; they aren't films in which there is anything very dramatic, for that matter. They are films in which a particular feeling is analyzed and where even the characters themselves analyze their feelings in a very introspective way. That's what constitutes a *Conte Morale*.

BC: *In* My Night at Maud's *and* Claire's Knee, *in particular, you show us some people around thirty-five to forty years old and also some who are very much* *younger. Do you think there was then, when these two films were made, a real disparity between such age groups, in the way that people often talked of the new generation's having a completely different set of customs and moral values?*

ER: My films are pure works of fiction; I don't claim to be a sociologist, and I'm not making investigations or collecting statistics. I simply take particular cases that I have invented myself; they aren't meant to be scientific: they are works of imagination. Personally, I've never believed very much in the idea of a difference between age groups. I don't think it's very strong and it's certainly not an opposition between one group and another. I also don't think it was so very much stronger in the late 1960s and early 1970s than it was before. And even if it is true, the subject doesn't interest me very much. It's not something I'm concerned with. The fact that the young generation at this time might as a whole have had a certain kind of mentality didn't interest me. What interested me was to show young people as they really were just then, but also as they might be if they were fifty years old or a hundred years old, and the events of the film were taking place in ancient Greece, for things haven't changed all that much. For me what is interesting in mankind is what is permanent and eternal and doesn't change, rather than what changes, and what's unchanging is what I'm interested in showing.

BC: *What do you think about what is happening in films at the present moment? Do you think a new kind of cinema is coming into being?*

ER: I've no idea. There may be people who are creating a "new" kind of cinema, but you have to ask how new it really is, and if it doesn't just form part of the "eternal avant-garde," which sometimes just rediscovers ideas that were avant-garde years ago. For me what is really new is an idea that never dates. It seems to me that it would be desirable to be able to see everything that is being made by young people in the cinema, even if it isn't completely successful. But I very seldom go to the cinema these days, I don't write criticism anymore, and I don't have enough knowledge to reply properly to your question. So I can't pass judgment on this new cinema, though the films I make myself haven't any of the characteristics of what is called the avant-garde, and I feel that this "traditional" avant-garde isn't the route the cinema ought to follow. I make films that are right for me, in any event, and other people can follow their own path and find their own public.

BC: *Have you ever wanted to make a film in the United States?*

ER: No. First of all I don't speak English well enough, and I couldn't work in a country where I don't know the language intimately. And second, I want to show the reality of life in France; I don't want to deal with a way of life I don't understand. Even if I admire American cinema enormously, I think that each nation should guard its cultural hegemony—otherwise, artistically speaking, things could get dangerous. On a moment's notice, I could make a documentary about life in a foreign country, but that's a different matter. Moreover, I have a very personal way of working and in France I have a great deal of freedom in this respect. I work with an extremely small crew; I have no assistant director, no script girl, so I take care of the continuity myself. Perhaps I make mistakes and put an ashtray here when it should be there, but that's just too bad. And as there usually are no special clothes for the actors and few objects of special importance, in the long run there are no problems with this way of working. I use very few technicians because there are very few camera movements, but those technicians that I have are excellent. In other countries you have crews that are terrifyingly large. I use five or six people and in other places you have sixty. That frightens me and I would be quite incapable of working in that way. I don't like to be the big boss who dominates everyone else; I like to be close to everyone, and I don't see how I could work under such conditions as those that obtain in the United States. Certainly what I've said applies only to traditional filmmaking in the United States; "underground" films would be a different matter.

In sum, I can show on the screen only those things I know about, and I think that there's still a lot to deal with in France. There's the question of language, too: I place a lot of importance on speech, on style, on voice quality and intonation, and that's very important. The French language counts for a great deal in my films. I'm a writer, too; I write my own scripts, and the French language is important to me. I couldn't write something and give it to someone else to translate, for I'm my own author in my films. So I could only make films in French and in France. But let me say that in the beginning, the public that sustained my career the most was not so much the French but the American one; *My Night at Maud's* was a big success in your country. Since then I've had quite a lot of success in Europe, particularly in Italy, Spain, and Germany, as well as in Japan. But it was the Americans, in a sense, who gave me my start.

BC: *What films or directors have most influenced your own work, in style or theme?*

ER: Silent films above all, though I don't know how direct the influence is. People say that there is a lot of talk in my films, that I express myself through speech rather than images, and yet in actual fact I learned about cinema by seeing the films of Griffith, Stroheim, Murnau, and the silent comedians. There are two directors after the silent period whom I like very much, and these are Jean Renoir and Roberto Rossellini; they are the filmmakers who most influenced me. As for the others, I admire Americans like Hitchcock, but I don't think I've really been influenced by them; if I have, it's quite unconsciously. I can tell you whom I admire, but influence is a different matter, for sometimes you don't even know yourself who has influenced you. Perhaps I'm not the right person to talk about such a subject; you need to ask your fellow critics and historians who has influenced Eric Rohmer!

BC: *How do you choose your actors?*

ER: By intuition, always. I audition one person, he or she reads the lines, and that's that!

BC: *Do you prefer to work for a small audience that will appreciate what you are doing, rather than for a large public?*

ER: Yes, certainly. If it depended only on me, instead of attracting people to my films, I would try to drive them away. I would tell them the films are more difficult than they really are, because I don't like to deceive people; I like to show my films to people who can appreciate them. I'm not interested in the number of spectators. Having said this, I have to say that it's true a film is a commercial undertaking and ought to recover its costs. But as my films don't cost much, and do receive some state subsidy, I don't think I need a very large audience, and I've always thought that my pictures should be shown in theaters that aren't too big. The intimate nature of my films doesn't suit a theater or an audience too large for them. And I don't think they call for a mass reaction or a collective reaction. It's better if the spectator feels he is experiencing a completely personal reaction to it. Each reaction should be unique, individual, different. I think a film by me is enjoyed more if the spectators aren't sitting too close to one another, if the theater isn't too full, and if they don't know each other. Then each has a different, truer reaction, which is better than a uniform reaction. I don't like watching one of my films in public and it distresses me if everyone laughs in the same place, as my film wasn't made with such a response in mind. I didn't write something just to make everyone laugh at the same time. It's all right if someone smiles, but everyone shouldn't at exactly the same place in the film. Perhaps this is because my films are more like reading than like watching a spectacle; they are made more to be read like a book than seen like something on the stage.

So it distresses me to see a collective reaction to my work. I owe my success in the end to a small but faithful public.

BC: *Would you agree that the endings of your films tend to be rather sad?*

ER: They are not what one is expecting to happen; they are to some extent *against* the person or character concerned. What happens is against the wishes of the character; it's a kind of disillusionment—not exactly a failure on his part but a disillusionment, an internal conflict. The character has made a mistake, and he realizes he has created an illusion for himself: a kind of world for himself, with himself at the center, and it seemed perfectly logical that he should be the ruler or the god of this world. Logically, everything seemed very simple, and all my characters are a bit obsessed with logic. They have a system and principles, and they build up a world that can be explained by this system. Then the conclusion of the film demolishes their system and their illusions collapse. It's not exactly a happy ending, but that's what the films are all about.

BC: *Do you think your twenty-first century films,* The Lady and the Duke *[2001] and* The Romance of Astrea and Celadon *[2007], will surprise audiences used to your* Contes Moreaux, *not to speak of your* Comedies and Proverbs *and* Tales of the Four Seasons?

ER: No, I don't think so. And besides, whenever I have made slightly different films, be they historical or political, like *The Tree, the Mayor, and the Media Center* [1993] and *Perceval* [1978], the audience has followed me. I wouldn't want to limit myself to overly psychological topics or romantic comedies, even if that's where I feel most involved on a personal level. I like to get out from time to time, you know.

Eric Rohmer Filmography

The Sign of Leo (1959)
La Collectionneuse (1967)
My Night at Maud's (1969)
Claire's Knee (1971)
Chloe in the Afternoon (1972)
The Marquise of O . . . (1976)
Perceval (1978)
The Aviator's Wife (1980)
Le Beau mariage (1982)

Loup y es-tu? (1983)
Pauline at the Beach (1983)
Full Moon in Paris (1984)
The Green Ray (1986)
Boyfriends and Girlfriends (1987)
Four Adventures of Reinette and Mirabelle (1987)
A Tale of Springtime (1990)
A Winter's Tale (1992)
The Tree, The Mayor, and the Media Center (1993)
Rendezvous in Paris (1995)
A Summer's Tale (1996)
Autumn Tale (1998)
The Lady and the Duke (2001)
Triple Agent (2004)
The Romance of Astrea and Celadon (2007)

Bibliography

Cone, Annabelle. "Misplaced Desire: The Female Urban Experience in Colette and Rohmer." *Literature/Film Quarterly* 24, no. 4 (1996), 423–431.

Crisp, C. G. *Eric Rohmer, Realist and Moralist.* Bloomington: Indiana University Press, 1988.

Fawell, John. "Eric Rohmer's Oppressive Summers." *French Review* 66, no. 5 (April 1993), 777–787.

Hammond, Robert, and Jean-Pierre Pagliano. "Eric Rohmer on Film Scripts and Film Plans." *Literature/Film Quarterly* 10, no. 4 (1982), 219–225.

Mann, Chris. "The Seasons in the Films of Eric Rohmer." *Australian Journal of French Studies* 36, no. 1 (1999), 101–109.

Mazierska, Ewa. "Road to Authenticity and Stability: Representation of Holidays, Relocation, and Movement in the Films of Eric Rohmer." *Tourist Studies: An International Journal* 2, no. 3 (2002), 223–246.

Rider, Jeff, Richard Hull, and Christopher Smith. "The Arthurian Legend in French Cinema: *Lancelot Du Lac* and *Perceval Le Gallois*." In Kevin J. Harty, ed., *Cinema Arthuriana: Essays on Arthurian Film*, 41–56. New York: Garland, 1991.

Spiegel, Alan. "The Cinematic Text: Rohmer's *The Marquise of O . . .*" In Andrew Horton and Joan Magretta, eds., *Modern European Filmmakers and the Art of Adaptation*, 313–328. New York: Ungar, 1981.

Warehime, Marja. "Eric Rohmer in the '90s: Seasonal Variations on the *Conte Morale*." *West Virginia University Philological Papers*, 47 (2001), 120–128.

Williams, Linda. "Eric Rohmer and the Holy Grail." *Literature/Film Quarterly* 11, no. 2 (1983), 71–82.

Alter Ego, Autobiography, and Auteurism

François Truffaut's Last Interview

The product of an unhappy, loveless home, François Truffaut (1932–1984) began using films to escape the exigencies of reality at age seven, virtually living in various Parisian movie houses. He left school to go to work at fourteen, and, one year later, founded a film club, which brought him to the attention of the influential cinema critic André Bazin. Over the next few years, Bazin both financed and protected Truffaut, helping the young cineaste weather such crises as his arrest for non-payment of debts and his 1951 public humiliation following his desertion from the army. In 1953, Bazin hired Truffaut as a critic for *Cahiers du cinéma*. And it was in the January 1954 edition of this influential periodical that Truffaut published his landmark essay "A Certain Tendency of the French Cinema," in which he attacked directors who merely ground out films without any personal cinematic vision; he also propounded the auteur theory, which opined that the only directors worth serious consideration were those who left their own individual signatures on each of their films.

Hoping to put his auteur theory to practical use, Truffaut decided to direct a short film, 1954's *Une Visite*. In 1957, he set up his own production company, Les Films du Carrosse (named in honor of the Jean Renoir film *Le Carrosse d'Or*), and in the same year garnered critical acclaim for his short subject *Les Mistons*. Two years later, in 1959, he made his first feature, the intensely autobiographical *400 Blows*. Cast as Truffaut's alter-ego Antoine Doinel was young Jean-Pierre Léaud, who went on to play Doinel at various later stages of his life in the director's four follow-ups to *The 400 Blows*. In 1961, Truffaut directed what many consider his masterpiece, and what not a few observers regard as the finest film of its year: *Jules and Jim*, a hauntingly beautiful tale of a lingering romantic triangle.

Though in the vanguard of the French New Wave (he contributed to the scripts of such groundbreaking films as Jean-Luc Godard's *Breathless* [1960]), Truffaut was never a hard-to-fathom aesthete but, instead, the most successful filmmaker in France, as popular with casual fans as serious film students. He also differed from his New Wave colleagues by avoiding overt political statements: even his most "politicized" film, 1980's *The Last Metro*, was more in the romantic tradition of Renoir than the tract-like pronouncements of Godard. In developing a style of his own, Truffaut was heavily influenced by his idols Jean Vigo, Jacques Tati, and especially Renoir, whom Truffaut admired for his ability to simultaneously depict the realities of life and "improve" upon them. Like Renoir, Truffaut endeavored to make films that approximated real life but were romanticized enough to be entertainment. Truffaut also admired such Hollywood directors as Alfred Hitchcock, Howard Hawks, and Orson Welles. Echoes of Hawks and Welles would persist throughout Truffaut's career, while Hitchcock was imitated outright in 1967's *The Bride Wore Black*.

As he matured professionally, Truffaut's previous attention-getting techniques grew less pronounced, and he began favoring the "invisible camera" à la John Ford. After finishing his Oscar-winning *Day for Night* (1973)—a film about the making of movies—Truffaut announced his retirement from directing, but, within a year, was back on the job. In addition to his directorial activities, Truffaut also produced the works of others, and occasionally dabbled in acting, first in his own films (*The Wild Child*, *Day for Night*, etc.) and later in the leading role of French scientist Claude Lecombe in Steven Spielberg's *Close Encounters of the Third Kind* (1977). In addition to his Oscar for *Day for Night*, Truffaut was honored with the Cannes Film Festival Best Director prize for *The 400 Blows*, a Best Director César for *The Last Metro*, and the Prix Louis Delluc and National Society of Film Critics Award for *Stolen Kisses* (1968).

The following interview was conducted both in English and French (translated by me) in late May of 1984 in François Truffaut's private office at Les Films du Carrosse, the production company in Paris he founded and ran. His last public appearance had been in a television interview on April 13, 1984, for the *Apostrophes* series hosted by Bernard Pivot. When Truffaut generously agreed to meet with me, for what was intended to be a print interview (which did not materialize at the time), he was clearly weak but unquestionably lucid. He died from brain cancer on October 21, 1984.

Bert Cardullo: *I'd like to focus our discussion today on the Antoine Doinel cycle, M. Truffaut—though perhaps we'll have time to treat some other films of yours as well. Could we begin by talking about your life prior to becoming a movie director?*

François Truffaut: Yes, of course. During the war, I saw many films that made me fall in love with the cinema. I'd skip school regularly to see movies—even in the morning, in the small Parisian theaters that opened early. At first, I wasn't sure whether I'd be a critic or a filmmaker, but I knew it would be something like that. I had thought of writing, actually, and that later on I'd be a novelist. Next I decided I'd be a film critic. Then I gradually started thinking I should make movies. And I think seeing all those films during the war was a sort of apprenticeship.

The New Wave filmmakers, you know, were often criticized for their lack of experience. This movement was made up of people with all kinds of backgrounds—including people like me who had done nothing more than write for *Cahiers du cinéma* and see thousands of movies. I saw some pictures fourteen or fifteen times, like Jean Renoir's *The Rules of the Game* [1939] and *The Golden Coach* [1953]. There is a way to see films that can teach you more than working as an assistant director, without the viewing process becoming tedious or academic. Basically, the assistant director is a guy who wants to see how movies are made, but who is constantly prevented from doing just that because he gets sent on errands while the important stuff is taking place in front of the camera. In other words, he is always required to do things that take him away from the set. But in the movie theater, when you see a film for the tenth time or so, a film whose dialogue and music you know by heart, you start to look at how it's made, and you learn much more than you could as an assistant director.

BC: *Which films first struck your attention when, as a boy, you began frequenting the cinema?*

FT: The first films I truly admired were French ones, like Henri-Georges Clouzot's *The Raven* [1943] and Marcel Carné's *The Devil's Envoys* [1942]. These are movies I quickly wanted to see more than once. This habit of multiple viewing happened by accident, because first I would see some picture on the sly, and then my parents would say, "Let's go to the movies tonight," so then I'd see the same movie again, since I couldn't say I'd already seen it. But this made me want to see films again and again—so much so that three years after the Liberation, I'd seen *The Raven* maybe nine or ten times. But after I wound up working at *Cahiers du cinéma*, I turned away from French film. Friends at the magazine, like Jacques Rivette, thought it absurd that I could recite all of *The Raven*'s dialogue and had seen Carné's *The Children of Paradise* [1945] fourteen times.

BC: *A little while ago, you mentioned two Renoir films that you had also seen a dozen or more times. Could you say something about Renoir's impact on you?*

FT: I think Renoir is the only filmmaker who's practically infallible, who has never made a mistake on film. And I think if he never made mistakes, it's because he always found solutions based on simplicity—human solutions. He's one film director who never pretended. He never tried to have a style, and if you know his work—which is very comprehensive, since he dealt with all sorts of subjects—when you get stuck, especially as a young filmmaker, you can think of how Renoir would have handled the situation, and you generally find a solution.

Roberto Rossellini, for example, is quite different. His strength was to completely ignore the mechanical and technical aspects of making a film. They just didn't exist for him. When he made notes in his scripts, he said all kinds of extravagant things, such as "The English army enters Orléans." So you think, "OK, he'll need lots of extras." And then you see *Joan of Arc at the Stake* [1955], where there are only ten cardboard soldiers jammed onto a small set. When Rossellini achieves serenity or even casualness in a film, like the one he did about India, it's phenomenal yet at the same time inexplicable. Such a film's minimalism, its humility before its subject, is in the end what makes it such a magnificent work. My favorite Rossellini film is *Germany, Year Zero* [1947], probably because I have a weakness for movies that take childhood, or children, as their subject. Also because Rossellini was the first to depict children truthfully, almost documentary-style, on film. He shows them as serious and pensive—more so than the adults around them—not like picturesque little figures or animals. The child in *Germany, Year Zero* is quite extraordinary in his restraint and simplicity. This was the first time in the cinema that children were portrayed as the center of gravity, while the atmosphere around them is the one that's frivolous.

Rossellini reinforced a trait already evident in Renoir: the desire to stay as close to life as possible in a fiction film. Rossellini even said that you shouldn't write scripts—only swine write scripts—that the conflict in a film should simply emerge from the facts. A character from a given place at a given time is confronted by another character from a very different place: and voilà, there exists a natural conflict between them and you start from that. There's no need to invent anything. I'm very influenced by men like Rossellini—and Renoir—who managed to free themselves of any complex about the cinema, for whom the character, story, or theme is more important than anything else.

BC: *What about the influence on you of American cinema?*

FT: You know, we owe so much, here in France, to American cinema, which Americans themselves don't know very well. Especially early American cinema, which Americans hardly know at all and even scorn. As for influential Americans around the time of the French New Wave, I'm thinking of Sidney Lumet, Robert Mulligan, Frank Tashlin, and Arthur Penn. They represented a total renewal of American cinema, a little like some of the New Wave directors in France. They were extremely alive, the first films of these men, like early, primitive American cinema, and at the same time they were quite intellectual. Their movies managed to unite the best of both qualities. At the time, Americans scorned these filmmakers because they didn't know them very well and because they weren't commercially successful. Success is everything in America, as you know far better than I.

BC: *Why was the French New Wave an artistic success?*

FT: At the start of the New Wave, people opposed to the young filmmakers' new films said, "All in all, what they're doing is not very different from what was done before." And in a sense these people were right. I don't know if there was actually a plan behind the New Wave, but as far as I was concerned, it never occurred to me to revolutionize the cinema or to express myself differently from previous filmmakers. I always thought that the cinema was just fine, except for the fact that it lacked sincerity. I'd do the same thing others were doing, but better.

There's a famous quote by André Malraux: "A masterpiece isn't better rubbish." Still, I thought that good films were just bad movies made better.

In other words, I don't see much difference between a film like Anatole Litvak's *Goodbye Again* [1961] and my picture *The Soft Skin* [1964]. It's the same thing, the same film, except that in *The Soft Skin* the actors suit the roles they play. We made things ring true, or at least we tried to. But in the other picture, nothing rang true because it wasn't the right film for Ingrid Bergman, Anthony Perkins, or Yves Montand. So *Goodbye Again* was based on a lie right from the start. The idea isn't to create some new and different cinema, but to make the existing one more true. That's what I had in mind when I began making films. There isn't a huge difference between Jean Delannoy's *The Little Rebels* [1955] and *The 400 Blows* [1959], either. They're the same, or in any event very close. I just wanted to make mine because I didn't like the other one's artificiality—that's all.

BC: *Everyone knows you were a film critic before you became a director. What film was your first article about?*

FT: Charlie Chaplin's *Modern Times* [1936], an old print of which I saw in a film club. It was seized afterwards by the police because it was a stolen copy! Then I started writing for *Cahiers du cinéma*, thanks to André Bazin. I did an incendiary piece in *Cahiers* against French films as typified by the screenwriters Jean Aurenche and Pierre Bost, the fossils of French cinema. That article got me a job at the weekly *Arts*, where I wrote the film column for four years.

I think being a critic helped me because it's not enough to love films or see lots of films. Having to write about films helps you to understand them better. It forces you to exercise your intellect. When you summarize a script in ten sentences, you see both its strengths and its weaknesses. Criticism is a good exercise, but you shouldn't do it for too long. In retrospect, my reviews seem more negative than not, as I found it more stimulating to damn rather than praise; I was better at attacking than defending. And I regret that. I'm much less dogmatic now, and I prefer critical nuance.

BC: *You were a film critic for four years, but all the while you were looking for an opportunity to make a film, right?*

FT: Oh yes, absolutely. I started making little movies in 16mm that weren't worth showing. They had all the same flaws as most amateur films: they were extremely pretentious; and they didn't even have a storyline, which is the height of conceit for an amateur. I probably learned something from this work, like how to suggest rather than show. But in the first of these shorts, there was nothing but doors opening and closing—what a waste!

My first real film, in 1957, was *Les Mistons—The Mischief Makers* in English. It had the advantage of telling a story, which was not common practice for short films in those days! It also gave me the opportunity to start working with actors. But *Les Mistons* also had commentary interspersed with its dialogue, so that made making it much simpler. The film met with quite a bit of luck. It was awarded a prize at a festival in Brussels, I believe. *Les Mistons* is based on a story by Maurice Pons; it's not my original script. I saw it as the first of a series of sketches. It was easier at the time, and would be even now, to find money for three or four different short films than to find enough financial support for a feature film. So I planned to do a series of sketches with the common thread of childhood. I had five or six stories from which I could choose. I started with *Les Mistons* because it was the easiest to shoot.

When it was finished, I wasn't completely satisfied because the film was a little too literary. Let me explain: *Les Mistons* is the story of five children who spy on young lovers. And I noticed, in directing these children, that they had no interest in the girl, who was played by Gérard Blain's wife, Bernadette Lafont; the boys weren't jealous of Blain himself, either. So I had them do contrived things to make them appear jealous, and later this annoyed me. I told myself that I'd film with children again, but next time I would have them be truer to life and use as little fiction as possible.

BC: *Is it awkward for a writer-director to have been a critic first? When you start a scene, does the critic in you tap you on the shoulder and say, "I don't think so!"?*

FT: It is indeed rather awkward, because not only was I a critic, I have also seen nearly 3,000 films. So I always tend to think, "But that was done in such-and-such a film," "Compared to X's movie, this is no good," etc. Plus, however necessary they may be, I'm very skeptical of storylines. So much so that I turn a script's narrative over in my head endlessly, to the point that often, at the last minute, I want to cancel the filming of it.

BC: *How, then, do you ever manage to complete a film?*

FT: Because the advantage of cinema over novels, for instance, is that you can't just drop it. The machine's in gear, contracts are signed. And besides, I like actors a lot, at least some of them—those I choose! There are promises to be kept, there is motivation to keep your word. But once you've begun, the problem of self-doubt falls away, even the problem of anxiety in general. Then there are just the daily problems of moviemaking, which are strictly technical and can be solved amid all the noise and laughter—it's really quite exhilarating. When the filming is over, though, the doubts come back.

BC: *What was the provenance of* The 400 Blows?

FT: When I was shooting *Les Mistons*, *The 400 Blows* already existed in my mind in the form of a short film, which was titled *Antoine Runs Away*.

BC: *What caused you to lengthen Antoine's story and make* The 400 Blows *longer?*

FT: It was because I was disappointed by *Les Mistons*, or at least by its brevity. You see, I had come to reject the sort of film made up of several skits or sketches. So I preferred to leave *Les Mistons* as a short and to take my chances with a full-length film by spinning out the story of *Antoine Runs Away*. Of the five or six stories I had already outlined, this was my favorite, and it became *The 400 Blows*.

Antoine Runs Away was a twenty-minute sketch about a boy who plays hooky and, having no note to hand in as an excuse, makes up the story that his mother has died. His lie having been discovered, he does not dare go home and spends the night outdoors. I decided to develop this story with the help of Marcel Moussy, at the time a television writer whose shows for a program called *If It Was You* were very realistic and very successful. They always dealt with family or social problems. Moussy and I added to the beginning and the end of Antoine's story until it became a kind of chronicle of a boy's thirteenth year—of the awkward early teenaged years.

In fact, *The 400 Blows* became a rather pessimistic film. I can't really say what the theme is—there is none, perhaps—but one central idea was to depict early adolescence as a difficult time of passage and not to fall into the usual nostalgia about "the good old days," the salad days of youth. Because, for me in any event, childhood is a series of painful memories. Now, when I feel blue, I tell myself, "I'm an adult. I do as I please," and that cheers me up right away. But, then, childhood seemed like such a hard phase of life; you're not allowed to make any mistakes. Making a mistake is a crime: you break a plate by mistake and it's a real offense. That was my approach in *The 400 Blows*, using a relatively flexible script to leave room for improvisation, mostly provided by the actors. I was very happy in this respect with Jean-Pierre Léaud as Antoine, who was quite different from the original character I had imagined. And as we improvised more, the film became more pessimistic, then—in brief spurts, as a contrary reaction—so high-spirited that it almost became optimistic.

BC: *Does the screenplay of* The 400 Blows *constitute in some ways your autobiography?*

FT: Yes, but only partially. All I can say is that nothing in it is invented. What didn't happen to me personally happened to people I know, to boys my age and even to people that I had read about in the papers. Nothing in *The 400 Blows* is pure fiction, then, but neither is the film a wholly autobiographical work.

BC: *Let me put my question another way: it has often been said that Antoine Doinel was you, a sort of projection of yourself. Could you define that projection, that character?*

FT: There is indeed something anachronistic or composite-like about Antoine Doinel, but it's difficult for me to define. I don't really know who he is, except that he is a kind of mixture of Jean-Pierre Léaud and myself. He is a solitary type, a kind of loner who can make you laugh or smile about his misfortunes, and that allows me, through him, to touch on sad matters—but always with a light hand, without melodrama or sentimentality, because Doinel has a kind of courage about him. Yet he is the opposite of an exceptional or extraordinary character; what does differentiate him from average people, however, is that he never settles down into average situations. Doinel is only at ease in extreme situations: of profound disappointment and misery, on the one hand, and total exhilaration and enthusiasm, on the other. He also preserves a great deal of the childlike in his character, which means that you forget his real age. If he is twenty-eight, as Léaud was in 1972, you look at Doinel as if he were eighteen: a naïf, as it were, but a well-meaning one for all that.

BC: *A related question: is it because Montmartre holds personal childhood memories for you that you came back to it in at least two of your Antoine Doinel films— the first two, as a matter of fact—*The 400 Blows *and* Love at Twenty *[1962]?*

FT: Yes, most likely. It's easier to orient myself when I shoot on familiar streets. Also, when you're writing, you tend to think of people and places you know. So you wind up coming back to these familiar places and people. As for my method of writing, I started making "script sheets" when I began work on *The 400 Blows*. School: various gags at school. Home: some gags at home. Street: a few gags in the street. I think everyone works in this way, at least on some films. You certainly do it for comedies, and you can even do it for dramas. And this material, in my case, was often based on memories. I realized that you can really *exercise* your memory where the past is concerned. I had found a class photo of mine, for example, one in the classic pose with all the pupils lined up. The first time I looked at that picture, I could remember the names of only two friends. But by looking at it for an hour each morning over a period of several days, I remembered all my classmates' names, their parents' jobs, and where everybody lived.

It was around this time that I met Moussy and asked him if he'd like to work with me on the script of *The 400 Blows*. Since I myself had played hooky quite a bit, all of Antoine's problems with fake notes, forged signatures, bad report cards—all of these I knew by heart, of course. The movies to which we truants went started at around ten in the morning; there were several theaters in Paris that opened at such an early hour. And their clientele was made up almost exclusively of school children! But you couldn't go with your school bag, because it would make you look suspicious. So we hid our bags behind the door of the theater. Two of these movie houses faced each other: the Cinéac-Italiens and the New York. Each morning around 9:45, there would be fifty or sixty children waiting outside to get in. And the first theater to open would get all the business because we were anxious to hide. We felt awfully exposed out there in the middle of all that. . . .

BC: *As a former critic, if you had had to talk about* The 400 Blows, *would you have spoken about it in the glowing terms used by most critics?*

FT: No, I don't think so. I honestly think I'd have liked it, because I like the ideas in the picture—they're good ideas—but I wouldn't have gone so far in praising *The 400 Blows* as the critics did. I couldn't have called it a masterpiece or a great work of art, because I can see too clearly what's experimental or clumsy about it.

BC: *Was the film received well in every country outside France?*

FT: No, it flopped in Italy, for one, maybe because it's too similar to Italian neorealist films, and *they* always flopped there, too! *The 400 Blows* didn't go over very well in Germany, either; and the Spanish didn't even want to distribute it despite the Catholic prize it won at Cannes. But the film worked in Japan, in Holland, in America, and of course elsewhere, too.

BC: *The* 400 Blows *drew some reaction from French censors, didn't it?*

FT: Yes, because of the situations in the film: adultery, a child seeing his mother with another man, escaping from reform school, things like that. Initially, the French censors rated *The 400 Blows* for sixteen-year-olds and over. But after the film was awarded not only the Catholic prize, but also the prize for best director at Cannes, the 16+ rating was rescinded.

BC: *Were the censors afraid they'd look like idiots?*

FT: I think that's it, yes.

BC: *I'd like to get back for a moment to the matter of Renoir's, as well as other filmmakers', influence on you—particularly in the instance of* The 400 Blows.

FT: Well, Jean Vigo's influence is obvious in *The 400 Blows*. But certainly *The 400 Blows* is also, if less obviously, influenced by Renoir's work, be it in a simple gesture or in some solution to an artistic or technical problem. For example, Renoir's secret is his casual style, as I've already indicated, yet that "styleless style" never prevents him from handling larger-than-life scenes. I had the problem of such a larger-than-life scene in *The 400 Blows*. The boy Antoine—who, to repeat, told the teacher that his mother had died to avoid having to hand in a note for his absence, and who is found out in the afternoon when his mother comes to the school—decides never to return home. And after school, he talks with his young friend about his plans. This was quite difficult dialogue to do, because it wasn't natural. These words weren't something a child would normally say; I'm very realistic and such moments, as originally written, went against the—or my—grain. It was hard, therefore, to find the right stance with which to direct Jean-Pierre Léaud in this scene. For some reason, the situation reminded me of a scene in *The Human Beast* [1938], where Jean Gabin, as Jacques Lantier, returns at the very end of the movie. He comes back to his locomotive the morning after killing Simone Simon's character, and he has to explain to the other conductor, played by Julien Carette, that he killed this woman. Renoir directed Gabin marvelously here, precisely by using the hallmark of his cinematic style: its utter casualness or offhandedness. Gabin says, "It's horrible. I killed her. I loved her. I'll never see her again. I'll never be by her side." He said all this very softly, very simply. And I used my memory of Gabin's performance to direct Léaud, who did his own scene exactly like Gabin's.

That was a tough scene. It was easier to coach Léaud in the scene where he goes to school without a note after a three-day absence and decides to say his mother died. In this instance there wasn't any question of someone's directorial influence on me, but only of my own directorial instinct. We don't know that Antoine has decided to tell this lie, only that he'll say something big. Of course, he could use a number of ways to say his mother had died. He could be shifty or sad or whatever. I decided the boy should give the impression that he doesn't want to tell the lie. That he doesn't dare say it but that the teacher pushes him to do so. The teacher asks, "Where's your note?" and the child replies, "It's my mother, sir." The teacher inquires, "Your mother? What about her?" It's only because the teacher badgers him that Antoine suddenly decides to fight back and say, "She's dead!" I told Léaud, "You say, 'She's dead!' but you think in your head, 'She's dead! What do you say to that?'" He doesn't say this but he thinks it, and that gives him the exact look and tone of voice I wanted—even the upturned head. There's a lie you can use only once!

Let me give you another example, returning once again to the issue of directorial influence—this time of someone other than Renoir. If in *The 400 Blows*, I had filmed the father coming to the classroom and slapping his son after the boy returned to school and said his mother was dead, then I'd have had problems editing because I would have wanted fast action here and could have gotten that only with a lot of cutting. But the rest of the film was just a matter of capturing a lot of situations, without an excessive amount of cutting. So I knew I'd have to create the drama in this scene within the frame itself, with little or no cutting, and I thought of Alfred Hitchcock. Otherwise I had no point of reference; I had no idea how to edit the scene in order to create the intensity I wanted. I knew now that I had to show the headmaster, then there's a knock on the door, the boy senses it's about him, and next you see the mother. I told the actress Claire Maurier that, instead of scanning the classroom for her son, as might be natural since she had never been to the school before, she was to look right away in the direction of Antoine's desk. I knew that this would create the dramatic effect I was looking for, and not the reality of her searching for her son's face amidst a sea of other young faces.

BC: The 400 Blows *was filmed on location but without direct sound, right?*

FT: Yes to your first question: we filmed in real locations. We found a tiny apartment on Rue Caulaincourt in Paris, but I was afraid that my cameraman, Henri Decaë, wouldn't want to film there. I showed it to him and he nonetheless accepted, knowing the numerous problems he would face. For example, when we wanted to show the father, the mother, and the boy around the dinner table, Decaë had to sit on the windowsill, on the sixth floor, with the whole crew waiting outside on the stairs. Things like that happened all the time.

I don't like studios, I have to say; I overwhelmingly prefer to shoot on location. And I've shot all my pictures on location, with the exception of *Fahrenheit 451* [1966], where we had to burn the set in the end! It's a simple question of reality. On location, there may be the necessity of going indoors *from the outdoors*, but even if that weren't an issue, what happens inside is truly different depending on whether you're in a studio or a real apartment. A real apartment would cost a fortune to create in a studio: the thickness of the wood in a door, say, the lock or set of locks, the way the door closes. You don't get these things in a studio, where everything's made of plywood.

As for your second question, yes again: *The 400 Blows* was shot almost entirely without direct sound. It was dubbed afterwards, except for one scene, where the psychologist questions Antoine. If this scene got so much notice, it's not just because Léaud's performance was so realistic; it's also because this was the only scene we shot with live sound. The shooting of such a scene, as you might guess, is heavily influenced by television. Although I believe TV is misguided when it attempts to compete with the cinema by trying to handle poetry or fantasy, it's in its element when it questions someone and lets him explain himself. This scene from *The 400 Blows* was definitely done with television in mind. Jean-Pierre didn't have a script. I gave him an idea of the questions and a basic sense of the answers so that they would match the storyline, but he used his own words, his own language—and, of course, it was much more interesting this way.

Aside from this scene with the psychologist, the dubbing worked rather well, because children are easily dubbed, and Jean-Pierre Léaud is dubbed so well you can't tell. With the parents in the film, the post-synchronization is not so good.

BC: *Why did you shoot* The 400 Blows *in CinemaScope?*

FT: Because I had the naïve feeling that it would make the film look more "professional," more stylized, and less naturalistic. CinemaScope has this strange quality of being an oblong window that hides many details, so that when a character moves through a room, he moves almost abstractly, as if he were in an aquarium. I shot *Shoot the Piano Player* [1960] and *Jules and Jim* [1962] in CinemaScope as well, and perhaps such stylization works better in these two "stylized" films.

BC: *Could you say something about the relationship, in your career, of* Shoot the Piano Player *to* The 400 Blows?

FT: *Shoot the Piano Player*, my second feature film, was made in reaction to *The 400 Blows*, which was so French. I felt that I needed to show that I had also been influenced by the American cinema. Also, after the exaggerated reception and publicity for *The 400 Blows*—its disproportionate success—I became quite agitated. So I touched on the notions of celebrity and obscurity in *Shoot the Piano Player*—reversed them, in fact, since here it is a famous person who becomes unknown. There are glimpses in this film, then, of the feeling that troubled me at the time.

I had made *The 400 Blows* in a state of anxiety, because I was afraid that the film would never be released and that, if it did come out, people would say, "After having insulted everyone as a critic, Truffaut should have stayed home!" *Shoot the Piano Player*, by contrast, was made in a state of euphoria, thanks to the success of *The 400 Blows*. I took great pleasure in filming it, far more than in *The 400 Blows*, where I was concerned about Jean-Pierre Léaud. I was wondering whether he would show up each day, or, if he did, whether he had had a fight the night before and would appear on the set with marks all over his face. With children, we directors worry more, because they do not have the same self-interest or self-regard as adults.

BC: *Is it true that you placed an ad in the newspaper* France Soir *to recruit the boy who would play the hero of* The 400 Blows?

FT: Yes. I didn't like the idea of finding a kid on the street and asking his parents, "Would you let him make a movie with me?" For this first feature film of mine about children, I wanted the children to be willing—both the children and their parents. So I used the ad to get them to come to a studio near the Champs-Elysées, where I was doing 16mm screen tests every Thursday. I saw a number of boys, one of whom was Jean-Pierre Léaud. He was more interesting than all the rest, more intense, more frantic even. He really, really wanted the part, and I think that touched me. I could feel during the shoot that the story improved, that the film became better than the screenplay, thanks to him.

Jean-Pierre Léaud as Antoine Doinel in Truffaut's *The 400 Blows*.

BC: *Léaud's work gave birth not only to* The 400 Blows *but to the whole Antoine Doinel saga, which I think is unique in the history of cinema: starting in 1959, to follow a character for twenty years, watching him grow older over the course of five films. Let's talk now about the other films in the cycle:* Love at Twenty, Stolen Kisses *[1968],* Bed and Board *[1970], and* Love on the Run *[1979]. At the end of* The 400 Blows, *we left Jean-Pierre Léaud on the beach. He had just escaped from a reform school, where he had been up to some mischief and had suffered various misfortunes.*

FT: When I brought him back, in *Love at Twenty*—which was really just a sketch, called "Antoine and Colette," as part of an anthology film—he was eighteen and perhaps living on his own. In any case, you no longer see his family in this film. Antoine is starting his professional life, working in a record company, and we see his first love affairs a few months before he must go into the army. *Stolen Kisses* is simply the continuation of the adventures of Antoine Doinel. It is the same character: like me, but not me; like Jean-Pierre Léaud, but not Léaud.

I must say that I like to start with more solid material than this. I like having two or three reasons to make a movie: say, the coming together of a book I want to adapt or an atmosphere I want to depict with an actor that I want to film. In *Stolen Kisses*, I admit, I just wanted to work with Jean-Pierre Léaud again; I more or less set a specific date by which I wanted to begin making a film with him. And, with my screenwriters Claude de Givray and Bernard Revon, I sat down and said, "What are we going to do with Léaud?" For his professional life, we adopted a perfectly simple solution. Leafing through a phone book, we found an ad for private detectives. We thought, "Here's a job you don't see in French films, usually only in American movies about a famous detective named Marlowe." But it should prove funny in France. For Doinel's romantic life, I suggested putting him opposite a girl his own age, even younger. We'd even suppose that he wrote her when he was in the army and therefore already knows her. We would then have him live what I think is every young man's fantasy: an affair with a married woman. I thought right away of Delphine Seyrig for the part of the married woman, because I didn't want this affair to be sordid, but instead a bit dreamlike or idealized.

BC: *Well, Seyrig was the perfect actress to achieve that end.*

FT: Exactly. We know that Jean-Pierre is in love with Delphine, but we also know that she knows, and that Léaud doesn't know that she knows, so the game goes three ways. The scene of their having coffee is thus not just between Jean-Pierre and Delphine. It's between Jean-Pierre, Delphine, and the audience. It's much stronger with three players, much more intense, which means in filmic terms that you can take your time. The long silences make you expect something unusual: perhaps he'll lunge at her for a kiss. We don't know what to expect, but we expect something. My only direction to the both of them was, "Stir the sugar not once but six times. Don't sip the coffee right away. We have all the time in the world in a scene like this, where the situation is so fraught with tension."

The anticipation comes to a climax when Léaud responds "Yes, sir" to Delphine's question, "Do you like music, Antoine?" The wrong way to do the scene at this point would have been to fade to the next scene. But this "Yes, sir" is like a moving locomotive. And to keep it on track, you have to keep up the momentum. As a director, your only salvation lies in flight, and flee Léaud does as the music becomes very frenzied. I asked Antoine Duhamel for something like the music you find in chase scenes in American movies—music, that is, that would sustain the tension and not dissolve or break it. And this music mustn't stop, even when there is dialogue. It's a total frenzy. Plus the camera is constantly moving.

This scene, or sequence, illustrates another lesson I learned from Hitchcock, who said: "You work hard to create an emotion, and once the emotion is created, you should work even harder to maintain it."

BC: *Why did the Antoine Doinel cycle come to an end?*

FT: I guess because the ideas I get about Antoine Doinel, and the way Léaud plays him, are closely tied to adolescence; there's something in the character that refuses to grow up. I'm like the silly father who continues to treat his twenty-three-year-old son like a child: "Blow your nose"; "Say hello to the nice lady." That's the problem with parents who won't allow their children to grow up. People who do comic strips have the same problem: they create a character who will be the same age forever. But starting with *Bed and Board*, the character of Antoine had actually reached adulthood, so there was no reason to go on much beyond that. That's why the cycle had to come to an end with *Love on the Run*. It has a deliberately, boldly, even desperately happy ending, unlike the endings of the previous four films in the cycle, all of which were open ended.

BC: *In* Bed and Board *you were examining the problems of romantic relationships. How did you approach them?*

FT: Not really as problems. More as a chronicle, with some happy scenes and some serious or dramatic scenes.

BC: Shoot the Piano Player *has similar changes of tone.*

FT: It does. They were planned in that film, since they were also in the American David Goodis's source novel—a *série noire* from 1956 called *Down There*—but the changes of tone were reinforced during the shooting because I realized I was faced with a film without a theme. The same thing happened spontaneously in *Stolen Kisses* and *Bed and Board*, themselves movies without clear subjects: some days during the shooting I stressed the comical side, other days the dramatic side. Compared to what I did in *Stolen Kisses*, though, in *Bed and Board* I tried to be much funnier when something was funny, and much more dramatic when something was dramatic. It's the same mixture in both films, but in *Bed and Board* I just tried, so to speak, to increase the dosage. And I did this in part by showing Antoine Doinel as a married man.

It was around ten years later that I made *Love on the Run*, which included flashback sequences from the earlier Doinel films and had the feeling of a conclusion for me. When the characters in *Love on the Run* talk about a memory, I was able to show that memory, while still telling a story happening in the present and with new characters. There is a summing up in this film, since I had already decided that, once it was finished, I would no longer use the character of Antoine Doinel.

BC: *I'd like to press you a bit more on why you used so much flashback material in* Love on the Run. *In some instances in this film it almost seems like padding.*

FT: Well, to begin with, there are only eighteen minutes—in a film of ninety-five minutes— borrowed from the earlier works in the Doinel cycle. In using these flashbacks, I felt I had to take advantage of an opportunity never afforded any previous movie director. When filming a story that involves the past, you always have the problem of finding a young actor who looks like the adult protagonist. When I made *The Man Who Loved Women* [1977], for example, I found, on the streets of Montpellier, and by sheer luck, a little boy who looked just like Charles Denner. We jumped at the opportunity to use him and included in the film two or three flashbacks of the Denner character as a child. But when you have the good fortune, as I did in the Antoine Doinel cycle, to shoot someone at the ages of fourteen, eighteen, twenty-four, and twenty-six, then to pick him up again at thirty-five, you have in your hands material that is precious. And I wanted to take advantage of having filmed this same boy at different stages of his life: by placing him in a new story that allowed him to be seen—simultaneously, as it were—as a man, an adolescent, and a child.

BC: *The editing of* Love on the Run *must have presented its share of continuity problems.*

FT: Yes, it is obviously a film in which editing is much more important than it was in such linear narratives of mine as *The Green Room* [1978] and *The Story of Adele H.* [1975]. This must be the film where I spent the most time—sixteen weeks, in fact—in the editing room since *Fahrenheit 451*, where all the book-burning scenes were played as flashbacks. The problem in *Love on the Run* was to homogenize very unrelated material, to retain the train of thought when we came back to the present after a flashback. And the more the visual material is unrelated, the more unity you have to preserve on the soundtrack: the sound bridges the gaps. Let's just say that when the image changes, the sound cannot change, or has to change as little as possible.

BC: *So, in the end, you were happy with this film?*

FT: To tell the truth, I wasn't happy with *Love on the Run*. This picture was, and still is, troubling for me. People may well enjoy it, but I'm not happy with it. It didn't seem like a real film to me. For one thing, the experimental elements in it are too pronounced. A movie often has an experimental feel in the beginning, but by the end you hope it feels like a real object, a real film, so that you forget it's an experiment.

BC: *But in defense of your own movie, it's a kind of diary on film. You watch a character through his evolution.*

FT: Yes, but did he really evolve? I felt that the cycle as a whole wasn't successful in making him evolve. The character started out somewhat autobiographical, but over time it drew further and further away from me. I never wanted to give him ambition, for example. I wonder if he's not too frozen in the end, like a cartoon character. You know, Mickey Mouse can't grow old. Perhaps the Doinel cycle is the story of a failure, even if each film on its own is enjoyable and a lot of fun to watch.

That said, Antoine Doinel's life is just a life—not an exhilarating or prodigious one, but the life of a person with his own contradictions and faults. When I have a man like this as the main character on screen, I focus on his weaknesses. I also did this outside the Doinel cycle: Charles Aznavour in *Shoot the Piano Player*, Jean Desailly in *The Soft Skin*, and Charles Denner in *The Man Who Loved Women* are not heroes, either. American cinema is great at depicting "heroes," but the vocation of European cinema may be to express the truth about people, which means to show their weaknesses, their contradictions, and even their lies.

BC: *The character of Antoine Doinel aside, it must have been an advantage to work with the same actor on five different occasions.*

FT: Yes, that's true. It's always nice to work with an actor more than once, because shooting goes by so fast that you really only get to know the actors in the editing room, after they've gone off to work on other films. There you watch them in slow motion, backwards, and forwards, taking your time to look closely at everything they say and do. I think a first film is like being introduced to an actor. It's only later that you get to know the actor better and enjoy writing for him.

BC: *Jean-Pierre Léaud is certainly the actor you know best. You've watched him grow, into a man as well as a film artist.*

FT: Yes, but I don't want him to be too closely linked with me or Antoine Doinel. As you know, he's made other films, like Jean-Luc Godard's *Masculine Feminine* [1966]. And he has worked not only with me and Godard, but also with Julien Duvivier, Jean Eustache, Jean Cocteau, Jerzy Skolimowski, and many other directors. I used him myself outside the Doinel cycle, in *Two English Girls* [1971] and *Day for Night* [1973]. But, obviously, the character of Antoine Doinel fit Léaud like a glove, because, as the cycle progressed, I wrote the character with him in mind. Indeed, I created some scenes just because I knew he would be funny in them—at least I laughed during the writing as I thought of him.

The problem is, I got a kick out of putting him in situations that were, if not degrading, then not to his advantage. The characters around him look strong, and Antoine therefore looks too weak. It's a high price to pay for the fun I had when writing or filming the cycle, and that Léaud had while acting in it—because he loved to play the part. But sometimes the public gets confused. They forget it's fiction and can form an inaccurate opinion of the actor. That happened in *Day for Night*, which is about shooting a film. I had this fabulous Italian actress, Valentina Cortese, who portrays an alcoholic prone to dramatic outbursts because her son is dying or for whatever reason. Now no one thought that Valentina Cortese was an alcoholic in real life. Léaud himself plays a young actor in *Day for Night*. At some point he jeopardizes the whole shoot because of a romantic problem he is having. And do you know what? People thought from this that Jean-Pierre Léaud was capable of walking off the set, of abandoning a film before the shooting is completed. This hurt Léaud a bit, this public reaction: he told me so.

BC: *There was a process of identification of the man with his character, going all the way back to* The 400 Blows.

FT: Yes, more with him than with Jacqueline Bisset or Valentina Cortese or Jean-Pierre Aumont in the same film: a director's perverse triumph, you could call it.

BC: *You once told a tale about going into a café the day after they showed one of the Antoine Doinel films on television. The waiter in the bistro said to you, "I saw you on TV last night." He had identified you with the character of Doinel.*

FT: He came to pour my coffee and said, "You must have made that picture some time ago." He saw the age discrepancy, at least.

BC: *But he saw a resemblance, too. When you think about it, is this amazing, disconcerting, or both?*

FT: There was a scene in *Day for Night* where Léaud and I were face-to-face, together for the first time in front of the camera. *That* was a strange feeling, for both of us, and for more than just a moment.

BC: *In 1957 you wrote the following: "The films of the future will be more personal than autobiographical, like a confession or a diary. Young filmmakers will speak in the first person in order to tell what happened to them: their first love, a political awakening, a trip, an illness, and so on. Tomorrow's film will be an act of love." If someone wanted to make movies today, would you tell that person, "Tell us about your life. There's nothing more important or more interesting." Or would you say, "The industry is tougher now. Conform to it and don't listen to what I said."*

FT: Very tactfully put, M. Cardullo. Yes, well done. My prediction was fulfilled beyond my wildest dreams—you know that. So I wouldn't say the opposite today. But I *would* say, "Talk about what interests you, but make sure it interests others, too."

BC: *What does that mean? How can you know your film will interest others?*

FT: I know the type of film I was reacting against when I wrote those sentences in 1957. I was thinking of films like—no, I don't really want to give negative examples. I'm not a critic anymore. Suffice it to say that I was thinking of films where you could put the following in the opening credits: "Any resemblance to real life is purely coincidental." These are films where everything is false: male/female relationships, the way people meet, *everything*. I'm not talking about Robert Bresson, Jacques Becker, and Max Ophüls. There were some filmmakers, like these, that we liked. But I am talking about the kind of movie in which the script was written by five or six people, who had been given the royal treatment for a month, at the Trianon in Versailles, as they put the screenplay together.

BC: *Or during filming on the Côte d'Azure.*

FT: Yes. This process produced really awful movies, which we still occasionally see on television. Time has lent them a sort of harmless homogeneity that they did not have at the time they were made. So back then it was only natural to call for more personal films. Films like *Bonjour tristesse* [1958], from the novel by Françoise Sagan, who was a teenager when she wrote this book. Basically we wanted films like that, or at least closer to that, and I think this is what happened, but to such a point that films eventually became more than personal: they became narcissistic. The makers of such films spoke very personally, but sometimes they could have benefited from having had a friend read their scripts first.

Many such films, for example, followed a single, often autobiographical character. In the Antoine Doinel cycle, of course, I followed just such a character. But at some point I felt that I had evolved—when I made *Stolen Kisses*, to be exact—because there I made myself add several substantial supporting roles. So I, and others, were gradually returning to a narrative tradition based more on observation and synthesis than subjectivity and self-exploration. Now we have both kinds of films. It's true there are no more powerful producers who send writers to work at St-Paul-de-Vence or the Trianon, and this is probably a good thing. Nowadays you write a script all by yourself, in your own little apartment—and perhaps this is perhaps not so good a thing as one might at first think.

BC: *Thank you so much for your time today, M. Truffaut. I know this was not easy for you. You have been a most gracious and giving host.*

FT: You're quite welcome; I enjoyed our talk. And I wish you luck in your own critical career. Do you want to remain a critic?

BC: *For now, yes.*

FT: Then at least stay as close to filmmaking as you can, if you do not become a director yourself. I mean through set visits, script advising, television commentary, and interviews like this one—which was nothing like the academic kind I am often called upon to give. Such activity will make you a better, or more complete, critic, and, especially if others follow your lead, it could ultimately make the cinema less self-directed, which is to say more honest. *Plût à Dieu!*

François Truffaut Filmography

The Four Hundred Blows (1959)
Shoot the Piano Player (1960)
Jules and Jim (1962)
The Soft Skin (1964)
Fahrenheit 451 (1965)
The Bride Wore Black (1967)
Stolen Kisses (1968)
Mississippi Mermaid (1969)
Bed and Board (1970)
The Wild Child (1970)
Two English Girls (1971)
Such a Gorgeous Kid Like Me (1972)
Day for Night (1973)
The Story of Adele H. (1975)
Small Change (1976)
The Man Who Loved Women (1977)
The Green Room (1978)
Love on the Run (1979)
The Last Metro (1980)
The Woman Next Door (1981)
Confidentially Yours (1983)

Bibliography

Allen, Don. *Finally Truffaut*. Rev. ed. London: Secker & Warburg, 1985.

Crisp, C. G. *François Truffaut*. New York: Praeger, 1972.

Holmes, Diana, and Robert Ingram. *François Truffaut*. Manchester, UK: Manchester University Press, 1998.

Ingram, Robert. *François Truffaut: Film Author, 1932–1983*. Köln: Taschen, 2004.

———. *Truffaut: The Complete Films*. Köln: Taschen, 2003.

Insdorf, Annette. *François Truffaut*. Rev. and updated ed. New York: Cambridge University Press, 1994.

Monaco, James. *The New Wave: Truffaut, Godard, Chabrol, Rohmer, Rivette*. New York: Oxford University Press, 1976.

Stam, Robert. *François Truffaut and Friends: Modernism, Sexuality, and Film Adaptation*. New Brunswick, N.J.: Rutgers University Press, 2006.

Truffaut, François. *The Early Film Criticism of François Truffaut*. Ed. Wheeler Winston Dixon. Trans. Ruth Cassel Hoffman, Sonja Kropp, and Brigitte Formentin-Humbert. Bloomington: Indiana University Press, 1993.

———. *The Films in My Life*. Trans. Leonard Mayhew. New York: Simon and Schuster, 1978.

———. *Truffaut by Truffaut*. Ed. Dominique Rabourdin. Trans. Robert Erich Wolf. New York: Abrams, 1987.

Walz, Eugene P. *François Truffaut: A Guide to References and Resources*. Boston, Mass.: G. K. Hall, 1982.

The Cinema of Resistance

An Interview with
Jean-Pierre and Luc Dardenne

Luc Dardenne (left) and Jean-Pierre Dardenne.

Ever since *The Promise* in 1996, the prospect of a new film from Belgian siblings Luc and Jean-Pierre Dardenne has been cause for rejoicing. Naturalistically shot, impeccably constructed, uncompromising and emotionally searing, the Dardenne brothers' films give voice to a population often despised or ignored: illegal aliens, slumlords, corrupt officials, and small-time criminals. To their characters the brothers bring a compassionate view born of the understanding that this underclass has, in part, been created by society's higher-ups. These are figures of limited material and social means who, under the most dire circumstances, must grapple with life-and-death decisions. And though the pair might deny it, their films also suggest an ingrained Christian vision through insisting on the transformative possibility of the most debased being.

The Silence of Lorna, their latest portrait (2008), which premiered in Cannes, failed to elicit the rapturous response received by some of the earlier work, such as the 2005 Palme d'Or winner *L'Enfant* (*The Child*). Yet despite an exposition that some found lengthy, the Dardennes bring great resonance to this fable of a young Albanian immigrant caught in a terrible dilemma who struggles to redeem herself. As in *The Promise*, the film focuses on the machinations forced on illegals hoping to grab a morsel of the world's wealth—in this case through fake marriages for citizenship. This time the brothers placed their camera in the more gentrified city of Liège, rather than in their grimy industrial hometown of Seraing. Lorna has become a Belgian citizen through her sham marriage to junkie Claudy (Dardenne regular Jérémie Renier). A local mobster who engineered the union is planning to kill Claudy with a staged overdose so Lorna can remarry a Russian mafioso. But when Claudy threatens to start using drugs again, the two have passionate sex and form a sudden bond. . . .

"Beyond *L'Enfant*: The Complete Dardenne Brothers," a retrospective that ran at the Film Society of Lincoln Center in late May and early June of 2009, showcased the Dardennes' fiction features and the documentaries on social and political subjects with which the brothers made their name in the 1980s, as well as two early works—1987's heavily theatrical *Falsch* and 1992's relatively conventional *Je pense à vous*. I caught up with the Dardennes at Lincoln Center in New York and had the following conversation with them.

Bert Cardullo: *Where is your office located?*

Jean-Pierre Dardenne: In Liège, quite close to the places where we make our films. These are all the same landscapes that were used when we shot our documentaries. They're places we know from childhood, part of our sense of place. In the fiction films, in fact, we've given the settings less importance because it's an industrial city—they're dangerous as backdrops, they engender a kind of fascination and we didn't want that to be at the expense of the characters.

BC: *You did documentary work for many years. Could you talk a bit about going from non-fiction to fiction? How did you negotiate the transition from documentary to feature filmmaking?*

JPD: With documentaries and features, the contract with the spectator is different. With a documentary, the viewer is aware that the characters are real people and the stories actually happened to them. If you're watching a fiction film and you see a character being killed, you know when they finished shooting that person got up and walked off. But it enables you to go in a direction that wouldn't be permitted: In *La Promesse*, for example, you see characters allowing a man to die and then burying him. That's certainly not something you could show in a documentary.

Luc Dardenne: The way in which we filmed the earlier films—there's no relationship between this and the way we work now. We haven't kept any of that. What we have kept are the people and characters we filmed in the earlier years. We filmed hundreds of people in the area where we lived, working in their daily lives. They were shot on video and have been erased, but we might say in making a fiction film, "Do you remember what that person said?" The earlier films were films of memory, films about the past. Very few records existed about the workers' movement in that area—we wanted to capture the way they spoke, how they believed society could be changed, the society they lived in. Those documentary films dealt with a working class in the process of disappearing. The groups that existed then no longer exist. Now, we're dealing with people who are alone in an area that's collapsing economically around them. How do they try to find a connection, to meet someone else, to come together with another person? It's as if there's been a major catastrophe and there are only a few survivors, and they try to make contact with each other to re-create some kind of society. The main moral question is, do I kill you to advance my own interests or not? Do I let you have your life or not?

JPD: Let me add, to draw a further connection between the documentaries and our fictional work, that in the documentaries that we used to make, you go to film a reality that exists outside of you and you don't have control over it—it resists your camera. You have to take it as it is. So we try to keep that aspect of documentary in our fiction, to film something that resists us. And we try not to show everything or see everything. The character and the situation remain in the shadows and this opacity, this resistance, gives the truth and the life to what we're filming.

BC: *How do you create a situation that resists the camera?*

JPD: We put limitations on ourselves. For example, when we shot the scenes in the trailer in *Rosetta*, we specifically didn't want the walls to be movable; we wanted the walls to remain as they are in any trailer. This is a way to proceed; it's really an attitude. We don't want to be God—we don't want to dominate anything. We want to remain on the level of things as they are and not impose on them.

BC: *Are there moments in* Rosetta *that came out of spontaneity?*

LD: We shot in super-16, which allows you to have very lengthy shots; some shots would be ten minutes, many were five to eight minutes. We rehearse the actors a lot and we don't put anything on the floor for the actors to follow. So even if you organize exactly what they are going to do, they are never going to do it the same way. For example, the very last shot in *Rosetta*, because we did it that way—open to changes and not marking everything down—things happen, tensions are created from that, because you really don't know what's going to happen when you shoot. In the last scene, we did maybe ten takes and chose the last one, because the more the actress did it, the more tired she got. And the moment when she falls is the moment where we improvised in the frame. We didn't plan it, so those are the happy accidents; however rehearsed you are, there's still spontaneity that you don't control and in a way you provoke.

BC: *Do you see film as social activism in any way?*

LD: No.

BC: *Then as entertainment?*

LD: A little.

JPD: Hopefully, it's also entertaining. It's difficult to say. What do you mean when you say "social activism"?

BC: *In making a film about this woman Rosetta, you've also made a film about unemployment. So is that part of your agenda, or does that theme just derive organically from telling her story?*

JPD: Yes, our first desire is to make this portrait of a woman who is a fighter, a survivor. She really believes that if she doesn't find a job and a place in society, she is going to die. So we had to put ourselves and put the camera in that state of mind. And once you've done that, you have to address the moral issues: to kill or not to kill, to commit suicide or not to commit suicide. Of course, by doing this, you are also going to depict society and unemployment. We know what we're doing, but social activism, as you call it, is not our first aim; that comes with it, but it's not the reason why we do it.

BC: *Were you politically active as young men?*

JPD: There was always a desire on our part to take people—*people*, not political ideas necessarily—from the margins of society and put them in the center of the images we make. We weren't active politically but the first documentaries we made were portraits of working-class people who were active in unions, or in Communist, socialist, or Christian movements.

LD: Seraing was once a vibrant working-class town, with a strong labor movement. But with the crisis that struck the steel mills in the early 1970s, suddenly, we saw people like Rosetta and *L'Enfant*'s Bruno and Sonia, cut off from each other and with no social ties to the previous generation.

BC: *Can you comment on the use of the handheld camera in* Rosetta? *It seems to mirror the character's obsession-compulsion.*

JPD: You're right. But how we do it doesn't matter. How you get it matters and you obviously got it.

BC: *With your previous film,* La Promesse, *and this film, a gritty, sort of low-budget style on your part emerged. Could you conceive of making a film with more equipment and a bigger budget—with a crane at your disposal, for example?*

Jérémie Renier as Igor in the Dardennes' *La Promesse.*

LD: This is a house that we like to live in. Filming is like a house: you have to feel comfortable in it.

BC: *Why have you chosen to make narrative films and strayed away from documentaries? Do you find it more fulfilling?*

JPD: It's more exciting, because you put together a group of twenty people, and every morning you get together and you start giving life to creatures that don't exist, characters that don't exist, and not only do they then start to exist in front of you, but they escape from you and you can't control them anymore. You can't exhaust the possibilities. In documentaries, you're confronted with reality, and you cannot manipulate or move it. It's given to you the way it is, and in narrative fiction you can manipulate a bit.

BC: *How long did it take to shoot* Rosetta?

JPD: Eleven weeks.

BC: *For such a simple film, that seems a rather long time.*

LD: We shot a lot of footage, because we film many versions of the same sequence. Sometimes we shoot the scene, look at the dailies, and aren't happy with them, so we go back and shoot it again. We keep all the sets until the end, until the editing is absolutely over. We'd rather have the opportunity to re-shoot a scene than to rent a crane.

BC: *Could you speak about the sound in* Rosetta *briefly? The motorcycle, her breathing, her steps . . . they're so important to the film. Did you conceive of such sound at the script stage? Was that always part of the film?*

JPD: On the set, we started hearing the sounds very clearly, then after a week or two, we started realizing how important it was. For us, that's the most beautiful part of making a film: when you're shooting and you find those actions, ideas, or simple devices and make them part of the film.

BC: *Speaking of ideas, how did you get the idea for* Rosetta?

LD: We thought of the character of K. from *The Castle*, by Kafka. K. doesn't have access to the castle, he's rejected by the village, and he begins to question his own existence. This gave us the idea of a girl who is cast aside, who wants to gain something that will allow her back into society, but she is always knocked back. We decided to make her obsessed by the idea of having a job, just like anybody else, and of having a normal life. We decided to give this fixed idea to the character and to see just where this would lead her. From this point on, we wrote a great deal, with numerous re-writes, before finding Rosetta.

JPD: We decided not to begin with a plot but with a character. The idea was to put the spectator in a position where he asks himself: "What will happen to her? How will she deal with what happens to her?"

BC: *You have said that Rosetta is a warrior.*

JPD: With or without work, it is a constant battle that people lead today. Not working, regardless of choice, places you on the margins of society. You lose your reference point, you are unstructured, you don't know your place anymore, or even if you still have one. Work gives you certain duties and rights. When you are no longer working, you lose your rights. Work becomes a rarity. There is nothing left. To get a job you have to take someone else's place, and you have to be prepared to do certain things to get that.

LD: Rosetta is a warrior who never gives up, who is always prepared to attack. She is a survivor who lives in a primary state: water, shelter, food. She has found her own weapons, a survival system: boots for the campsite, shoes for work, a box for bait, bottles for fishing. She tinkers about, constantly obsessed by the search for a job.

BC: *Why did you make her live on a campsite?*

LD: We wanted to place Rosetta in living conditions where she feels she has almost reached rock bottom.

BC: *How did you create the character of Riquet?*

LD: We took more time to find him than we did with Rosetta. He is a straightforward thinker. He tells only one story. Rosetta is the opposite: she spies, she suspects, she peers through doorways, she always fears a conspiracy against her. With Riquet, it is the story of someone helping someone else. Riquet says: "I'm here for you," but Rosetta doesn't understand that.

JPD: When he reappears at the end it's because he can't accept what she has done. He comes back to haunt her. She has become a little like his prey. By harassing her, he keeps her alive. This tense, stubborn, hardened girl will finally open up and accept someone's help.

LD: From the first shot of the opening scene—with our obsessive-compulsive camera, as you call it—the spectator is disoriented.

JPD: The first scene of the film had to be both simple and violent, to introduce Rosetta, her situation, and her reaction to things. This scene reveals her character in its entirety. It shows the violence to which she's subjected, and it shows how violently she herself reacts. If you've understood everything from that point, then everything that follows should fall into place.

LD: Giving too much away prevents the character's existence. The less you say about a character the more the character exists. So we try not to give away too much. Everything is done in that way, including the mise-en-scène and the editing. Rather than give too much away, we try to find the essential movement of the character. What's touching and moving is that Rosetta doesn't pretend to live. She fights, ready to do seemingly unacceptable things under any other circumstance. She refuses to pretend, as her mother does: Because Rosetta's constantly waging a battle, she becomes withdrawn, she becomes hard. She isolates herself from others; there's something inside her that's stronger than she is, that inhabits her, something over which she has no control. Rosetta's attitude towards her mother is surprising. Her mother represents decay, and the daughter is scared of that.

BC: *How soon after* Rosetta *did you begin work on* Le Fils?

LD: We always need a bit of time after finishing a film before we start up again. After *Rosetta* we had the beginnings of two stories, and we were hesitating between the two. And then we started working on *Le Fils*, but we abandoned it twice and had a rest for a while. Then finally we did go back to it and made it our next project.

BC: *What is so special, if I may ask, about Olivier Gourmet as an actor?*

JPD: What is special about him is that there is nothing special. He's an Everyman figure; he could be anybody. He's neutral. If he were among ten people you probably wouldn't recognize him or pick him out. What interests us is his body. He's got a certain weight about him and yet at the same time he's very agile. He was very sporting when he was younger. Also his glance, his look is very particular, and we played with his eyes in *Le Fils*. In certain positions, whether it's sideways or face-to-face, you can virtually eliminate his eyes. It's very particular the way his eyes are hidden by the rim of his glasses. His eyes are actually very small.

BC: *Has Olivier Gourmet asked you why you are interested in him?*

LD: He does say that he likes to work with his body and he is very manual. He is a man who doesn't speak very much. He's from the countryside and he likes the fact that we don't speak very much on set. The work on set is quite quiet. Our films don't have that much text. The films have an understanding, an entente, which doesn't rely on words.

BC: *How did you develop* Le Fils?

JPD: It didn't develop from an idea. Initially, once we had a few fixed images, our main object was to think how Olivier would welcome into his workshop the killer of his son, and how the two bodies would react in such a confined space. Olivier is attracted to Francis and he's also scared, and that's what interested us. At that point we decided that Olivier would be a carpenter. That helped us enormously in terms of the storyline and the scenes. That's how we got the scenes with tape measures or the one with ladders. And all the while, with the bodies unbalancing the equilibrium. The small camera allowed us to give the impression that Olivier's body was permanently un-balanced, as though he didn't have two feet on the ground—unlike Rosetta, who had both feet planted on the ground.

BC: *Why do you make your films so minimalist? There are no back stories, so to speak; the narrative is pared down, and there's no music.*

LD: You could say it's a formula. The more you take off materially, the more spiritually the disarray can appear. It's only a point of view, but what interests us is to go immediately to the essential and for us the essential in this story is the doubt, the hesitation, the oscillation about whether to kill or not to kill. That was what was working in our heads, that was the underlying ques-tion in the film. I'm not sure, but that's what makes a lot of things no longer seem necessary. We explored silence in a different way in *Rosetta*. There she mustn't speak, so as to preserve her energy. Here the silence is more about waiting. You're waiting for something or somebody to say, "I regret," or "I killed your son." We cleared out more in this film than in other films. For example the color in Olivier's apartment was the same as in the carpentry workshop—there are no photos in the flat. It's a film that's more abstract than *Rosetta*.

BC: *Your films are often parsed as spiritual allegories. Were you raised Christian?*

JPD: Yes, we had a strong Catholic upbringing, until we were in our teens and rejected what our father had imposed on us. But despite the coercive, puritanical elements of religion, our education taught us to acknowledge other people as human beings. We were forbidden to watch TV or movies, though—our father thought they were the devil incarnate.

BC: *To what extent can we read* Le Fils *itself as a religious parable?*

JPD: Such a thing is often said to us about this film, so there must be some truth in it! We hope, though, we haven't illustrated the script of the Passion. It's true that if you want to read it in a certain way, there is a religious dimension. When Olivier is in the lumberyard, at one point he climbs up to the top and drops one of the planks. I don't know how, it must have been a fluke—I think one of the actors must have been in profile—but we had the father, the son, and the cross. And we yelled "Cut" because it was too much.

BC: *But you could have made Olivier a plumber.*

LD: Death is ever present in the film. We never see it but death is there. Wood remains a material that is alive. For a few months Olivier was going to be a cook. But we couldn't quite grasp that—we need to have an image even if it's slightly out of focus compared to what the film is actually going to be like. Often on location or set, we play the characters ourselves to see how things are going to happen, and to try different camera angles. The tape measure wasn't just an idea—it was in the matter. Then we were able to articulate the story and the mise-en-scène in a way we couldn't if the setting were a kitchen.

BC: *Bruno Dumont, the director of* L'Humanité, *has said that a film should be a dialogue between himself and the viewer. Is that valid for you as well?*

JPD: We think about that the whole time. If somebody asks us if the audience is present, and are you scared whether the audience is going to like your work or not, we answer that we want our film to love the audience, which doesn't mean love or seduce in that sense, or make them more stupid. Within the frame we have a little spare space for the spectator to enter the film and do his own work. The camera is close in *Le Fils*, as in *Rosetta*. But in *Rosetta* the audience knows what she is going to do, or what she's looking for. Here Olivier doesn't know; the spectator himself will assume he wants to take revenge against Francis for killing his son. It's a sort of moral experience that the spectator undergoes through Olivier. Sometimes I've heard people say that at one point they felt close to the boy Francis, because he was weak. It's a shame, one woman said, that he didn't say "sorry" for what he did.

BC: *Your recent films have been almost obsessively focused on their main characters.*

LD: For *L'Enfant*, it was an image. While shooting *Le Fils*, we would see this young woman pushing a baby carriage, very violently, as if she were somehow trying to get rid of the child. When we got around to thinking about our next film, this vision reappeared. Eventually, the missing character, the child's father, became the main character. We had discussed before the idea of a father selling his baby, but we didn't want that actual act to become the central element. We wanted to tell the story of a man who, to accept paternity, has to sell his child first.

JPD: As I implied in my remarks about *Rosetta*, it's important for us that the characters don't become prisoners of the story. They should retain a sense of autonomy. They're not pieces on a chessboard.

BC: *Do you always know ahead of time how you're going to end a film? Your last few films have very potent final scenes. Since your characters are, as you say, autonomous, they may indeed sometimes lead you in unexpected directions.*

JPD: For *Le Fils*, on the last day we came up with a different ending. Since we shoot chronologically, we have a sense as we go of how the story is developing. In *L'Enfant*, we knew what we wanted from the start. We always had in mind this reconciliation. There were other endings that we considered—one of them had a longer chase scene and a shooting—but they seemed a little bit too "adventure," too much like a crime or action film.

LD: We also don't like to kill our characters—we love them too much. Shooting our films is such a physical ordeal for the actors that we want to save them at the end.

BC: *The main character of your new film, Lorna, is played by an actress from Kosovo. How did you find her?*

JPD: One of our assistants went to Pristina, Skopje, and Tirana in order to audition about one hundred professional and non-professional young actresses. We selected Arta Dobroshi. We had seen her in two Albanian movies a few weeks before. We went to Sarajevo, where she lives, to meet her and we filmed her with our DV camera for a whole day. We filmed her walking, running, singing, and also playing in scenes like those in our movie. Then she came over to Liège and we filmed her acting with Jérémie Renier and Fabrizio Rongione. She was amazingly beautiful and natural. In the evening, before she flew to Sarajevo, we told her that we had selected her for the role of Lorna and that she would have to come back to Belgium a few months before the shooting to rehearse and learn French.

BC: *Unlike your previous films, which were shot in super 16mm, this one is shot in 35mm with a less mobile camera and wider frames. Why did you make this change?*

JPD: We tested five digital cameras, a 35mm, and a super 16mm. The images shot at night with the 35mm were closest to what we wanted for this project. Plus, we had decided that this time around, the camera would not be constantly moving, would be less descriptive and limited to recording images. Because of its weight the 35mm was best suited for us.

BC: *In your previous works, the camera focused very closely on the characters, whereas in this film it seems to maintain a certain distance. You could say that* The Silence of Lorna *is characterized by an understated directorial approach, and that ever since* Rosetta *your camera has steadily been "calming" down in this way.*

LD: We used a more distant, static camera because we wanted to watch this mysterious Lorna, to observe her. It was a case of not moving with her and mimicking her energy; we wanted to replicate rather than write with the camera. This film's storyline is, without doubt, the most complex we have ever written. Lorna is surrounded by four men and each represents a different story—which is another reason for the "observational," removed approach.

BC: *All your previous movies were set in Seraing, the industrial town where you spent your childhood. In this instance, you decided to set your story in Liège, which is a big city, although it's just a few miles away from Seraing.*

LD: We agree that Liège is a bigger city, with plenty of people in the streets during the daytime as well as in the evening. For Lorna, the main character, who comes from Albania, a big European city embodies all sorts of hope. We also wanted to see Lorna in the midst of the crowd, with people physically close to her but who knew nothing of her secret. Placing Lorna and her secret amidst people who know nothing about her makes her even more strange and conveys a greater sense of fear and solitude.

BC: *Despite the dramatic dimension of* The Silence of Lorna, *your film has an almost sensual, even sweet, quality.*

JPD: We owe it to Arta, the actress—her face, her voice, the way she moves, the way she speaks French with her special accent. It's probably also because of our camera's perception of things, and let's not forget that the movie is a kind of love story.

BC: *Did Lorna have a source in real life?*

LD: Someone among our acquaintances told us the story of a real-life Lorna, who made a false marriage—but we took her story in a different direction.

BC: *How do you apportion the directing of your films?*

LD: We discuss the script. We both do the casting. On the set we work solely with the actors for a long time, without any crew. Then the crew and the director of photography come on board, and one of us goes to the monitor. Once we take a shot, we discuss it in front of the monitor and evaluate it. Then we discuss it with the cinematographer. We both edit. It's really not more complicated than if there were only one person.

BC: *Do you rehearse a lot before shooting?*

JPD: Yes, we do—so we can be at our most free when we shoot. We're free when we're very familiar with the work. In fact, the rehearsals are the best period of the whole business—*le plus beau* moment. We don't discuss the psychology of the characters. It's something more instinctual. Rehearsals are like soccer camp. Then when we shoot, it's the championship.

BC: *The first shot of* The Silence of Lorna *is bills being handed over at the bank. The physical circulation of money, in fact, is very present in the film. Could you talk a bit about the omnipresence of money in your films?*

JPD: Money governs our relations with others to a certain extent, which is not necessarily negative. Money gives you the means to change your life, and in this film, all the characters want to change *their* lives—and the only way of achieving this in our day and age is with money. Unlike many films, ours don't treat money as if it were something shameful: we show it for what it is. It's just there. And we want to depict human characters whom viewers won't judge as they do in real life. Money, after all, can permit as well as immoral moral behavior. When Lorna opens a bank account to deposit money for Claudy's child—her unborn child—it's beautiful money.

BC: *I found something in Lorna's transformation rather mysterious. Through much of the exposition she seems irritated by strung-out Claudy and wants only to blow him off. What triggers the change in her feelings for him?*

LD: Not one thing alone. When she starts to help Claudy—for instance helps him get up from the floor—she starts to change as a human being. She undresses to keep him from leaving in pursuit of drugs; she makes an extreme gesture . . . and also at the same time feels desire. Claudy shows her he can stop, she admires that, and she feels guilty that they plan to kill him. But, bottom line, her gesture toward him is mysterious and can't be explained—in fact, it mystifies her, too. It's as mysterious to her as it is to us.

BC: *Was the whole script planned in? Or were there changes as you went along?*

JPD: As in all our work, we tend to augment the physical aspects, to add gestures when we shoot and reduce dialogue. And the actors bring something of themselves to it; the shoot is organic and changes with the circumstances. Even so, the film you see in this case is very close to the script.

BC: *There's an enigma at the heart of this film: is Lorna's baby real or imaginary? Of course, the doctors say there's no child. Yet the question remains. . . .*

LD: We first had the idea for the imaginary pregnancy when we decided not to show Claudy's corpse. This absence for Lorna is filled by the baby, though the baby is an absence, too. You know, if you want to believe she's pregnant, you can. An interesting thing: even with an added scene in which a doctor shows her she's not pregnant, audiences persist in believing she is. I think it's because the viewer wants her to redeem herself and protect a new life. She was careless with Claudy's life, but she'll be careful with the life of the baby, which represents the future and hope.

BC: *The film offers a harsh vision of Europe.*

JPD: Even though the film is set in Western Europe, what interested us essentially was the story of people who come from elsewhere, how they arrive, and what methods (which are not to be praised) they are willing to use in order to realize their dreams. Lorna is a human being with her own paradoxes, a woman who mistrusts everybody but learns to have faith at a certain point. In order for the story to work, she had to come from a country outside the European Union. She is Albanian, but she could just as well have been Brazilian or Russian. We can't fight against waves of migration as we thought we could ten years ago. Today, we have to adopt a more fraternal and human approach in dealing with these people, without lapsing into naïveté, either, for those who hire clandestine workers will only take advantage of the situation.

BC: *You gradually reveal information as the film unfolds. How did you manage to withhold information for so long from the audience, and to what extent do you risk losing the viewer by doing this?*

JPD: We didn't want to lose the viewer but instead create a sense of anticipation and encourage the audience to ask questions. It's the first time that we've made a film driven by suspense and we played with the rules of the genre, notably by using jump cuts, which were there from the start.

BC: *Examined closely, the plot of Lorna is worthy of any American thriller. It deals with the Mafia, false identity papers, marriages of convenience, and murder. You nonetheless succeed in maintaining your own distinctive outlook. How did you manage to stay within the realm of a certain "cinema of the real"?*

LD: One of the most important aspects is that Lorna and Fabio do not conform to the stereotyped image of the film noir heroine and gangster. Lorna and her boyfriend are immigrants who yearn for a normal life. We can't speak of Lorna as a femme fatale; we show her leading an ordinary, everyday life. There are, however, elements of genre film in the aesthetic composition: the night, the city, and the rain.

BC: *Each character is distinguished by a prop or an item of clothing: for instance Lorna's jacket and red trousers, Fabio's taxi, and Claudy's envelope.*

JPD: Some were more obvious than others. Fabio's taxi was there from the outset; it's his status and his home, and it took on even more significance during the shoot. Claudy's envelope is the prop that symbolizes his relationship with Lorna. As for the costumes, after a month's work, we decided that Lorna would have a skirt and two pairs of trousers, including the red one, which makes her instantly recognizable when she walks around the city!

LD: She was a bit heavier as well, so we asked her to lose weight. The settings, the walls, the colors—all this is carefully studied and thought out, so it takes time. Even the floor of the apartment is "designed," if you will.

BC: *Here is a question related to the one I asked you earlier about* Rosetta *and social activism. Is immigration one of the themes of the film, or is it simply a vehicle for telling your character's story?*

LD: Again, more of the latter. Obviously we're not drawing parallels between immigration and "the underworld," but the Russian and Albanian mafias do exist. Our heroine is part of this world, yet at the outset she's primarily an economic refugee. To her, Liège is paradise. It's possible to find work, she makes marriage plans and saves money to buy a snack bar, etc. Unfortunately, she finds herself at the center of a scheme that takes place at the expense of someone considered to be of little worth, because he is a junkie.

BC: *The film explores a subject found throughout your works: guilt.*

JPD: In a word, I'd say that this subject interests us because it's when we feel guilty that we become more human. In all our films, it's thanks to feelings of guilt that the character breaks his or her routine and changes.

LD: But I'd say the idea of guilt, of what we're prepared to do in order to guarantee our place in the sun, has become simply a human question in our society. Take note that, for us, there is nothing morbid in this; guilt is not narcissistic because it enables us to work towards something better.

BC: *You've distanced yourselves from your first two features. How would you introduce them to viewers familiar with your later work?*

JPD: *Falsch* was like a continuation of doing a documentary. It was the first time we worked with real actors and we were a little afraid. Looking back on *Je pense à vous* from the perspective of now, we consider it a happy failure.

We were very conscious as we moved from documentaries to features that we hadn't gone to film school. It was as if we were very-well-brought-up children who didn't want to go against the usual way of doing things, so we tried to respect the usual ways of filming. We were afraid, and we were afraid of our fear as well. Sometimes fear can motivate you and get you to move on, but here it paralyzed us. In the end it was fortunate—it enabled us to see that this was not the route we wanted to take. That gave us the freedom to find out what we wanted to do next.

LD: I think our style—this freedom we have in our way of working—really came with *La Promesse*. It was there that we developed our technique. We begin on the first day with the first shot and work through chronologically. We try to act as though we had never filmed anything before and are starting again; we try to ask, "What are we trying to do? What are we trying to show?"

BC: *There's also a shift in subject matter from the explicitly political Cold War–era documentaries to your recent features about atomized twenty-first-century individuals.*

JPD: It's true that the documentary films we made took place in the second half of the twentieth century and dealt with questions of class and the post-war generation's coming to terms with the struggle between the communist East and the capitalistic West. In *La Promesse* and *The Silence of Lorna* in particular, there are characters new to the traditional idea of Western Europe. They want to have better lives. One of the characteristics of the past twenty years is this enormous change in the idea of Western Europe. A lot of people are coming and trying to find a place, but it's not going to be very easy—there's this fortress mentality of the old Europe. This is really the most important challenge for Europe now: How do we incorporate these migrations, find a place for these groups of people so that they can contribute towards developing the wealth of Europe?

BC: *What's your next project?*

JPD: We've already spoken about quite a lot of projects, but they are always the same ones! Something will come forward with a bit more weight. We're lucky in that we can get on with the films we want to make—not the ones your average viewer wants to see.

Jean-Pierre and Luc Dardenne Filmography

Falsch (*False*, 1986)
Je pense à vous (*You're on My Mind*, 1992)
La Promesse (*The Promise*, 1996)
Rosetta (1999)
Le Fils (*The Son*, 2002)
L'Enfant (*The Child*, 2005)
Le Silence de Lorna (*The Silence of Lorna*, 2008)

Bibliography

Belant, Lauren. "Nearly Utopian, Nearly Normal: Post-Fordist Affect in *La Promesse* and *Rosetta*." *Public Culture* 19, no. 2 (2007), 273–301.

Cooper, Sarah. "Mortal Enemies: Reading Levinas with the Dardenne Brothers." *Film-Philosophy* 11, no. 2 (August 2007), 66–87.

Crano, R. D. "'Occupy without Counting': Furtive Urbanism in the Films of Jean-Pierre and Luc Dardenne." *Film-Philosophy* 13, no. 1 (April 2009), 1–15.

Hessels, Wouter. "*Rosetta*." In Ernest Mathijs, *The Cinema of the Low Countries*, 239–247. London: Wallflower, 2004.

Mosley, Philip. *Split Screen: Belgian Cinema and Cultural Identity*. Albany: State University of New York Press, 2001.

O'Shaughnessy, Martin. "The Dardenne Brothers and the Emergence of Raw Revolt." In Martin O'Shaughnessy, *The New Face of Political Cinema: Commitment in French Film since 1995*, 47–55. New York: Berghahn Books, 2007.

———. "Ethics in the Ruin of Politics: The Dardenne Brothers." In Kate Ince, ed., *Five Directors: Auteurism from Assayas to Ozon*, 59–83. Manchester, UK: Manchester University Press, 2008.

Rosello, Mireille. "Protection or Hospitality: The Young Man and the Illegal Immigrant in *La Promesse*." In Mireille Rosello, *Postcolonial Hospitality: The Immigrant as Guest*, 136–148. Palo Alto, Calif.: Stanford University Press, 2001.

Spaas, Lieve. "Luc and Jean-Pierre Dardenne." In Lieve Spaas, *The Francophone Film: A Struggle for Identity*, 37–43. Manchester, UK: Manchester University Press, 2000.

Thyss, Marianne, and René Michelems. *Belgian Cinema*. Ghent, Belgium: Ludion, 1999.

NEAR EAST, FAR EAST,
MID-CONVERSATION

"I Am Simply a Maker of Films"

A Visit with Akira Kurosawa, the Sensei of the Cinema

Akira Kurosawa (1910–1998) was a Japanese film director, producer, screenwriter, and editor. In a career that spanned fifty-seven years, Kurosawa directed thirty films. He is widely regarded as one of the most important and influential of all filmmakers. In 1989, he was given an Academy Award for Lifetime Achievement "for cinematic accomplishments that have inspired, delighted, enriched, and entertained worldwide audiences and influenced filmmakers throughout the world."

The great irony of Kurosawa's career is that he was far more popular outside Japan than inside his native country. The son of an army officer, Kurosawa studied art before gravitating to film as a means of supporting himself. He served for seven years as an assistant to director Kajiro Yamamoto before beginning his own directorial career with *Sanshiro Sugata* (1943), a film about the nineteenth-century struggle for supremacy between adherents of judo and jujitsu that so impressed the military government, he was prevailed upon to make a sequel in 1945.

Following the end of World War II, Kurosawa's career gathered speed with a series of films that cut across all genres, from crime thrillers to period pieces. Among the latter, his *Rashomon* (1950) became the first postwar Japanese film to find wide favor with Western audiences, and simultaneously introduced leading man Toshiro Mifune to viewers around the world. It was Kurosawa's *Seven Samurai* (1954), however, that made the largest impact of any of his movies outside Japan. Although heavily cut for its original release, this three-hour-plus medieval action movie, shot with painstaking attention to both dramatic and period detail, became one of the most popular Japanese films ever in the West, and every subsequent Kurosawa film was released in the U.S. in some form, even if many—most notably *The Hidden Fortress* (1958)—had their running time significantly reduced.

In his later years, despite ill health and problems getting monetary backing for his more ambitious projects, Kurosawa remained the most prominent of Japanese filmmakers. With his Westernized style, he always found a wider audience and more financing opportunities in Europe and America than he did in his own country. A sensitive romantic at heart, with a sentimental streak that occasionally rose forcefully to the surface, Kurosawa the artist probably resembles the American John Ford more closely than he does any of his fellow Japanese directors.

The following interview took place in the spring of 1992 after the New York premiere of *Rhapsody in August*.

Bert Cardullo: *Could you talk a bit about all the aspects that go into the making of a film?*

Akira Kurosawa: There are many aspects to a film: cultural, philosophical, musical, visual, and so on. But the most important thing is for these elements to come together and make a movie. When this is done well, it is only then that the audience can perceive a truly beautiful film. I have been trying to capture this throughout my career, but it's actually quite difficult. For example, in any one of my films there are only a few cuts that I am fully satisfied with.

BC: *At the Academy Awards, you said, "I don't really understand moviemaking yet." What did you mean by saying that, since no one could quite believe it?*

AK: What I really meant by saying that is that I don't possess a logical mind, so it's difficult for me to explain how films are supposed to be made. All I am capable of doing is actually creating them.

BC: *How did you learn to make films?*

AK: In the 1930s, I started out by working as an assistant to Yamamoto Kajiro, but I was completely free to do whatever I wanted. At the time, our company, P.C.L., was quite small—only two buildings, with very little ground space. The company's policy was to regard assistant directors as cadets—a kind of élite-to-be. Assistants like me were supposed to involve themselves in every stage of production; then they would be promoted to chief assistant, whereupon they were supposed to learn leadership, how to guide a team in one direction. A chief assistant had to do every imaginable kind of job, including that of producer.

There were two pillars in Yamamoto's training policy: scenario writing and editing. He considered that a good director must be a scenario writer, too, and he let me write a lot—scenarios were my main source of income at the time. He also let me do a lot of editing; in the latter part of his career, I edited almost all his films. That naturally was very helpful to me. Our relationship was less that of teacher and student than that of elder brother and younger one; Yamamoto's greatness was that he tried to remain open to all sorts of talent—in this case, whatever talent he saw in me at this point in my career.

This period, the 1930s to the early 1950s, was the springtime of Japanese filmmaking. There was growth as well as optimism. The top management of the film companies itself consisted of film directors, and they didn't try to restrict you for commercial reasons. But in the late 1950s and the 1960s the climate changed. It was tragic when men like Mizoguchi, Ozu, and Naruse all died, because we began to lose our standing as directors and the companies themselves took over the power. After that came the Dark Ages.

BC: *Have you ever taken on a project simply offered to you by a producer or a production company?*

AK: No, my films emerge solely from my own desire to say a particular thing at a particular time. The root of any film project for me is this inner need to express something. What nurtures this root and makes it grow into a tree is the script. What makes the tree bear flowers and fruit is the directing.

BC: *You have spoken in the past of "cinematic beauty," and I'd like you to elaborate on that phrase if you will.*

AK: Cinematic beauty, of course, can only be expressed in a film, and it must be present in a film for that film to be a moving work. When it is very well expressed, one experiences a particularly deep emotion while watching that film. I believe it is this quality that draws people to come and see a film, and it is the hope of attaining this quality that inspires the filmmaker to make his film in the first place. In other words, I believe that the essence of the cinema lies in cinematic beauty.

Let me try to answer your question by asking another and then answering it. What is cinema? The answer to this question is no easy matter. Long ago the Japanese novelist Naoya Shiga presented an essay written by his grandchild as one of the most remarkable prose pieces of his time. He had it published in a literary magazine. It was entitled "My Dog" and ran as follows: "My dog resembles a bear; he also resembles a badger; he resembles a fox as well. . . ." The essay proceeded to enumerate the dog's special characteristics, comparing each one to yet another animal, and developing into a full list of the animal kingdom. However, the essay closed with the statement, "But since he's a dog, he most resembles a dog."

I remember bursting out laughing when I read this essay, yet it makes a serious point. Cinema resembles so many other arts. If cinema has very literary characteristics, it also has theatrical qualities, a philosophical side, attributes of painting and sculpture, and musical elements. But cinema is, in the final analysis, cinema, and cinematic strength—or beauty—derives from the multiplier effect of sound and image being brought together.

BC: *Color, of course, has something to do with such beauty, as does black and white—however infrequently used it is these days. Why had you not used color in your films up to 1970, when you made* Dodeskaden *in color?*

AK: In its state at the time, color cinematography was too strong or loud to represent properly the subdued color that is peculiarly Japanese. By strict standards even Teinosuke Kinugasa's *Gate of Hell* [1953] was not truly Japanese; its color was a little different in quality, I think. Then, too, the photosensitivity of color used to be so low, I couldn't close down my iris enough to capture the detail I like to get. And, in any event, shooting simultaneously from several different camera positions, as I like to do, would in the past have made the cost of color prohibitive. But there's something to be said for black and white, and I harbor the hope of returning to it someday. A black-and-white film has a special quality. It's difficult to describe, but that quality is still very much alive for me today. On *Rashomon* my cameraman was Miyagawa Kazuo, and I think black-and-white photography reached its peak with that film.

BC: *You always work out the continuity for a film in advance, don't you?*

AK: Yes, but that sequence may not necessarily be the most interesting way to shoot the picture. Things can happen without warning on a shoot that produce a startling effect. When these can be incorporated into the film without upsetting the balance, the whole becomes much more interesting. This process is similar to that of a pot being fired in a kiln. Ashes and other particles can fall onto the melted glaze during the firing and cause unpredictable but nonetheless beautiful results. Similarly unplanned but interesting effects arise in the course of directing a movie, so I call them "kiln changes."

Actually, I have to say that it's very, very important to me *not* to film the movie exactly the way it's written or exactly the way I have worked it out ahead of time. That takes all the fun out of it. Because you're dealing with actors and circumstances of nature, a lot of things can change, and it's important to be able to take advantage of those things at the moment they occur. A director's job is like a general's: you have to be prepared for lots of unexpected occurrences—especially anything to do with nature. But that's what makes me happy about filmmaking: the possibility of getting something different and better than what I had conceived at an earlier stage.

Even in the writing stage, I think a lot of directors conceive of their characters in such a way that they just sort of set them out there to carry forth the drama like puppets. The director pushes them this way and then that way, and they do what they're programmed to do. But when I conceive of a character, it's very important to have that character develop his own life. When he does, then I feel *I'm* being led around like a puppet by the character. That's where my interest in film comes from.

BC: *Let me ask the same question in a different way. What, for you, is the relationship between a script and the film made from it? That is, what role does the script play in determining the finished film's quality?*

AK: With a good script a good director can produce a masterpiece; with the same script a mediocre director can make a passable film. But with a bad script even a good director can't possibly create a good film or a truly cinematic expression. The camera and the microphone must be able to cross both fire and water: that is what makes a real movie. And the script must be something that has the power to launch this crossing, if you will.

Something else you have to take into account is the fact that the best scripts have very few explanatory passages. Adding explanation to the descriptive passages of a screenplay is the most dangerous trap you can fall into. It's easy to explain the psychological state of a character at a particular moment, but it's very difficult to describe it through the delicate nuances of action and dialogue. Yet it is not impossible to do so. A great deal about this subject can be learned from the study of the great plays, and I believe that the "hard-boiled" detective novels can also be very instructive.

BC: *What's your favorite cinematic structure?*

AK: I like the structure of a symphony, with its three or four movements and differing tempos. Or one can use the Noh play with its three-part structure: *jo,* or introduction; *ha,* or destruction; and *kyu,* or haste. If you devote yourself fully to Noh and gain something good from this, it will emerge naturally in your films. The Noh is a truly unique art form that exists nowhere else in the world; by comparison the Kabuki, which imitates it, is a sterile flower. But in a screenplay, I think the symphonic structure is the easiest for people of today to understand.

BC: *Where do you get the initial inspiration for a screenplay?*

AK: I've forgotten who it was that said creation is memory. My own experiences and the various things I have read remain in my memory and become the basis upon which I create something new. I couldn't do it out of nothing. For this reason, since the time I was a young man I have always kept a notebook handy when I read a book. I write down my reactions and what particularly moves me. I have stacks and stacks of these college-style notebooks, and when I go off to write a script, these are what I read. Somewhere they always provide me with a point of breakthrough. Even for single lines of dialogue I have taken hints from these notebooks.

At the beginning of the writing process, something very ambiguous comes into my mind as an idea; I let it mature by itself, and it goes in several specific directions. Then I go away somewhere to immerse myself in writing the scenario. It's less a matter of working within a defined structure than, again, of letting myself be moved by the characters I've chosen to work with. I do this even with the very first scene. I myself don't know what direction it will take from there; I leave everything to the natural development of the characters. Even if a collaborator suggests that we should do something specific the next day, it never works out as foreseen. As I said a little while ago, the spontaneous development of the characters is the most interesting part of the writing process for me.

Still, the writing is also the hardest part—creating something from nothing—and it's a very, very lonely job. Once you start shooting, there are lots of people about and it's quite enjoyable.

BC: *Tell me about your demeanor on the set.*

AK: During the shooting of a scene, the director's eye has to catch even the minutest detail, but this does not mean glaring concentratedly at the set. While the cameras are rolling, I rarely look directly at the actors; instead I focus my gaze somewhere else. By doing this, I sense instantly when something isn't right. Watching something does not mean fixing your gaze on it, but being aware of it in a natural way. I believe this is what the medieval Noh playwright and theorist Zeami meant by "watching with a detached gaze."

BC: *What about the* actor's *gaze, by which I mean his relationship with the camera?*

AK: The worst thing an actor can do is show his awareness of the camera. Often when an actor hears the call "Roll 'em," he will tense up, alter his sight lines, and present himself very unnaturally. Such self-consciousness shows very clearly to the camera's eye. I always say, "Just talk to the actor playing opposite you. This isn't like the stage, where you have to speak your lines out to the audience. There's no need to look at the camera." But when the actor knows where the camera is, he invariably, without realizing it, turns one-third to halfway in its direction. With multiple moving cameras, however, as I like to film, the actor has no time to figure out which one is shooting him!

BC: *How do you deal with your actors before the actual shooting begins?*

AK: I push. Some directors seem to "pull" performances out of actors, but I'm always pushing them, nudging them to try new or different things. We rehearse a scene or bit of action over and over again, and with each rehearsal something new jumps out at them and they get better and better. Rehearsing is like making a sculpture of papier-mâché: each repetition lays on a new sheet of paper, so that in the end the performance has a shape completely different from when we started. I make actors rehearse in full costume and makeup whenever possible, and we rehearse on the actual set. In costume, the work has an on-camera tension that vanishes whenever we try rehearsing out of costume.

The samurai prepare for battle in Kurosawa's *Seven Samurai*.

Let me add that my regular group of actors consists mostly of personal friends. I've never consciously built up my own repertory group. I try to select actors on the basis of my friendship with them, or the potential for friendship. I also consciously try to use two or three new faces in each film, as well as giving the regulars a new challenge. I try not to typecast them. For instance, Seiji Miyaguchi, who played Kyuzo in *Seven Samurai*, normally used to play very mild-mannered, gentlemanly parts, so in that film I intentionally cast him as a powerful swordsman.

BC: *Is it true that you discovered Toshiro Mifune and taught him how to act?*

AK: No. All I did was see what others had seen, take Mifune's acting talent, and first show it off to its fullest in *Drunken Angel*. Mifune possessed a kind of talent that I had never encountered before in the Japanese film world. It was, above all, the speed with which he expressed himself that was astounding. The ordinary Japanese actor might need ten feet of film to create an impression; Mifune needed only three feet. The speed of his movements was such that he said in a single action what took ordinary actors three separate movements to express. He put forth everything directly and boldly, and his sense of timing was the keenest I have ever encountered in a Japanese actor. And yet, with all his quickness, he also had surprisingly fine sensibilities. Anyway, I have to say that I'm a person who is rarely impressed by actors, but in the case of Mifune I was completely overwhelmed from the first time I saw him perform.

BC: *I've heard that you are very exacting about sets and properties. Is this true?*

AK: It's true that I am often accused of being *too* exacting with sets and properties, of having things made, just for the sake of authenticity, which will never appear on camera. Even if I don't request this, my crew does it for me anyway. The first Japanese director to demand authentic sets and props was Mizoguchi Kenji, and the sets in his films are truly superb. I learned about many aspects of filmmaking from him, and the making of sets is among the most important. The quality of the set, for one thing, influences the quality of the actors' performances. If the plan of a house and the design of the rooms are done properly, the actors can move about in them naturally. If I have to tell an actor, "Don't think about where this room is in relation to the rest of the house," that natural ease cannot be achieved. For this reason, I have the sets made exactly like the real thing. Such a process does restrict the shooting, but it encourages that necessary feeling of authenticity.

BC: *Has your thinking about musical scores remained the same throughout your career?*

AK: No, I changed my thinking about musical accompaniment from the time Hayasaka Fumio began working with me as the composer of my film scores. Up until that time, film music for me was nothing more than underlining or italicization—for a sad scene, for instance, there was always sad music. This is the way most filmmakers use music, and it is ineffective—or perhaps I should say *too* effective. But from *Drunken Angel* onward, I used light music for some key sad scenes, and in general my way of using music began to differ from the norm—I just don't put it where most directors do. Working with Hayasaka, I began to think in terms of the counterpoint of sound and image as opposed to the seamless union of the two.

BC: *You said earlier that all you are really capable of doing is creating films, not explaining them or how they are supposed to be made. And, of course, someone like me comes at films from the opposite perspective. Could you say a bit more on this subject?*

AK: Critics take my work and say things about it such as, "This scene in Kurosawa's film means such-and-such." But it's not true! I was not thinking of that at all! Really, my films are created in a totally natural way; I just film them as I go along. They may turn out to affect people in a certain way, but I don't create films by rationalizing my thoughts and then putting them on celluloid. My way of creating, my style if you want to call it that, is something I was born with: it comes naturally. For that reason, it's not something I'm overly aware of while I'm doing it. I don't force any picture of mine to be a Kurosawa film. I just tell the actors to be honest with themselves and true to their feelings, not to think about unnecessary things, and to let their actions flow naturally. This is my philosophy of film art, and it's an aesthetic principle that I hold dear—it comes from the heart. I am simply a maker of films.

In sum, I don't think the "messages" of my films are very obvious. Rather, they are the end products of my reflection; my views are thus implicit in any finished work simply because I, the creator, am a living, thinking human being who lives now, in the present. I am not consciously trying to teach a lesson or convey a particular message, to express any philosophical or political views, since audiences don't like that. They are sensitive to such things, to such "sermons," and rightly shrink from them. People go to see films to enjoy themselves, and I think that I have made them aware of certain problems without their having had to learn about them so directly. In any case, I believe that the world would not change for the better even if I made a direct statement in one of my films: do this and that, and watch the positive result. Moreover, the world will not change unless we steadily change human nature itself and our very way of thinking. We have to exorcise the essential or primordial evil in human beings, rather than depicting our social problems and trying to present concrete solutions to them. In other words, we have to treat the human cause, not the social symptom.

BC: *One can divide your films schematically into two categories: gendai-geki [modern film stories] and* jidai-geki *[historical film stories]. Is this distinction connected to a precise intention on your part in the formulation of a scenario and in the filming of it?*

AK: I myself do not perceive any difference. After making a modern film story, I try to make an historical film story, or vice versa. For example, after making *Ikiru* I wanted a change of style: this genre of human inquiry required a great concentration of spirit on my part and left me exhausted. I wished in my next project, quite naturally, to make a lighter, more lively film, a simple and detached one . . . so I made *Seven Samurai.*

The only advantage of historical film stories, with the possible exception of *Throne of Blood*, comes from their greater potential for spectacle. I would not say that this element is indispensable to the cinema, but it certainly creates great appeal. Moreover, it was present at the very onset of cinema. There are, of course, a thousand notions of what constitutes a spectacle. For myself, action-adventure is spectacle in the historical film story, whereas adventure in a modern film story is more often of a metaphysical, moral, and social kind.

What really interests me is the interior or exterior drama of a person and how to represent that person through his particular drama. To describe a person effectively, for instance, a social or a political context is necessary. Moreover, I don't think that one should depict events of the present day in a coarse manner; the public is shocked if it is plunged coarsely into contemporary reality. One can only make the public accept such a reality through indirect means: the story of a person living in this world. I would make a similar remark with regard to your classification: it is somewhat schematic. *Gendai-geki* and *jidai-geki* are different genres, but the subject always determines the form. And there are subjects that one can treat more readily in the form of *jidai-geki*.

BC: *Like* Rashomon, *which some have called a "modern" film that has an "historical" context.*

AK: Yes. To repeat: I, Kurosawa, live in modern society. Thus it is normal that my "historical" films contain "modern" dimensions.

BC: *For you, isn't* Rashomon *an "historical" film in the cinematic sense, too?*

AK: Yes, I think it is, and the historical reference here is silent film. Since the advent of the talkies in the 1930s, I felt at the time of *Rashomon's* conception, we had forgotten what was so wonderful about the old silent movies. I was aware of this aesthetic loss or displacement as a constant irritation. I sensed a need to go back to the origins of the motion picture to find once again the particular beauty of silence, if you will. In particular, I believed that there was something to be learned from the spirit of the French avant-garde films of the 1920s. Yet in Japan at this time we had no film library. I had to forage for old films, and try to remember the structure of those I had seen as a boy, ruminating over the aesthetic qualities that had made them special.

Rashomon would be my testing ground, the place where I could apply the ideas and desires growing out of my silent-film research.

BC: *Could you give one example of the imagistic application of such an idea or desire?*

AK: Well, for one thing, I had to figure out how to use the sun itself. This was a major concern because of the decision to use the light and shadows of the forest as a keynote for the entire film. I determined to solve the problem by actually filming the sun. These days, especially, it is not uncommon to point the camera directly at the sun, but at the time *Rashomon* was being made, such a shot was still one of the taboos of cinematography. It was even thought that the sun's rays shining directly into your lens would burn the film in your camera! But my cameraman, Miyagawa Kazuo, boldly defied this convention and created superb images. The introductory section, in particular, consisted of magnificent camerawork, as it led the viewer through the light and shadow of the forest into a world where the human heart loses its way.

Through *Rashomon*, by the way, I myself was compelled to discover an unfortunate aspect of the human heart. This occurred when the film was shown on television for the first time ten years ago or so. The broadcast was accompanied by an interview with the president of Daiei, and I couldn't believe my ears. This man, after showing so much distaste for the project at the outset of production, after complaining that the finished film was "incomprehensible," and after demoting both the company executive and the producer who had facilitated the making of *Rashomon*—this man was now proudly taking full and exclusive credit for its success! He boasted about how for the first time in film history the camera had been boldly pointed directly at the sun. And never in his entire discourse did Daiei's president mention my name or the name of the cinematographer whose achievement this was, Miyagawa Kazuo.

Watching that television interview, I had the feeling that I was back in the world of *Rashomon* all over again. It was as if the pathetic self-delusions of the ego, those failings I had attempted to portray in the film, were being exhibited in real life. People do indeed have immense difficulty talking about themselves as they really are. I was reminded once again that the human animal suffers from the trait of instinctive self-aggrandizement.

BC: *Could we move to a discussion of your adaptations of Shakespeare? Why, for example, did you think of filming* Macbeth?

AK: Well, in the age of civil wars in Japan, there are plenty of incidents like those portrayed in *Macbeth*, aren't there? They are called *gekokujo*, which means that a retainer murders his lord and deprives him of his power. The age of Japanese civil wars—starting from 1460 and lasting for about 100 years—is itself named *gekokujo*. For this reason, the story of *Macbeth* appealed to me very much, and it was easy for me to adapt as *Throne of Blood*.

BC: *What about your additions to your version of* King Lear, *titled* Ran, *specifically your giving the characters a past or a history that Shakespeare doesn't provide?*

AK: What has always troubled me about *King Lear* is precisely that Shakespeare gives his characters no past. We are plunged directly into the agonies of their present dilemmas without knowing how they got to this point. How did Lear acquire the power that, as an old man, he abuses with such disastrous results? Without knowing his past, I have never really understood the ferocity of his daughters' response to Lear's feeble attempts to shed his royal power. In *Ran* I tried to give Lear a history. I tried to make clear that his power must rest on a lifetime of bloodthirsty savagery. Forced ultimately to confront the consequences of his misdeeds, he is driven mad. But only by confronting his evil head-on can he transcend it and begin to struggle toward virtue.

I started out, you know, to make a film about Motonari Mori, the sixteenth-century warlord whose three sons are admired in Japan as paragons of filial virtue. What might their story be like, I wondered, if the sons had not been so good? It was only after I was well into writing the script about these imaginary unfilial sons of the Mori clan that the similarities to *Lear* occurred to me. Since my story is set in medieval Japan, the protagonist's children had to be men; to divide a realm among daughters at that time would have been unthinkable.

And then there was the issue of medieval Japan itself, which also attracted me. At that time, if a man was strong enough to fight, he could make something of his life. Even a fighting peasant could do it, though the competition was fierce. People this far back in history could express their personalities much more so than they ever could today.

BC: *Is it true that you were working on the adaptation of* King Lear—*the production costs of which nearly prevented you from turning it into a film—when you came upon the idea for* Kagemusha?

AK: Yes, that is true. I was researching the Sengoku Jidai period—the clan wars of the late sixteenth century. I grew very interested in the Battle of Nagashino, which remains a question mark in history. No one has satisfactorily explained why all the *taisho* of the Takeda clan should have died, while not one of the Oda or Tokugawa clans did. I started to consider ways of tackling this interesting question. It occurred to me that Takeda Shingen was known to have used many *kagemusha*, or doubles, and I thought that by approaching this historical enigma through the eyes of one such *kagemusha* I might keep the subject to manageable proportions. Once I'd hit on the idea of making the *kagemusha* a petty thief, I had to consider how this man could become so immersed in the character of Shingen that he would actually "become" him. I decided that it must be because of the strength of Shingen's own character. Then I conjectured that the *taisho* who died in battle must also have been charmed or enchanted by Shingen. In effect, they committed suicide at Nagashino: that is, they martyred themselves for Shingen. They must have been in love with him, as it were.

BC: *Was* Ran *influenced by Eisenstein's* Ivan the Terrible?

AK: No, I've never been influenced in such a way. I like *The Battleship Potemkin*, but by the time of *Ivan the Terrible*—by that point in Eisenstein's career—I had stopped looking at his films.

BC: *You have filmed* The Idiot, *written by Dostoyevsky, and* The Lower Depths, *written by Gorky. So I guess that one can say you are deeply attached to Russian literature.*

AK: Yes, I greatly admire Russian literature, particularly Dostoyevsky and Tolstoy. Tolstoy, above all in *War and Peace*, is the only writer to create a piece of literature both extraordinarily visual and almost cosmically visionary. He is thus a wager lost in advance! It is impossible to create filmic images more alive and forceful than his.

As for Dostoyevsky, it is difficult for me to speak of him. He is even more singular. On the whole, he is—how should I say—more psychological than visual. At the same time that he deepens characters and action through psychology, this author strives for surface representation that is rigorously objective. It is an objectivity that is total, even fatal, in that it attempts to present everything nakedly. But nakedness, if you will, can still be put into images. For this reason I was led to adapt Dostoyevsky to the screen, but the effort was a veritable battle that left me exhausted.

I must say, however, that I think *The Idiot* is wonderful; I rank it among Dostoyevsky's masterworks. At the end of the novel, Rogozhin murders Nastasya and goes mad, and the other suitor, Prince Myshkin, becomes an "idiot" again—in what, if I may say so, is a cinematographic passage. The scene is to my thinking the most beautiful, the most agonizing, the most profound, and finally the most hallucinatory in the history of literature. But there is one big problem: how to interpret this novel. How can one comprehend the work of Dostoyevsky? In effect, each critic and each artist gives his own interpretation. I have given one myself in this instance, by translating into images the truth most compelling to me. Yet I have been reproached for making a difficult and heavy picture. Myself, I think I simply rendered a simple truth in cinematic terms.

BC: *On what Russian work did you base* Dersu Uzala?

AK: It's based on the book *In the Thickets of the Ussuri Taiga,* by the Russian traveler and writer Vladimir Arsenyev. As you know from the film, it portrays the life of the hunter Dersu in far eastern Russia early in the twentieth century and his friendship with Arsenyev, who, as a soldier-scientist, was mapping the wilderness. The Russian word is *taiga,* which is better, because it means "infinity." However far you travel, the wilderness just does not seem to end. But these boundless expanses were hard to convey on the screen. I should have liked to follow the actual route Arsenyev took in his travels, but every frame took so much equipment to shoot. For instance, the light of a bonfire is quite sufficient to illuminate the faces of the people sitting around it and the *taiga* landscape. But to get even some of that effect on the screen we had to use many, many floodlights. If we had had the sort of equipment that could see things exactly as a man sees them, we could have literally recreated Arsenyev's travels. Unfortunately, such film and equipment did not exist at the time.

BC: *So one of the film's themes is man's harmony with nature—when he achieves it—and how such harmony can only help his relations with other men.*

AK: Precisely. People today have forgotten that man is a part of nature and, as a result, they are rapaciously destroying their natural environment. The air is becoming unbreathable, and, in twenty years or even less, Japan will be an unfit place to live. We are on the eve of disaster—something that should be shouted from every rooftop. I myself can't do such shouting in words, so I am doing it in pictures by showing in *Dersu Uzala* a man in harmony with nature. Though I have to add that, after his eyesight fails and Dersu moves to the city with Arsenyev, it is the city that kills him—in the form of a thief and murderer. Trying to visit his grave ten years later, Arsenyev cannot even locate it because of urban expansion and the destruction of the cemetery where Dersu's body lay.

BC: *Is your film entirely faithful to the book?*

AK: Yes, except for one incident I really hated to skip. Arsenyev describes a gray spot moving up the slope of a hill and says he took it for a cloud. But when, at Dersu's suggestion, he approached it, he saw it was a great herd of wild boar. That would have made a great scene, but of course there was no chance of finding such a herd.

My biggest difficulty, however, came when I decided to shoot a scene of golden autumn. I didn't realize that autumn lasted only three days there! I climbed a mountain to see what I would film, took in the beautiful view, and by the time the equipment arrived the weather had changed. It rained cats and dogs, and then the snow began. We waited and kept hoping, but the weather only got worse. In the end the cameramen were soaking wet and chilled from the cold and the terrible wind.

The next day we went up again, and I looked down and saw that the trees had lost all their leaves. The wind and rain had destroyed the golden autumn. But I *had* to show that autumnal view; this part of the narrative could not be changed. So what you see in the final film is not real: the golden leaves are in fact pieces of material that we attached to the trees. Nature, alas, had defeated me.

BC: *But technology in this case did triumph: the picture still got made.*

AK: It did indeed. I am a filmmaker, after all; films are my true medium. And I think that to learn what became of me after *Rashomon*—which I mention in this instance because it was the gateway for my entry into the international film world—the most profitable procedure would be to look for me in the characters of the films I made after *Rashomon*. Although human beings are incapable of talking about themselves with total honesty, it is much harder to avoid the truth when you pretend to be other people. *They* often reveal much about themselves in a very straightforward way. And, as their very auteur, I am certain that I did, too. After all, there is nothing that says more about its creator than the work itself.

Akira Kurosawa Filmography

Sanshiro Sugata (1943)
The Most Beautiful (1944)
The Men Who Tread on the Tiger's Tail (1945)

Sanshiro Sugata, Part II (1945)
No Regrets for Our Youth (1946)
Those Who Make Tomorrow (1946)
One Wonderful Sunday (1947)
Drunken Angel (1948)
The Quiet Duel (1949)
Stray Dog (1949)
Rashomon (1950)
The Idiot (1951)
Ikiru (a.k.a. *To Live*, 1952)
Seven Samurai (1954)
Record of a Living Being (a.k.a. *I Live in Fear*, 1955)
The Lower Depths (1957)
Throne of Blood (1957)
The Hidden Fortress (1958)
The Bad Sleep Well (1960)
Yojimbo (1961)
Sanjuro (1962)
High and Low (1963)
Red Beard (1965)
Dodeskaden (1970)
Dersu Uzala (1975)
Kagemusha (a.k.a. *The Shadow Warrior*, 1980)
Ran (1985)
Dreams (1990)
Rhapsody in August (1991)
No, Not Yet! (1993)

Bibliography

Desser, David. *The Samurai Films of Akira Kurosawa*. Ann Arbor, Mich.: UMI Research Press, 1983.

Erens, Patricia. *Akira Kurosawa: A Guide to References and Resources*. Boston: G. K. Hall, 1979.

Goodwin, James. *Akira Kurosawa and Intertextual Cinema*. Baltimore: Johns Hopkins University Press, 1994.

———, ed. *Perspectives on Akira Kurosawa*. New York: G. K. Hall, 1994.

Kurosawa, Akira. *Something Like an Autobiography*. Trans. Audie E. Bock. New York: Alfred A. Knopf, 1982.

Prince, Stephen. *The Warrior's Camera: The Cinema of Akira Kurosawa.* Rev. and expanded ed. Princeton, N.J.: Princeton University Press, 1999.

Richie, Donald. *The Films of Akira Kurosawa.* 3rd ed. Berkeley: University of California Press, 1996.

Yoshimoto, Mitsuhiro. *Kurosawa: Film Studies and Japanese Cinema.* Durham, N.C.: Duke University Press, 2000.

~

Master of Art

An Interview with Satyajit Ray

Satyajit Ray (1921–1992) was a Bengali-Indian filmmaker. He is regarded as one of the greatest auteurs of twentieth-century cinema. Ray was born in the city of Calcutta into a Bengali family prominent in the world of arts and letters. Starting his career as a commercial artist (art director of an ad agency and book illustrator), he was drawn to independent filmmaking after meeting French filmmaker Jean Renoir and viewing the Italian neorealist film *Bicycle Thieves* (1948) during a visit to London.

Ray directed thirty-seven films, including feature films, documentaries, and shorts. He was also a fiction writer, publisher, illustrator, graphic designer, and film critic. His first film, *Pather Panchali* (1955), a story of village life, won an award for "Best Human Document" at the Cannes Festival. *Pather Panchali*, *Aparajito* (1956), and *The World of Apu* (1959) form the Apu Trilogy, which brought Ray—and Indian cinema—to world attention. He later won acclaim for *The Goddess* (1960), *Three Daughters* (1961), *The Big City* (1963), *The Lonely Wife* (1964), *The Chess Players* (1977), *The Home* and the World (1984), and The Stranger (1991). Ray wrote all his own screen-plays and often composed the music for his films, in addition to casting and editing them. He received many major awards during his career, including thirty-two Indian National Film Awards, a number of prizes at international film festivals, and an Honorary Academy Award in 1992.

I met Satyajit Ray on a hot morning in the summer of 1989 at his home in Calcutta, up two flights of stairs in an old building on Bishop Lefroy Road. At the time, he was working on a new feature, his twenty-sixth: Ganashatru, based on Henrik Ibsen's An Enemy of the People.

Bert Cardullo: *How do you feel when some of your films do not get a favorable critical, or box-office, response?*

Satyajit Ray: Actually, I've been amazed and heartened by some of the critical reaction to my films. One of my favorite films, for example, is *Days and Nights in the Forest*. It was rejected in India. No box-office success, no critical success here, but it's considered one of my best films abroad. *Days and Nights in the Forest* had a very long run in London and was widely praised in America. I mean, that's the way it is. You learn about people, their likes and dislikes and their response to things Indian, and some of the Western criticism itself has been most beneficial. To speak of India, I think that, over the years, I have built up a following in Calcutta, certainly. Any film I make will play for six to eight weeks in three separate theaters in the city. There is definitely always an anticipation of my next film from a very large section of the Calcuttan public.

BC: *Not just other movie people and the intelligentsia but a larger—*

SR: Yes, my audience is getting to be bigger and bigger now. It's spreading out to the suburbs, and that is good.

BC: *Do you secretly dream of something you want to do that you haven't done yet?*

SR: Oh, there are lots of things that I'd love to do, but some of them cost a lot of money and others maybe are too complex. I would like to do some-thing, for instance, from the epics. I would like to do some more folk tales in a very different style. Not in the conventional narrative style that I've used so far, but with a simple, stylized type of approach. I'm not sure whether there's an audience for such a film, but one has to do it to find out. Perhaps

I could do a segment as well from one of our two national epics—you know, the *Ramayana* and the *Mahabharata*. The *Mahabharata* particularly fascinates me: the epic itself, the incidents, the characters, all so human and time-less. I'd also like to do more historical films, on the Mughals perhaps. I'm fascinated by certain characters from the Mughal period. I would also like to do something on the English adventurers who used to come to India in the eighteenth and nineteenth centuries. Some of the foreign painters were very interesting—the ones who left records of India, like Daniell or Forbes or Hodges. I mean, these men did marvelous work. Without them we wouldn't know what the India of the eighteenth or nineteenth century looked like. And they came here as adventurers. They were real adventurers, out to make money, which they made in the most extraordinary ways. I'd be interested in filming something like that.

BC: *Do you think the British influence is still significant in India, and is it good or bad?*

SR: Well, you see, we all admit that we owe a lot to the British. After all, I think I myself am a product of East and West, and I think that my filmmaking reflects that. We've been exposed to Western literature, the cinema has done a lot, and BBC radio has done quite a bit. You can't help it: you're part, not just of India, but of the whole world; the world has shrunk. And my style of film reflects that. As a director, I can't deny the influence of the West. But, at the same time, one still feels rooted to one's own country, to one's own culture. It's a question of absorbing what you think is good and what you think you can use. For example, I've been trying through my films to explore the history of Bengal over the years: the British period, the nineteenth century, independent India, the end of feudalism. The death agony of a particular class, from any country, fascinates me. There's a poignancy to it. One has to take a sympathetic attitude to something that is dying after so many years. *The Music Room* itself is a film that shows a sympathetic attitude even to Indian noblemen, who were useless people, really. But to tell a story about one such character, one has to take a sympathetic stance. From his point of view, it's a major tragedy; to us, it's the folly of trying to cling to something that is inevitably going to vanish. These noblemen, though idlers, were great patrons of music and the arts, and all that is gone now. The subject of class has fascinated me all along, the fact that such social contrasts could exist side by side—and continue to exist today. This conflict between old and new has been one of the major themes of my films over the years.

BC: *You have been criticized by some people in India for not dealing more with social problems. Do you want to say anything about that?*

SR: That's not strictly true. I think I have dealt with a lot of social problems in my films. Maybe not in the way some people would like me to treat them. They want solutions to the problems at the end of the film, but I don't know the solutions myself in most cases. I like to present problems as clearly as possible, and let the audience think for themselves.

BC: *As you speak, I think of* Distant Thunder, *which seems to me to make your point in its treatment of the Bengal famine.*

SR: Yes, I think you're right. Let me give you some context. At the time of the famine, 1943, I had just got my new job as an advertising designer, and I was living in Calcutta. Hundreds and even thousands of people, from the villages, were streaming into Calcutta. I remember the railway stations were just jam-packed with refugees. People were at the point of death, or they would have died in a few days' time at the most. We would come out of the house on our way to work and step across dead bodies, just lying all over the place. Ten, fifteen years later, I read this novel by a writer whom I admire greatly, Bibhuti Bhushan Banerjee. He was actually living in a village at the time of the famine, and he had written the book from his own experience. This was around 1958 or '59. And I decided immediately to turn this material into a film. But I couldn't find the right actors to play the parts, and then all sorts of things happened—including the fact that I went on to make other films. Finally, in 1972, I decided that I had to make the famine film: *Distant Thunder*.

But I approached the famine from a paradoxical angle: that of the extreme generosity in the villages to a guest, particularly from the city. You can go to a village, anybody's house, and they will offer you a meal. On an hour's notice you will get a meal there. They have very little themselves, but a guest is treated like a god. This, by the way, is called for in the Indian scriptures. In *Distant Thunder*, a very old man appears at the height of the famine, and the wife says, "We must give him a meal." Her husband is clever at this point, but he is gradually changing. He says, "No, he's a scrounger. I know he's come to beg, so we must be very cautious; we must think of our own meal first." She responds, "I'll go without it. I'll go without lunch *and* dinner, but let's give him a meal." The husband is a priest, he's a schoolmaster, he's a doctor. He knows nothing very well, but he has status because he's the only Brahmin in a village of peasants. Then he goes to perform a ceremony to ward off cholera; but before he goes, he reads his book on hygiene and performs the appropriate ritual. He says, "By the way, don't drink the river water, don't eat food where flies have settled," you know, that kind of thing. He believes, in a way, in what we call progress and science.

Fine, excellent. But in the beginning he is a bit of a racketeer, because he's exploiting the ignorance of these poor village people. At the end, when death, through famine, comes to an Untouchable woman, and nobody will touch her body, it is the husband, the Brahmin, who declares, "I'll go and do something about this. I'll perform the cremation myself." So he is liberated enough in the end to be able to do that. His humanity then emerges.

BC: *Is censorship a serious problem in India?*

SR: Politically it is, yes. Every film is censored.

BC: *Have you run into any problems?*

SR: I haven't, perhaps because of my special position. *The Middleman*, for instance, had a fairly outspoken scene. If somebody else had made this film, its political references probably would have been censored. But for a while now, I have been able to get away with a few things.

BC: *Have you ever actively participated in politics or worked with a political party?*

SR: No. Although most of my friends are leftist minded, I've become disillusioned with politics and don't think about such matters any longer. Now I've almost stopped discussing politics altogether, even reading newspapers. I take account of the man; I don't care about his politics.

Having a political consciousness, though, can also mean having a consciousness of the failure of politicians, like our Indian ones. I find politicians and their game of politics extremely dishonest and puerile. They change colors like chameleons, so much so that it's difficult to keep pace with them. Besides, the brain has a rather limited number of compartments, and I have no vacant compartment to take in all that's happening on the political front.

BC: *Can political involvement obstruct creativity?*

SR: It has happened—take the filmmakers in the Soviet Union. Whenever they try to make films about modern life in their country, their work becomes simplistic and two-dimensional. At the same time, they make very good films based on their literature from the past. The filmmakers themselves feel constricted. At the Moscow Film Festival once, Grigori Chukhrai told me that he didn't make a film for seven years after *Ballad of a Soldier*, because about eighty of his scripts had been disapproved for political reasons. He sat in a studio watching other people work. And Mark Donskoi asked me, "What do you think of our films? Why don't you just say they are all rubbish?"

BC: *What kinds of political opinion can an artist hold in contemporary society, then?*

SR: As an artist, I only want an environment in which I will be free to work as I like. I have no other opinions.

BC: *Yet it is commonly felt that you are sympathetic to the left. Perhaps this was because your first film,* Pather Panchali, *was about the lives of poor Indian villagers.*

SR: At the same time, many have said that I upheld feudalism in *The Music Room*—that since I didn't condemn feudalism, I was sympathetic to it.

BC: *What were the aesthetic and reactive impulses that prompted you to make* Pather Panchali?

SR: Well, I felt that if I made the film, then Bengali cinema would take a different turn. I was inspired, I have no doubt about that. I thought I had found an ideal subject for a first film. One must keep in mind that before I made *Pather Panchali*, I had been to London and had seen some Italian neorealist films. But even before I went to England, I had spoken to a number of professional people about this project. They told me that it was not possible to make a film in the way I proposed. You cannot shoot an entire film outdoors, I was told. Nor can you make a film just with new faces. It is difficult, they said, to make a film without makeup or to manage your camerawork outside the studio. Thus was I dissuaded from even attempting to make *Pather Panchali*. But I made it independent of the commercial set-up, which enabled me to ignore conventional audience expectations. However, I did have to keep my own estimate of the potential audience in view, as it was not my intention to make an esoteric film.

BC: *As one of the most creative forces in world cinema today, you must have certain ideas fermenting within you when you start thinking about a new film.*

Subir Banerjee as Apu in Ray's *Pather Panchali.*

What draws you most when you start a new work: a persistent image, a certain location, a particular character?

SR: It's everything combined, really. But I would say the dominant factor is the characters, the human relationships. Then come the setting and the possibility of telling the story cinematically—in motion. Other aspects that engage me are the structure of the picture, its internal contrasts, and its dramatic rhythm. These are all integrally related to the creation of film art. Then again, I also feel that the element of *rasa*—the concept of *nava rasa* as specified in Indian aesthetics—is quite important. *Rasa* is best described as the interplay of moods as expressed by various characters in a work of art.

There is also the element of numbers. I feel that I need an odd number of characters. If you analyze my films carefully, you will see that, most often, three, five, or seven characters come into play. The triangle, as you know, unquestionably plays a role here as well. In *Charulata*, for instance, there are five characters. If I had used four, I would have had problems; the use of five characters, I think, enhanced the dramatic possibilities of this film a bit.

BC: *Elsewhere, you have said that everything you learned as a student of fine arts has gone into your films. Can you specify how your training has shaped your visual style? For instance, you once drew an analogy between your films and painting—the paintings of Pierre Bonnard in particular.*

SR: Yes, I have drawn such an analogy, but it's not to be taken literally, of course. I love Bonnard, the way everything has the same uniform importance in his paintings. The human figure is no more or less important than objects like chairs and tables, a bowl of fruit, or a vase full of flowers. There's one single blend, and everything is expressed through it. I have tried to achieve the same effect in some of my films: to mix all kinds of things together, so that they are all related and equally important. You have to understand the characters in context, in relation to everything—objects, events, little details. They all mean something *together.* You can't take a single element out of this mix without disrupting the whole. And you can't understand one small thing without taking into account the film in its entirety.

I find this organicity in Henry Cartier-Bresson's photographs all the time, even in his portraits. The one of Sartre shows him off-center so that you can see everything around him: the bridge, the lamppost, the shape of the building behind him. You cannot ignore all this because it makes the photograph what it is, and it expresses the man. Similarly, Matisse sits among his pigeons in another Cartier-Bresson portrait, and the elements of bird and man are perfectly integrated.

BC: *How important has Cartier-Bresson been to your work, then?*

SR: Cartier-Bresson has been a major influence on my work from the very start. There is a wonderful shaping power in his photographs, a unity that in the end can only be called organic. He can create perfect fusion out of all kinds of diverse things, and, at the same time, achieve a precise sense of form. I also enjoy his wit very much. Most of all, I am drawn to his humanism, his concern for man—always expressed with sympathy and understanding.

BC: *Is there any specific reason why you write your own scripts—be they adapted or original—though you never write for another director?*

SR: I have always proceeded in this way. I did once write a screenplay for an assistant of mine who was promoted to full-fledged director, and he wanted me to do his first script. But that is the only time I have ever worked as a screenwriter for someone else. I think a script can best be turned into a film by the writer himself. Otherwise there is every chance the script will not be understood properly, or that the maximum will not be extracted from it. I think that, as a rule, directors should write their own screenplays.

A lot of directors, even abroad, say that they can compose their own scenario yet not write the dialogue. But then they have a different idea from mine about writing: they think that dialogue is something very literary, full of flourishes and puns and whatnot. I personally think that what one needs to write dialogue is a good ear, a sense for the rhythm and content of normal, everyday speech. For if you know what you want to say through your scenario and ultimately your film, why can't you put the words into the mouths of your characters?

BC: *What do you think is basically wrong with the Indian cinema? Why are Bengali films more artistic than the Bombay ones?*

SR: Well, not all Bengali films are that good. We hardly produce twenty films a year, whereas in Bombay they make something like 150 films or so. Naturally, the proportion between good and bad is probably higher here: out of our twenty films, there may be five or six a year that are worthwhile.

I think one important factor here in Bengal is that the directors are more aware of their roots. In Bengal it is the Bengalis who make the films, whereas in Bombay people have migrated from all sorts of places and consequently do not have the feeling of being rooted there—at least not in the sense that we feel rooted in Bengal. Bombay directors view filmmaking as an entertainment industry, and the stories they concoct do not have very much basis in reality.

But if you take the regional industry—in Marathi, for instance—you will find a certain amount of affinity with Bengal. This is how significant art becomes possible: if you are making films about people you know, the people who belong to a particular region, you will make more valuable and artistic films. But if you make a film about people who belong to no particular place, no particular country really, but who exist instead in a world wholly concocted by the cinema—an upper-class world with certain rarefied mores and morals—then you can only make entertainment, never art.

It is important, let me reiterate, that stories have their roots in reality. For a Punjabi director the reality is that of the Punjab, and yet he finds himself working somewhere other than the Punjab. There are a lot of directors in Bombay who originally come from the Punjab and, if given a story about their native region, they might be able to produce something worthwhile— something that they feel belongs to them, something that acquires a certain integrity along with its regional characteristics. But since Bombay is such a hybrid and cosmopolitan place, the only world these directors want to depict is a kind of cosmopolitan hybrid with certain qualities and values that have no relation to the qualities and values of the existing world. I can understand a satirical film that comes out of this kind of set-up, but if you take this world seriously, then you can only make very ineffective films from an aesthetic point of view.

Nonetheless, I don't know how many more years I can go on making films in Bengal. In my position, maybe I can make Bengali films for the international market for a few more years. But Bengali films today don't have much of a future, in my view, given the market and the overall expenditure that such a film requires. Making Hindi-language films or films in English seems to be the only solution. Even I have to make a Hindi film once in a while; there seems to be no other way out. This is purely a matter of circumstance, since I don't *want* to make films in Hindi very much because I do not know the language well.

BC: *That was one of the things I wanted to ask: when you make films in a language other than your own, do you feel there are barriers that you must overcome?*

SR: Yes, absolutely. In *The Chess Players*, for example, when I came to the English-language portion, I was much more at ease, for my Hindi is not as good as my English. So, although I wrote the English dialogue for *The Chess Players* myself, in *Sadgati* my English script had to be translated into Hindi dialogue. And I never knew whether that dialogue was good or right. Even the coaching of actors—where I often act out the pieces myself in advance—becomes impossible during the making of a Hindi-language film. Since I do not have enough knowledge of the language, I can only give a certain amount of verbal direction to the actors; what I *cannot* do, however, is act out the parts myself. So for Hindi films I can't even go in search of new faces; I must work with experienced actors only.

BC: *Will you ever make films in a language apart from Hindi?*

SR: No, never.

BC: *What about English?*

SR: Perhaps I will, but even then, the story I select must be a story from my own country. I really don't have any desire to make films abroad. A film in which the use of English sounds logical—where, say, people from different provinces in India come together and speak English so that they can all communicate—I might make such an English-language film in my own country.

BC: *Could you tell me something about the image of Indian cinema abroad? And then, has the Indian cinema as a whole been able to serve the cause of the common man?*

SR: I don't know what image the Indian cinema has abroad. Actually, it is mainly my films that have been playing in the West. But in the Middle East, where my films are not screened but where a lot of Bombay films are shown, I don't know what particular image they have of Indian cinema. A lot of people regret that there are not more export-worthy films, by directors other than me, produced here. But it seems that people in the Middle East enjoy the Indian films they see, which to them are highly entertaining and colorful. After all, India has lots of beautiful actresses and handsome actors, and there are good singers as well. But it is impossible to get an idea of the country from these films, and if Middle Easterners try to draw their conclusions about India from Hindi films, I am afraid they will arrive at a dead end.

As for your second question, I doubt very much that the Indian cinema has been able to serve the cause of the common man, because films—particularly Bombay films—give the impression of great affluence and the country is made to look very attractive, with lavish homes, gorgeous costumes, and the like. This gives an incorrect notion of India as a whole, but I don't think that intelligent people abroad have any delusions about India's wealth. They know this is a country that has to beg for aid from the international community. They accept the Bombay films as a kind of phenomenon, as a kind of habit of filmmaking, and they go to see these movies to be entertained—not to learn anything about the country of India.

BC: *Well, you know the country—the countryside—intimately, and yet you're a city person.*

SR: Yes I am, but I love the countryside. As an advertising man, I would go for excursions by train into the countryside to sketch or take photographs. So I feel deeply rooted in Bengal and its traditions; I love, for example, the country bazaars and village fairs.

BC: *Then again, I was surprised to see so many traces of the American gangster film appearing in your supposed children's fantasy,* The Golden Fortress.

SR: That picture was designed to reach audience members who loved my books but had had little opportunity to see my "serious" films. But there *are* levels to *The Golden Fortress* other than the one aimed at children. As for the gangster references, my connections to urban American cinema precede the influence of Renoir and Rossellini on my work. I enjoyed and appreciated many American films during the 1940s. I remember seeing films by Raoul Walsh, Howard Hawks, and John Huston—especially Huston's *Beat the Devil*, which is a marvelous take-off on gangster pictures.

BC: *What do you think of Japanese cinema?*

SR: I am a great admirer of Japanese cinema; they are really great masters. I don't know Ozu's early films, but at the end of his career he was totally Japanese—not at all influenced by Hollywood. He subverted all conventions: cinematic, spatial, rhythmic, etc. I have repeatedly seen some of his films and thought, "My God, he doesn't follow at all the Hollywood model or grammar." Ozu has another approach, which one can call a devotion to the geography of actors in their setting. This form of his is original, and it is fundamental enough to necessitate a thorough reassessment of the so-called first principles of filmmaking.

BC: *How about Renoir's* The River? *What's your view of this film?*

SR: I can't say that *The River* was a film about the real India. The background was Indian and it was marvelously used: the riverside, the boats, the fishermen, and the general landscape. But the story itself was a bit idealistic or idealized and not terribly interesting—about an English jute-mill manager and his family, adolescents mainly. It was certainly not an Indian story, and even as a Western story in an Indian setting, it did not come close to telling the truth. There are characteristic Renoir touches here and there, to be sure, and I enjoyed *The River* overall. But it doesn't compare with his French films.

BC: *From your point of view, what has been one of the most discouraging developments in the history of cinema?*

SR: The commercial dominance of color and wide-screen imagery, and the consequent asphyxiation of the intimate black-and-white cinema. But color now is much better than it was several decades ago, when they didn't know how to control it. Color back then tended to make everything look too beautiful, too pretty, but the advantage of color today is that it can give more subtlety, more detail. It must be used very carefully, however, and you can't allow the laboratory to change anything. If I choose the costumes for their color, I want the final film to show those colors. If I have emphasized blues and yellows, for example, I don't want the laboratory doing any "color corrections."

BC: *Do you always shoot your films on location?*

SR: I also shoot in a studio, but I am very careful about the art direction and the use of light in a studio setting. I don't want the audience to be able to tell whether it is a studio or not. Shooting in a studio is much easier, of course; location shooting in Calcutta, by contrast, is extremely difficult. There are always crowds and noise all around you. Sometimes, of course, one has to go outdoors, but when we do, we work very fast and with handheld cameras. We arrive, we shoot, we go away. There can be problems if you have a long sequence to photograph. We can't even use the police, who don't have a very good image in India; the police attract an even bigger crowd because people come to ask what is happening. So we do our own policing, because everybody in the crowd wants to be in the shot—they don't want to be there just to watch.

BC: *I'd like to follow up with a related question: What's your relationship with your cinematographer?*

SR: Well, I started out with a very good cameraman, but after each shot he would say, "We must take another." I asked him why, but he was never precise. Multiple takes are very dangerous when one is shooting on a small budget, so I decided to operate the camera myself. Sometimes during a tracking shot in which there is a lot of action, a slight shake—inevitably caused by me—is not important if the action is good. But this man thought only about the shake; he wanted smoothness at any price.

As the camera operator, I have realized that when I work with new actors, they are more confident if they don't see me: they are less tense. I remain behind the camera, I see better, and I can get exactly the framing that I want. If I am sitting over to the side, by contrast, I am dependent on the cameraman. He frames the shot, he does the panning, the tilting, the tracking—he does everything, in fact. Then it's only when you see the rushes that you know exactly what you have. I am so used to doing my own framing, my own visual composing, now that I couldn't work in any other way. It's not that I have no trust in my cameraman's operational abilities; it's just that the best position from which to judge the acting is from behind the camera, and therefore I must be the one looking through the lens.

So I turned to another man to be my lighting cameraman: Subrata Mitra, who was a real beginner. He was twenty-one when he took over the shooting of *Pather Panchali*; he had never handled a movie camera in his life. But I had to use somebody like this, because all the professionals said that you couldn't shoot in rain, and that you can't shoot out of doors because the light keeps changing, the sun goes down too fast, and so forth. When I got my new cameraman, we decided on certain basic things after a great deal of discussion, one of them being that I would compose the images in my own mind beforehand and that we would work from those. Later on, in the case of my color films, every color scheme was so decided, and the choice of each costume piece as well—the material for which I would go out to purchase myself. My cameraman and I also agreed on the use of available light; and we aimed at simulating available light in the studio, when we had to be there, by using "bounced light"—or light bounced off a big piece of stretched cloth.

BC: *What kind of cloth?*

SR: Just white sheets, what we call long-cloths. We had framed pieces of white cloth, enormous things, and we bounced light back from them—except during night scenes, of course. And once your source of light is established, you follow that source as much as possible. If it's a candle, a lantern, or an electric light, you follow the source. It simplifies matters.

You know, about seven or eight years after *Pather Panchali* was made, I read an article in *American Cinematographer* written by Sven Nykvist—at the time of Bergman's *Through a Glass Darkly*, I think—claiming the invention of bounced light. But we had been using it since 1954.

BC: *Is it true that these days there are more and more directors emerging in India who do their own camerawork?*

SR: Actually, there are very few cameramen-directors. And let me be clear: what I do is just guide the camera; I simply operate it. And a director who can operate the camera has a great advantage, because he gains greater confidence. In my case, the lighting portion is taken care of by my lighting cameraman under my guidance—the lighting, of course, being the main aspect of cinematography. I don't think there's anything wrong with my guiding the camera and the cameraman; it helps me to leave my imprint or personal point of view on the work. But I don't ever actually call myself a cameraman.

Moreover, as far as I can recall, none of the major directors, Indian or otherwise, are cameramen themselves. Yet, certainly, all the really great directors have a distinctive camera style: you can recognize their work right away on the basis of the photography, the use of color, the deployment of chiaroscuro. So obviously these directors are guiding their cameramen, and they ought to be able to do so as far as possible: it's to the advantage of any film. In my country, alas, there are not yet any cinematographers of the caliber of the best Europeans or Americans—say, Sven Nykvist and Gregg Toland.

BC: *You would say, then, that a good cameraman does not necessarily make a good director?*

SR: That's right, because the two activities are not really connected. But a good director must know how the lighting and composition should be done. And if he can guide the cameraman in his work—after all, the visual style is very much a part of the film director's statement—it is all the more desirable. Let me be even more blunt: the mastery over tools and technique—how to use the camera, where and how to place it, how to manage sound and lighting—if you don't have *that*, however much social commitment or aesthetic sensitivity you may display, I don't think you can make a successful film.

BC: *What, in your view, is the essence of film art?*

SR: I would say that the cinema's characteristic forte is its ability to capture and communicate the intimacies of the human mind. Such intimacies can be revealed through movement, gesture, vocal inflection, a change in the lighting, or a manipulation of the surrounding environment. But there doesn't have to be literal movement at all—of the camera or the character—in a succession of shots. All the same, the character can appear to unfold and grow. To describe the most important characteristic of the film medium, I would even use the word "growth" rather than "movement." The cinema is superbly equipped to trace the *growth* of a person or a situation. And to do that—to depict a social situation with the utmost truth and to explore human relationships to the utmost limit—one must eschew all the shortcuts that have been artificially imposed over the years by non-artistic considerations. I should also like to banish from my films every last trace of the theatrical and even the pictorial or prettified—two of the most common cinematic impurities.

BC: *How do you think, then, that intellectually speaking you have changed—from the way you thought earlier in your film career to the way you think now?*

SR: I don't know about my ideas, but my technique—my film grammar—has changed, and the French New Wave was responsible for that. Godard especially opened up new ways of . . . making points, let us say. And he shook the foundations of film grammar in a very healthy sort of way, which is excellent. Indian directors as a result have become much more clipped—fades and dissolves are used much less, for instance; we mostly depend now on cuts. But the audience has also progressed, for they accept this change. Our storytelling had been more American earlier. European influences came later: French, Swedish, German, all kinds of influence. So, if we compare an Indian film from the 1950s to one from today, we find the narrative much sharper in the later film.

A related matter: something that has always been difficult is how to express character *without* using speech, through the use of gestures, looks, actions, etc. The best example of that kind of expression in my work probably comes in *Charulata*, but I wasn't able to depict character in this way until after I had completed the Apu Trilogy. When I started directing, I just couldn't handle such "silent speech" as well.

BC: *As you look back at these early efforts of yours, what do you think? Could you say more about how far and in what direction you have traveled with regard to your approach to filmmaking, your method of handling actors, everything?*

SR: In writing dialogue, above all else, I have progressed the most. For *Pather Panchali* and *Aparajito*, I wrote only about fifteen to twenty percent of the dialogue; the rest came from the original novels. I never thought I'd be able to write dialogue myself, and the little dialogue that was my own in my first two films was neither significant nor particularly pointed. Now I have a lot more confidence in the writing of dialogue, a greater facility. It was during the making of *Kanchenjungha* that I realized for the first time that I *could* write my own dialogue entirely; and that, even as I created a character, I could conceive how that character would speak as well as act.

But insofar as pure cinematic ideas are concerned, those that appeared in *Pather Panchali* and did not come from the book—such ideas are still there today in my films. The main strength of that first film, however, lay in certain peculiar moments of inspiration, like the death of Indir, Durga's death, the incident concerning the snake at the end, or the sequence in which the train passes by as Apu and Durga watch. None of these were in the novel, and even today I enjoy watching these scenes. But in both *Pather Panchali* and *Aparajito*, I overshot a lot—so much, in fact, that quite a bit of it had to be discarded. That sense of proportion or tightness of construction came much later on my part. I have gradually gained confidence about my choice of lens, selecting the right camera position or movement—all such choices have become easier to make with experience. The whole process of filmmaking has become much faster and surer for me.

BC: *To get back to the subject of writing dialogue, may I ask you if you have ever thought of writing or directing a play? You used to read a lot of plays, I know, and you still do; you also are an avid theatergoer, I've learned. I ask this question as someone who himself received much of his formal college education in drama.*

SR: Well, there are so many wonderfully talented people working in the theater today, so what's the use of swelling the crowd? In the cinema, I must say, there isn't so much artistic talent—perhaps because it's such a technological medium. In any event, I felt quite early on that film was my province, not theater. Maybe because the cinema was in such a backward state in India, but perhaps I shouldn't put the matter so negatively. I've just never thought of writing or directing a play; it's the writing of screenplays that comes to me straightaway, and then of course the filming of them.

BC: *Hadn't you ever thought of making a film out of a play?*

SR: Until *Ganashatru*, not really, because then the film depends too much on speech—and I am not interested. To me the peak moments of a film should be wordless, whereas in a play the words are of primary importance. At times the situation in a play can be film-like or adaptable to the screen, but there also one should see exactly how far one can go without words—as I trust I have done in *Ganashatru*. The best source for an adaptation, however, is not a play and not even a novel, but rather a long short story. For a film of two hours or so, the long short story is the most suitable form. You simply cannot do justice to a novel that contains 400 to 500 pages with a film that is less than four or five hours, even if you run it in two or three parts.

BC: *What do you think of the filmed plays of Shakespeare?*

SR: Whatever else Laurence Olivier may have achieved in his adaptations, his Shakespeare films were never filmic. Grigori Kozintsev is the only director who has ever brought a different kind of vitality to a Shakespeare film with his use of backgrounds, peasants, etc. But apart from him, I don't think anyone else has been able to do this; it's very difficult, you know.

BC: *I find it interesting that, time and again, you draw from the non-professional or amateur theater for your actors. Do you find any extra advantage in using such performers?*

SR: Not really, because those who act in the theater, be they professional or non-professional, sometimes don't feel comfortable acting in films, where they don't get instant feedback or appreciation from a live audience. Theater actors also dislike the discontinuity of film acting; they have to do a role in small parts, over a relatively long period of time, with the continuity between shots left to the editing table.

BC: *Have you ever found a person quite suitable in appearance but totally unable to act, and who therefore had to be discharged?*

SR: No, I have been very lucky in this area. You do a screen test before the actual shooting begins, and then you find out who can act and who cannot. Only sometimes with children I have encountered difficulty on the set, as in the case of the boy who played Apu in *Pather Panchali*. His name was Subir Banerjee, and he looked so right, but he couldn't act at all; he was also inattentive. I made him act only after a lot of hard work—including tricks that I devised with the help of the camera. Some children, you see, are born actors, but not Subir-Apu in *Pather Panchali*.

BC: *In your films, one of the persistent themes has been growing up under different circumstances or conditions, at varying levels of society and even in different time periods. Why are you drawn to this theme to such an extent?*

SR: It's true that earlier in my career I did treat this theme, but now narratives with a long span—the ten to twelve years during which a person grows up—do not attract me very much. These days I prefer a short time span during which the character undergoes a change or transformation on account of a traumatic experience—this is the "growth," the development, the movement. A good example of it can be found in *Jana Aranya* [*The Middleman*], where the time span is no more than one or two months. During this short period of time a totally honest, innocent boy becomes totally corrupted— and, ironically, then and only then can he stand on his own two feet. This movement from a certain state of character to another state—this complete inner change—quite fascinates, I must say. Even in an older film of mine, like *Mahanagar*, you can find such an inner change. Here a woman who does not want to work, starts working at her husband's insistence, becomes successful, encounters her husband's envy, and even comes to dominate when he loses his job; then ultimately there is a reconciliation between the two. There are several stages of development in this film, almost a zig-zag, up-and-down movement—and if you don't have something like this, with all your action, you're not making my kind of motion picture.

BC: *What you are saying, then, is that, over the years, you have gotten interested more and more in the psychology of a situation.*

SR: Let's say that I am interested in psychology itself, and have been at least since I made *Devi*. Now "psychology" is of capital importance to me.

BC: *If you found a story where the extraneous details are important, would you be interested in filming it?*

SR: Yes, if the extraneous details are genuinely important, but I would want to know what is happening to the actual human beings in the story as well. If the characters aren't interesting or aren't growing internally, I am not interested.

BC: *From 1961 onwards, starting with* Teen Kanya, *you have composed the music for your own films. Before concluding, could you address the subject of music in general and film music in particular?*

SR: Yes, of course. Music has been my first love for many, many years—perhaps from the time I was thirteen or fourteen. As a child, I had a toy gramophone and there were always plenty of records in our home. Then later, at Presidency College and while I was at the University of Santiniketan, I became seriously interested in Western classical music. I did not have very much money in those days, so obviously it was a question of collecting slowly, one movement of a symphony or a concerto at a time.

When I started working, I began to take music even more seriously. I not only began to collect records, but I also got into the habit of buying musical scores. I remember there was a shop in Bombay in those days—S. Rose and Company—which used to sell miniature or pocketbook German scores. These became bedside reading for me. During the day I would listen to the records with the scores in hand, and then when I read the scores again at night, the music would all come back to me. This is also when I started to become familiar with staff notation.

BC: *Why primarily the interest in Western classical music?*

SR: You see, our home has always had a tradition of listening to Rabindra-sangeet and Indian classical music. My uncle was a great music lover, and the promising new musicians in those days would come regularly to our place and perform. So, since I was familiar with Indian music—from these private performances and from going to public concerts—I did not feel that there was anything more I needed to do in order to learn about it.

With Western music, on the other hand, I experienced the excitement of discovering something new, completely uncharted territory: Beethoven and others whom I had only read about, doing something that did not exist in our music. I shared this enthusiasm with several friends, and I remember that the salesmen at Bevan & Co., in Dalhousie Square, used to be quite astonished that three or four young Bengalis could be so interested in Western classical music.

BC: *In 1966 you said, "Of all the stages of filmmaking, I find it is the orchestration of the music that requires my greatest attention. At the moment, it is still a painstaking process."*

SR: Well, you know, I get involved in the composing of music only once a year or so. If I were a professional composer, perhaps I would have a greater facility for this work. You also have to remember that I was completely self-taught in the area of music. I would jot down musical ideas for a film in shorthand form, so scoring became quite a trial. Now, with experience, the whole process has become somewhat easier for me. Even so, I can't put a musical idea on paper as quickly or as smoothly as a professional composer can. And this work, for me, is very time consuming and tension inducing. The tension is sometimes increased when the musicians don't play as I want them to, because they are used to playing very differently—especially here in Bengal.

BC: *Did this sense of not being too sure of yourself musically, early on, have anything to do with the fact that, in* Pather Panchali, *Ravi Shankar was one of the few professionals you used?*

SR: I thought of using Ravi Shankar not primarily because he was a close personal acquaintance with whom I would feel comfortable working. I thought instead that it would be a good idea to work with someone like him, who would be able to introduce a fresh approach—quite unlike conventional Bengali film composers at the time.

BC: *How was it to work with a famous musician like Ravi Shankar?*

SR: Even at that time, Shankar was quite busy with his foreign tours. I had written to him in Bombay—or was it Delhi?—that I was thinking of making *Pather Panchali* and would like him to do the music. Then I went to see him when he came to Calcutta. He sort of hummed for me a melodic line—a folk tune of sorts—and I thought it was just right for *Pather Panchali*. So that became the film's musical theme—entirely Shankar's contribution.

BC: *Despite your interest in Western classical music, then, you have an aversion to using it in your films.*

SR: Oh, yes, that's right. A lot of films have used Western classical music, and not always with success. You know that Bo Widerberg's *Elvira Madigan* uses, again and again, parts of Mozart's Concerto 453 in G Major. Later on, I found the LP called *The Elvira Madigan Concerto*. That's terrible! Scandalous, even. Because, you see, then you are assuming that the film will rise to the level of the music; but what often happens is that the music is brought down to the level of the film! Particularly in this case, the two don't mix—like water and oil. Yes, I know that Stanley Kubrick used the Ninth Symphony played on a synthesizer in *A Clockwork Orange*; and I suppose it works for this film, though I wouldn't want to possess a record of it. And Kubrick has done some other daring musical things that just come off—like his use of *The Blue Danube* in *2001: A Space Odyssey*. I myself wouldn't mind using a relatively unknown piece of Baroque music—something by Couperin or Scarlatti, for instance—in a film if I can find the right subject.

I hate films, by the way, that are drenched with over-romantic music of the kind you find in some of those lush Hollywood films from the early 1940s. You got someone expensive for your music director, like Max Steiner or Alfred Newman, so you let him drown the film in music. You see, most of the American directors—with the exception of four or five, like William Wyler, Billy Wilder, Frank Capra, and George Stevens—had no control over a film after they finished shooting it. I asked John Huston, whose films are so wonderful, about his *Treasure of the Sierra Madre*, which is absolutely ruined by its music. And he said he had no control over the score; perhaps also, he's not musical, as some directors aren't, and the producers took advantage of this fact.

BC: *So I gather that you feel background music is really an extraneous element in films—that one should be able to express oneself without it.*

SR: My belief is that, yes, a film should be able to dispense with music. But half the time we are using music because we are not confident that certain changes of mood will be understood by the audience—so we underline these changes with mood music. I would like to do without music if such a thing were possible, but I don't think I'll ever be able to do it. I will say that I have used very little music in my contemporary films and as much natural sound as possible.

Initially, I did feel that film needed music partly because long stretches of silence tend to bore the audience: it's as simple as that. With music, the scene becomes "shorter" automatically. And in certain types of films, music is a must unless you have a very rich natural soundtrack. Then there's the type of film where music is needed just to hide the rough edges. You know, De Sica's earlier pictures—*Bicycle Thieves, Miracle in Milan, Shoeshine, Umberto D.*—were very grainy films, shot at a time when they were using five different kinds of black-and-white stock, and when shooting conditions were terrible, right after the Second World War. Not that the cutting or camera movement is bad—De Sica's a master in those departments—but some "rough" scenes simply cried out for music, and he had a marvelous composer, Cicognini, who provided it.

In general, let's just say that whether you are going to use music or sound effects depends on the mood of a scene. If a specific sound effect is crucial, I don't even think of using music in its place. And when you are trying to control time, to maintain real or chronological time, I would say the less music there is, the better, though sound effects can help a lot in this instance. When time is broken up, by contrast, music helps to preserve a linear flow.

BC: *Which score from one of your films would you re-do if you could?*

SR: All of them! Whenever I see an old film of mine, I say to myself: Given the chance, I would re-edit it and do the music all over again. Today recording quality has improved enormously, but what used to happen in the old days is that immediately after the shooting was over and the rough cut was done, we were faced with a deadline to deliver the finished film—as a result of which everything was done in a rush and everything suffered. Sometimes we used to mix through the night, keeping just one step ahead of the editor, who was probably laying the tracks of reel four while we were mixing reel three! That's the way we used to work, on the music as well as everything else. There was no possibility of getting total precision, exactly what I wanted, etc.

Today, things are a little easier. One even develops improvised methods of one's own. For instance, now I record all the dialogue in my films on a cassette, *with the silences*. Then I make a chart of each character's lines so that I can work out precise timings and know exactly what music to put where. And I can do this because, as the director, I have every little detail of the film in my head. So I can even work at home, and I can work faster here. Everything I know about musical scoring—indeed, filmmaking as a whole—I learned as I went along. There were no rules; one had to make up one's own.

BC: *Could you give an example of a scene in one of your films that calls for music but doesn't have any?*

SR: *Aparajito*, after Harihar's death. It's the very first day that Sarbajaya and Apu arrive in the village; it is also dusk and there's practically nothing happening, nothing to see—almost nothing to hear—in that long sequence. I feel so awkward when I see it now. But Ravi Shankar hadn't provided any music here, and I didn't have the confidence at this point to write any.

BC: *Which of your early films, above all the others, needed strong orchestration to strengthen the main theme?*

SR: *Jalsaghar*, which I knew would have long passages of silence, called for a fairly extensive use of background music.

BC: *I am certain that you have your own musical favorite among your films. Which is it?*

SR: If you judge just by the background score, I would say *Charulata* is my best "musical film." Here everything was right, everything worked. The music in this picture had a lot to do with theme and context. Charulata's loneliness is established visually at the start, but it had a special quality. I had to explain that there was also a youthfulness, even a restlessness, about her loneliness. And as soon as something new or "connective" occurs—when Amal comes along, for example—she is revitalized, as it were. So I needed something that was both playful and wistful. And I got it, for the musical theme that finally emerged is one of the best I have done.

Then consider the context: we're dealing with a liberal, progressive, Westernized family here, so I knew I needed a Western element. In two of the songs, I got both the Western and the Indian elements. In a sense, the possibilities of fusing Indian and Western music began to interest me from this point on. I began to realize that, at some point, music is one, though on the whole I have to say that Western music is better able to reflect mood changes.

It does this through transition from key to key, from major to minor, and so on. In Indian music, such transitions can only be accomplished through a sudden shift, from raga to raga—which itself can, in the right instance, be quite thrilling.

BC: *One final question, Mr. Ray. What do you feel are the main fears or crises confronting filmmakers today—I mean contemporary, serious filmmakers?*

SR: I'm afraid I don't know much about the others. I can only talk about myself. Obviously anyone who makes movies is concerned about the financial aspect. There possibly are directors who are not really concerned whether the producer gets his money back or not. But I put myself among those directors who are extremely aware of the fact that somebody else is making it possible for you to be creative. Without somebody else's help you are helpless, and you can never be creative in films. Making even the simplest of pictures costs money, and you don't always have that kind of money yourself. So you have to depend on others. Thus the need for communication, particularly of the economic kind.

Moreover, I don't think India is the place to be obscure, avant-garde, or abstract in the cinema. That is, unless you are making a film in Super-8 or using your own funds. Then you can do whatever you like. And it's good to conduct experiments from time to time. But when you consider yourself to be part of the commercial set-up, as I do, subconsciously you always think of an "ideal" audience. You are not necessarily thinking of the lowest common denominator in audiences; still, you are thinking of an audience for your film. And you expect this audience to respond to what you are doing. After a degree of experience, you know more or less what that audience is capable of responding to—which is what one endeavors to keep in mind.

BC: *One last thing, really. What truly amazes me is your utter accessibility. I mean, one has only to venture climbing a big flight of stairs to reach you, virtually unannounced. It's incredible, and I am so grateful to you for taking the time to talk to me.*

SR: Yes, I am in the phone book, and you can knock on my door. Everybody has access to me, anyone who wants to see me. In fact, the people who come to visit on Sunday mornings are often very ordinary folks. Not big stars or anything like that. Some are my old colleagues from advertising days. Others are those who simply feel friendly towards me as a result of the films of mine they have seen. In the end, I think it's rather stupid to raise a wall around oneself. This way of doing things—as we have done today—is much more interesting, rewarding, exciting.

Satyajit Ray Filmography

Pather Panchali (1955)
Aparajito (1956)
The Music Room (1958)
The Philosopher's Stone (1958)
The World of Apu (1959)
The Goddess (1960)
Rabindranath Tagore (1961, documentary)
Three Daughters (1961)
The Expedition (1962)
Kanchenjungha (1962)
The Big City (1963)
The Lonely Wife (1964)
Two (1964, short)
The Coward and the Holy Man (1965)
The Hero (1966)
The Zoo (1967)
The Adventures of Goopy and Bagha (1968)
Days and Nights in the Forest (1969)
The Adversary (1970)
Company Limited (1971)
Sikkim (1971, documentary)
The Inner Eye (1972, documentary)
Distant Thunder (1973)
The Golden Fortress (1974)
The Middleman (1975)
Bala (1976, documentary)
The Chess Players (1977)
The Elephant God (1978)
Kingdom of Diamonds (1980)
Pikoo's Day (1980, short)
The Deliverance (1981)
The Home and the World (1984)
Sukumar Ray (1987, documentary)
Ganashatru (1989)
Branches of the Tree (1990)

Bibliography

American Film Institute. *Satyajit Ray: A Study Guide*. Washington, D.C.: Author, 1979.

Bandyopadhyaya, Surabhi. *Satyajit Ray: Beyond the Frame*. New Delhi, India: Allied Publishers, 1996.

Biswas, Moinak, ed. *Apu and After: Re-visiting Ray's Cinema*. London: Seagull Books, 2006.

Cooper, Darius. *The Cinema of Satyajit Ray: Between Tradition and Modernity*. New York: Cambridge University Press, 2000.

Das, Santi, ed. *Satyajit Ray, An Intimate Master*. New Delhi, India: Allied Publishers, 1998.

Das Gupta, Chidananda. *The Cinema of Satyajit Ray*. 1980. Rev. and enl. ed. New Delhi, India: National Book Trust, 1994.

Ganguly, Suranjan. *Satyajit Ray: In Search of the Modern*. Lanham, Md.: Scarecrow Press, 2000.

Nandi, Alok B., and Ghosh, Nemai. *Satyajit Ray at 70 as Writer, Designer, Actor, Director, Cameraman, Editor, Composer*. London: Art Books International, 1991.

Nyce, Ben. *Satyajit Ray: A Study of His Films*. New York: Praeger, 1988.

Rangoonwalla, Firoze. *Satyajit Ray's Art*. Delhi, India: Clarion, 1980.

Ray, Satyajit. *Childhood Days: A Memoir*. New York: Penguin Books, 1998.

Robinson, Andrew. *Satyajit Ray: A Vision of Cinema*. London: Palgrave Macmillan, 2005.

———. *Satyajit Ray: The Inner Eye; The Biography of a Master Filmmaker*. New York: St. Martin's Press, 2004.

Sarkar, Bidyut. *The World of Satyajit Ray*. New Delhi, India: UBS Publishers' Distributors, 1992.

Satyajit Ray: An Anthology of Statements on Ray and by Ray. New Delhi, India: Directorate of Film Festivals, Ministry of Information and Broadcasting, 1981.

Sen, Jayanti, ed. *The Art of Satyajit Ray*. Calcutta, India: Oxford Bookstore Gallery, 1995.

Seton, Marie. *Portrait of a Director: Satyajit Ray*. Bloomington: Indiana University Press, 1971.

The Accidental Auteur

A Dialogue with Abbas Kiarostami

Abbas Kiarostami (born 1940) is the most influential and controversial post-revolutionary Iranian filmmaker and one of the most highly celebrated directors in the international film community of the last decade. During the period of the 1980s and the 1990s, at a time when Iranians had such a negative image in the West, his cinema introduced the humane and artistic face of his people. Kiarostami has been involved in the making of over forty films since 1970, including shorts and documentaries; he first attained global critical acclaim for directing the Koker Trilogy (*Where Is the Friend's House?* [1987], *Through the Olive Trees* [1992], and *Life and Nothing More . . .* [1994]), *Taste of Cherry* (1997), and *The Wind Will Carry Us* (1999).

Kiarostami belongs to a generation of filmmakers who created the so-called New Wave, a movement in Iranian cinema that started in the 1960s, before the revolution of 1979. Directors such as Forough Farrokhzad, Dariush Mehrjui, Sohrab Shaheed Saless, Amir Naderi, Bahram Beizai, and Parviz Kimiavi were the pioneers of this movement. These filmmakers had a number of techniques in common, including the use of poetic dialogue and of allegorical narrative as a way of dealing with complex political and philosophical issues. They were followed not only by Kiarostami, but also by Mohsen Makhmalbaf, Bahman Ghobadi, Jafar Panahi, and Hassan Yektapanah.

In his own movement toward an elliptically compressed, nearly plotless cinema, Kiarostami not only breaks away from conventional or mainstream narrative, he also questions the audience's role—playing with audience members' expectations and provoking their critical thinking as well as creative imagination. In addition, he has a reputation for using child protagonists, for filming stories that take place in rural villages and that therefore emphasize landscape and architecture, and for employing small crews, non-actors, and often no script. Kiarostami's documentary feature A.B.C. Africa (2001) signaled the emergence of yet another new approach, as it was his first film shot outside Iran and on digital video.

The following interview took place in Istanbul, Turkey, in May of 2005 at the Istanbul Film Festival, where Kiarostami was an honored guest.

Bert Cardullo: *Jean-Luc Godard famously said, "Film begins with D. W. Griffith and ends with Abbas Kiarostami." What do you think of that?*

Abbas Kiarostami: Well, Godard doesn't believe this anymore, especially since I diverted cinema off its course a bit when I made *Ten*.

BC: *Let me give you another quotation. Anthony Minghella said that "If Samuel Beckett had made films, he would have made them like Kiarostami." Do you agree?*

AK: Maybe. Beckett did make one film, actually, with Alan Schneider directing and Buster Keaton in the leading role: *Film*. So there is some evidence if anyone wants to prove or disprove Mr. Minghella's thesis.

BC: *How did you become a filmmaker?*

AK: It's all because of my friend Abbas Cohendari's shoes that I became a filmmaker! At the time I had passed my baccalaureate and had failed the entrance exam in painting at the School of Fine Arts. So I became a traffic cop. One day I was in Abbas Cohendari's dry goods shop and he asked me to go with him to the Tajreesh Bridge. I told him that I'd rather not because I had sandals on. So he gave me a pair of new shoes, just my size, and we set off for Tajreesh Bridge. Then we went over to Farhad Ashtari's, where I met a certain Mohaqeq who ran a painting workshop. So I enrolled in his classes and took the entrance exam for the Fine Arts School over again—this time I passed. I then began working in advertising. I had left my parents' home when I was eighteen and had to earn a living. In the beginning, I worked as a painter and graphic artist in a number of studios; I did book covers, posters, etc. Then I went to Tabli Film, which, at the time, was the main production center for commercials. When I offered my services as a director, they asked me to write a sketch about an isothermal water-heater. I spent the night writing a poem about water-heaters. Three evenings later, to my great astonishment, I saw a commercial on TV with my poem in it. That was how I got into commercials. Little by little, I made progress. I wrote more sketches and started directing commercials. From 1960 to 1969, I must have directed more than 150. I really enjoyed those commercials. You have to condense the introduction, the story itself, and the message into one minute; you must broach a subject, explain it quickly to everyone, and make the public want to go out and buy the product. I learned about cinema from commercials and graphic art: in a graphic project, you have a page, a column, or an insert on which to draw something that will immediately grab the reader's attention. I think graphics is the father of all arts. By its very limitations, this kind of commissioned work forces you to use your imagination. During the last few years of my work in advertising, I designed credit sequences for a few Iranian films; this was the turning point between my graphic work and my directing of non-advertising films. I discovered the camera during my work on these credit sequences.

BC: *Are you yet at a point yet where you regard yourself chiefly as a filmmaker?*

AK: I have many professions, and none of them appeases me. There are filmmakers who, when they are making one film, are thinking about the next. This kind of filmmaker tends not to be an artist. I am not like that. I am a vagabond. Being this vagabond leads me to all sorts of places and leads me to do all sorts of things. I spend a lot of time doing carpentry, for instance. Sometimes there is nothing that gives me the contentment that sawing a piece of wood does. Working in quiet gives me inner peace.

BC: *You are nearly as well known for your still photography as you are for your films.*

AK: For me, still photography, video, and film are all elements of one spectrum. The question is how we can best get close to our subjects. And, where that goal is concerned, the future belongs to digital video. The non-actors I like to use, for example, feel more comfortable in front of a digital camera, without the lights and the large crew around them, and we therefore arrive at far more intimate moments with them. Moreover, because of the requirements of the 35mm camera and the mode of production that comes with that camera, there were a lot of people who just couldn't afford to use it. Now, this digital camera makes it possible for everybody to pick it up, like a pen. If you have the right vision, and you think you are an instinctive filmmaker, there is no hindrance anymore. You just pick it up, like a pen, and work with it.

I photographed *Ten* and *Five* in digital video, but I did return to 35mm for the episode I shot in the three-episode anthology film made in Italy called *Tickets*. (The other two episodes are by Ken Loach and Ermanno Olmi.) If you are not going to take full advantage of digital, I must say, then 35mm is a better medium—especially for shooting dramas.

BC: *Could you say something about the paintings you still do?*

AK: Let me start by saying that I do not call myself a painter even though I do painting. It is more important to engage in painting than to label oneself a painter—I simply feel comfortable painting. When people ask me to judge their paintings, I decline and remind them that what is important is that they have been engaged in the activity of painting. Engaging in the art of painting itself is the worthwhile activity, and so I paint.

BC: *Though you say you aren't a painter, one of the extraordinary things about your films is the way you picture and frame the landscape. But painting is a solitary activity. You couldn't find something more socially and even artistically opposite from filmmaking, which involves so many people, and a big metaphorical canvas as opposed to a small, actual one.*

AK: I have gotten used to looking at reality in an artistic way, especially through the viewpoint of painting. When I look at nature, I see the frame of a painting. I see everything from an aesthetic angle. Even when I am in a taxi looking out the window, I put everything in a frame. This is the way I see painting, photography, and film—all interrelated and connected because they capture reality in frames. All interconnected, also, because they take advantage, or should, of mistakes, accidents, chance. I take my lead from Renoir the painter, who said that if you drip paint on your canvas, don't get too worried about it; instead try to use the drip as an element and evolve something else out of it.

BC: *Let me introduce a subject that couldn't be farther from such fortuitousness, which itself is a kind of artistic freedom. What is the relationship between censorship and filmmaking in Iran?*

AK: The government has not shown any of my films for the past ten years. I think they don't understand my films and so prevent them from being shown just in case there is a message they don't want to get out. They tend to support films that are stylistically very different from mine—melodramas. The government doesn't just own the cinemas, but also the means of production, so I have to work around them. The government is not in my way, but it is not assisting me, either. We lead our separate lives. Two things you have to keep in mind: one, an Iranian official hardly ever remains in his position for a very long time; when one goes and another comes, that is the best time to try again. Two films of mine have escaped the sharp censorship scissors, probably because the censors did not quite understand what they *should* censor in them! A movie is good, I think, when the censor does not understand what should be censored. If a film is made from which a censor cuts some parts, then those parts should have been cut, because he understood them!

Let me add that the Iranian cinema today is distinctive from that of the rest of the world not only because of its unique vision and perspective, but also because it reflects the way in which each filmmaker has come to terms with, and found ways of expressing himself within, the limitations that exist. I like to use the phrase "restrictive" to describe the conditions I work under rather than "oppressive," as some people do; and I understand that oppressive means many different things in many different contexts, but for us as artists and filmmakers what we are dealing with are the realities of restrictions, and I like to approach the subject of censorship from that angle. I look at these restrictions not in the context of the cinema alone but in the broader context of life. For me these restrictions exist everywhere and have always been there. Life in the East has never been without them. We have always had to live within certain boundaries. Life is the combination of, and the movement between, restriction and freedom—the field of action is limited, and the field of power is limited. When we were kids we were always told what we could do and what we couldn't, and how far we could go in doing things we could.

The best example I can give for this concept comes from the classroom, when our teacher told us to do a composition. When he gave us a topic, we would write about that topic and come up with something worthwhile. But when he did not specify the topic and left us free to choose our own, we usually couldn't come up with something worth writing about. We needed to be told what the boundaries and restrictions were. This has been the nature of our society and has been replicated in the realities of our film industry. For instance, during the first four years of the Iranian Revolution, there was a great deal of chaos in the film industry because not many rules were set yet. Interestingly enough, most of the Iranian moviemakers didn't produce much during this time, though a great deal could have been done. No one used the opportunity because everyone was waiting to find out what the restrictions were!

I don't want to imply that these limitations are good and should be there, but we have been brought up with them and it is in our mentality. This is not limited to my profession—it's in every profession: limitation makes people more creative. I have a friend who is an architect. He tells me that he is at his best professionally when he designs structures for odd lots, because these pieces of land do not fit into the normal pattern and he has to work within a framework of great limitation. So, he must be creative and he enjoys this. It is these restrictions that provide an opportunity for people to be creative.

BC: *Just before* Taste of Cherry *was to have been shown at Cannes, there was speculation that the Iranian authorities might stop it because it dealt with suicide. But afterward some reports said its subject matter had not been a problem. Did that film run into difficulties with the censors because of its subject?*

AK: There was controversy about the movie, but after I talked with the authorities, they accepted the fact that this is not a movie about suicide—it's about the choice we have in life, to end it whenever we want. We have a door we can open at any time, but we choose to stay, and the fact that we have this choice is, I think, God's kindness: God is kind because he has given us this choice. The authorities were satisfied with that explanation. A sentence from the Romanian-French philosopher E. M. Cioran helped me a lot: "Without the possibility of suicide, I would have killed myself long ago." *Taste of Cherry* is about the possibility of living, and how we have the choice to live. Life isn't forced on us: that is the main theme of the movie.

BC: *Why, may I ask, did you decide to remain in Iran after the 1979 revolution, unlike many Iranian filmmakers of your generation?*

AK: When you take a tree that is rooted in the ground, and transfer it from one place to another, the tree will no longer bear fruit. And if it does, the fruit will not be as good as it was in its original place. This is a rule of nature. I think if I had left my country, I would be the same as the tree.

Homayoun Ershadi as Mr. Badii in Kiarostami's *Taste of Cherry*.

BC: *Do you think your films genuinely depict the reality of Iranian life after the revolution?*

AK: No, I'm not sure of this at all. I'm not sure that my films show the reality of life in Iran; I show different aspects of life. Iran is a very extensive and expansive place, and sometimes, even for those of us who live there, some of the realities are very hard to comprehend.

BC: *Are you yourself religious?*

AK: I can't answer this question. I think religion is very personal, and the tragedy for our country is that the personal aspect has been destroyed. It would be the easiest thing in the world for me to say that I am religious, but I won't. This most personal aspect of our lives has become the tool of the government's power. The value of people is equated with their religiosity.

BC: *Does restrictive religion have anything to do with the fact that almost all of the protagonists in your films are male?*

AK: Such restrictions aside for the moment, I simply don't like the role of women as mothers, or as lovers for that matter. Or the role of women as victims, beaten and long-suffering. That's not my experience. Or women as exceptional. I don't like showing exceptions. Especially women as heroes, since it doesn't correspond to the real situation. And there's another role, women as decorative objects—not only in Iranian but in world cinema as well. So what am I left with? I did feature a woman in *Ten*, though.

BC: *Was the film drawn from your own marital experiences, may I ask?*

AK: Definitely. I never reflect or convey that which I have not experienced myself. I divorced twenty-two years ago. In Iran, while women can sue for divorce—only, I might add, if they charge their husbands with abuse or drug addiction—they are not economically able to look after their children afterwards and, as a result, often see their children only rarely. Women, after divorce, lose what little independence they had, and therefore they are less and less able to take responsibility for their children. It often results in tragedy for all concerned, and I was trying to explore that in *Ten*.

The woman in the film, who has divorced her husband, drives around Tehran with various passengers: her son, a friend, a prostitute, and an old woman. And I try, especially, to depict the consequences of her divorce in the person of her aggressive young son, who treats his mother disrespectfully from the passenger seat. He thus seems, already at the tender age of seven, to have internalized the masculine license of my patriarchal—some would say "sexist"—society.

BC: *Why have you consistently chosen to populate your films with non-actors, who more or less play themselves?*

AK: Working with non-professionals has got an advantage for me, in that they correct my script. That's the reason I use them. If I write something and it does not sound right coming from the mouth of the non-professional actor, if he cannot say it naturally, then I know it's wrong. The non-professional actors "interfere" during the entire period of filming. And finally, that helps me to produce a better movie. I do not want to make it sound as if using professional actors is negative, but I am able to create the personality of the characters of the film by working in my way. Usually directors bring stars to play the role of the normal people, but I bring normal people to play the role of themselves. And they cannot play any other role except their own. There is a saying that every person can be a romantic writer if he writes about his own love life. Therefore, these non-professional actors are performing very well, because they are playing themselves. Once you explain the scene to them, they just start talking, beyond what I would have imagined. It is like a cycle, and I don't know where it starts and ends: I don't know whether I am teaching them what to say, or they are teaching me what to receive!

BC: *What is the relationship of such actors to the filmgoing audience?*

AK: Non-professionals "do" less, and that fits my scripts, which do not spell things out so clearly. And both of these—the use of non-professionals and the writing of pared-down scripts—help the viewer to participate more in the filmmaking process. I am in favor of the "half-made film," which the spectator must complete with his mind. The cinema of the future is the cinema of the director *and* the viewer. I make one film as a filmmaker, but the audience, based on that film, makes 100 movies in their minds. Every audience member can make his own movie. This is what I strive for. Sometimes, when my audiences tell me about the mental movies they have made based on my movie, I am surprised, and I become the audience for their movies as they are describing them to me. My movie has only functioned as a base for them to make their movies. There is a Persian expression that captures this notion: the translation is "seeing with borrowed eyes," which defines my desire to have the audience both see what is in a given scene and imagine, with their "borrowed eyes," what is outside that scene. Let me put this in another way. The usual way in film is to show—and to say—something. But my aim is to create a cinema in which we see how much we can do without actually showing, or saying, it. How much use we can make of the imagination of the spectator. You must be able to imagine what is going on beyond what is physically shown, because the filmmaker is actually only showing a corner of reality. It is a good idea when pictures and action guide you to something that is outside the story without actually showing it. I believe in Bresson's method of creation through omission, not through addition.

BC: *Is this the reason your films are often consciously "un-concluded," as in the case of* Taste of Cherry?

AK: Yes. The idea not to end movies with some kind of conclusion occurred to me several years ago. Most of the time, people go to see a film with the expectation that a story will be told. I do not like this arrangement where there is a dichotomy between me, as the storyteller, and the spectator, as the one sitting there and watching the story as such. I prefer to believe that the spectators are much more intelligent and actually see it as unfair that I get the chance to captivate them for two hours telling them the story, ending it the way I say it must end, and so on. So I actually want to give them more credit by involving them and distributing the sense of belonging or creation between myself and the spectator. Some artists like their movies to be perfect as they describe it, but I don't seek that kind of perfection. To me perfection is defined by how much the spectator can engage in the movie, and so a good movie is one that involves the spectator as a part of it and not as a captive person.

BC: *Could you elaborate both on how you get your non-actors to be so natural and on how you go about creating scripts for your films?*

AK: I do not have very complete scripts for my films, as I have already indicated. I have a general outline and a character in my mind, and I make no notes until I find the character in reality who's in my mind. When I find that character, I try to spend time with him and get to know him very well. Therefore my notes are not from the character that I had in my mind before, but are instead based on the people I've met in real life. It's a long process and may take six months. I only make notes; I don't write out dialogue in full. And the notes are very much based on my knowledge of that person. When we start shooting I don't have rehearsals with the actor-characters at all. So, rather than pulling them towards myself, I travel closer to them; they are very much closer to real people than anything I could try to create. I give them something, it's true, but I also take from them.

There is a Rumi poem from about 1000 years ago that helps to explain this—it goes something like this: You are like the ball subject to my polo stick; I set you in motion, but once you're off and running, I am the one in pursuit. You are making me run, too! Therefore, when you see the end result of the filmmaking process, it is difficult to know who is the director, the actor-characters or I. Ultimately, everything belongs to the actors—I just manage the situation. This kind of directing, I think, is very similar to being a football coach. You prepare your players and place them in the right places, but once the game is on, there is nothing much you can do—you can smoke a cigarette or get nervous, but you can't do much else. While shooting *Ten*—which, as you know, consists of ten scenes set in the front of a car—I was sitting in the backseat, but I didn't interfere. Sometimes, I was following in another car, so I was not even present on the "set," because I thought the actors would work better in my absence. Directors don't always create—they can also destroy with too many demands. Using non-actors has its own set of rules and really requires that you allow them to do their own thing.

BC: *Do you think you prefer this method because of the way you started out at Kanoon [Iran's Institute for the Intellectual Development of Children and Young Adults], working very often with children, where you probably had to work in this manner?*

AK: This practice is very much rooted in that period of my life. If I hadn't started with children, I would never have arrived at this style. Children are very strong and independent characters and can come up with more interesting things than Marlon Brando, and it's sometimes very difficult to direct them or order them to do something. When I met Akira Kurosawa in Japan, one question he asked me was, "How did you actually make the children act the way they do? I do sometimes have children in my films, but I find that I reduce and reduce their presence until I have to get rid of them because there's no way that I can direct them." My own thought is that if one is very grand, like an emperor on a horse, it's very hard for children to relate to that; you have to come down to below their level in order to communicate with them. Actors are also like children.

BC: *Can you talk about your relationship with cars, since they feature so prominently in a number of your films?*

AK: My car is my best friend. My office. My home. My location. I have a very intimate feeling when I am in a car with someone next to me. We are in the most comfortable seats because we are not facing each other, but sitting side by side. We don't look at each other constantly, but instead do so only when we want to. We are allowed to look around without appearing rude. We have a big screen in front of us and we have side views. Silence does not seem heavy or difficult. Nobody serves anybody. And there are many other aspects to this experience, as well. One most important thing is that the car transports us from one place to another.

BC: *I'm an American and I'm sometimes appalled by the anti-Iranian bias in the American media. I'd like to think that your films—particularly your cinematic love affair with the automobile, which may not be so different from Americans' own such love—can create more understanding between Americans and Iranians, but I fear that the U.S. news media encourage Americans to think in somewhat simplistic ways about your country. What are your thoughts on this?*

AK: Thank you for your very positive view on the issue. Unfortunately, film critics like you are very few in America, but there are many, many critics of

Iran. It is very important for us film people to find common ground between cultures, and maybe that's less the case for politicians, who benefit more from finding the conflicts and differences between peoples. One of the mandates of art cinema, as you well know, is to show the universal reality behind the daily headlines.

BC: *Let's continue with the reception of Iran, and Iranian cinema, in America. In major U.S. cities, the films of yours that have been released commercially have come and gone in the blink of an eye. And it's puzzling when you consider that there was a time when films by the great filmmakers of the world—Bergman, Fellini, Godard—regularly received healthy international distribution, and caused crowds to line up around the block. You might be the first of an entire generation of similarly talented filmmakers whose work will be known almost exclusively within the constricted world of film festivals.*

AK: Thank you for comparing me with those three filmmakers. I, too, think they were making great films, but, at the same time, the Hollywood cinema wasn't as dominant then as it is now. It is a more formidable competitor today, and that's the reason its movies don't leave any audience for us. The fact is that movies train the eyes of their audience, and when they have been trained on these types of Hollywood movies, it is very difficult to then convert them to our films. But, sort of unknowingly, the Hollywood cinema is going in a direction that may end up helping our kind of cinema. Audiences are being left dissatisfied now. The viewers leave a film unfulfilled, hungry and uncertain as to the experience they have had; and this is where the genuine filmmaker has the chance to ensnare them, to win them over.

BC: *My feeling is that people don't expect very much today. They don't expect great pleasure; they expect action or something like that.*

AK: It's because the films have gotten them used to expecting action and not pleasure, because the technicians are making the films and not filmmakers. We are going to get to a point where that will become clear and the situation will have to change.

BC: *Does serious art always create in the spectator the desire for some other reality?*

AK: Yes, I believe so, because otherwise art would have no purpose. Should religion not prove successful at accomplishing that mission, art always can attempt it. They both point in the same direction. Religion points to another world, whereas art points to a better existence. One is an invitation, an offering to a faraway place, the other to a place that is closer by but nonetheless difficult to reach.

BC: *Who are other filmmakers you feel might be working on a similar wavelength?*

AK: Hou Hsiao-hsien is one. Tarkovsky's works separate me completely from physical life, and are the most spiritual films I have seen. What Fellini did in parts of his movies—bringing the dream life into film—Tarkovsky did as well. Theo Angelopoulos's movies also achieve this type of spirituality at certain moments.

BC: *You've spoken in the past about a desire to create a kind of "poetic cinema"—more indebted to poetry than to novels or theater. Indeed, the title of* The Wind Will Carry Us *comes from a poem by a woman named Forough Farrokhzad—a poem that is recited by the character of the engineer during one scene—and the film also features the* Rubáiyát of Omar Khayyám.

AK: Well, the cinema has been referred to as "the seventh art," and you can interpret that in two ways: either it includes the other arts and is some sort of summation of them; or, maybe, it is the most complete art form. But even if the cinema is the seventh art, it's ironic that all other art forms, such as painting and music, have gone through stages of evolution and have changed. For the cinema, however, this has not happened yet; the cinema is the same as it always was: it relies too much on storytelling. When I talk about "poetic cinema," I'm not talking about sending a humanistic message. I'm talking about the cinema's being like poetry, possessing the complicated qualities of poetry, and also having the vast potential of poetry—having the capabilities of a prism.

This kind of cinema—the prism-like cinema—has an enduring capability, and, in any given situation, in any given time period, you can relate to it in a different way and people can discover themselves in it. I think cinema should follow the other arts, go through the same process of development, and assume the same outlook that they do. But the viewers have to make a concession, in the sense of not expecting only entertainment from films, in the same way that, when they don't understand poetry, they don't fault the poetry for being bad poetry. They live with it. And when they go to hear music, they don't expect to hear a story. When they are looking at an abstract painting, it brings other things than a narrative to mind; it is through imagistic association that they "get" the meaning of it, not through the apprehension of immediate or linear reality. I wish they would do the same in front of a movie screen.

BC: *You're giving them a chance to do that with* Five, *where you shun storytelling in favor of five single-take short films shot on the shores of the Caspian Sea.*

AK: Yes, *Five* is at the crossroads between poetry, photography, and film. It's an experimental work of art. It has to be, since it features waves breaking, ducks waddling, walkers promenading, a pack of dogs, and, finally, moonlight on waves!

BC: *One of the differences between a film and a poem is that most people assume they can see a film once or twice and "get it," which is very different from the attitude you suggest toward poetry, which we return to over and over again. Will there always be problems reaching audiences with a poetic form of cinema, since people aren't accustomed to seeing a film again and again? Do you expect people to watch a given film of yours many times, or do you at least hope they will?*

AK: I would be too selfish if I said everyone should see my movies more than once. I know one thing, however. Many viewers may come out of the theater not satisfied, and yet they won't be able to forget the movie. I know they'll be talking about it during their next dinner. I want them to be a little restless about my movies, and keep trying to find something in them. In that sense, they will be seeing my movies more than once.

BC: *Like the "poetic" or "abstract"* Five, *the documentary* A.B.C. Africa *was shot in digital video as well, wasn't it?*

AK: Yes, that was the first film in which I used this new format. At first I didn't use the digital camera as a serious work tool. I took it with me more like a still camera, to take some notes with it. But when I actually started using it—and when I realized its possibilities and what I could do with them—I realized that I have wasted, in a way, thirty years of my career using the 35mm camera, because, as I argued earlier in our conversation, that camera, for the type of intimate, immediate work that I do, is more of a hindrance than a communication tool.

BC: *Which made the journey for you between making* The Wind Will Carry Us *and* A.B.C. Africa *not unlike the journey of the engineer in* The Wind Will

Carry Us, *who goes from filming with a big crew to capturing snapshots, surreptitiously, with his still camera.*

AK: Yes, actually. I was lucky that this new medium appeared to me between these two films. Because I also had that same sense of exhaustion that the engineer has in *The Wind Will Carry Us*; this new camera appeared to me, in a sense, like an angel and saved my artistic life. Not necessarily in terms of my mental approach to making a film, but in terms of the ease of making one.

BC: *How did the A.B.C. Africa project originate?*

AK: The United Nations, since they knew that I had made films for children for so many years, decided to invite me to make a film about the children orphaned by AIDS in Uganda. Their intention was a sort of general mobilization to attack this problem, and this movie became an invitation to the rest of the world to help these orphaned kids in their plight.

BC: *Could you speak a bit about your experience in Uganda? Why did you go there as opposed to some other African state?*

AK: I went to Uganda because it had less civil strife. Sometimes we drove for hours at night without there being a flicker of light. And people would be lining the road, dressed in white. There was no light at all. No electricity, no candles, no light at all. During the day, everything there is very green and beautiful. I saw people who are poverty stricken but extremely rich within. They are very happy people—something I've almost never seen anywhere. I asked a friend why these people were so happy. He said it was because of the three things these people do not have: pollution, tension, and competition. The competition that they do have, however, is a big one, between life and death. And that's why their lives have so much meaning, because death, in the form of AIDS, is so close at hand. They're happy just to be alive.

BC: *Is the subject of AIDS of any interest or concern to an Iranian audience?*

AK: They have kept the whole question of AIDS under the rug in Iran; it is like a secret illness. There was an attempt in 2001 to bring it out into the public arena for discussion, but this attempt was aborted. To me, AIDS is an international epidemic and every country potentially can be affected by it.

Therefore, it should be discussed on an international level. Unfortunately, AIDS doesn't require a visa.

BC: *Were you eager to accept the UN invitation, or did you have initial reservations about making the film?*

AK: I didn't quite officially accept the invitation, but I agreed to go to the area for a visit. So, the trip was a sort of location scouting, but we had cameras with us and we started shooting—not for the purpose of making the actual film. Then, when we finished shooting, we looked at the footage we had and decided that maybe we could make the movie out of this footage.

BC: *This is hardly alien to you: this idea of making a movie on the spot, as you did in* Homework *and* Close-Up *previously. And yet, most movies endure long and arduous pre-production processes—only to produce an end result that is, in terms of clarity and sense of purpose, frequently inferior to your own impromptu films.*

AK: I agree with you about this style of working. A good movie is made by an initial burst of energy that contributes to the quality of the work. When I talk to some of the younger filmmakers, they are so worried about their films that, eventually, this state of being worried reflects itself in, and actually helps, the final work. Whereas, with projects that are meticulously planned, you look at the end result and it is full of emptiness.

BC: *There is a lot of corruption in the film industry—all of it related to money— and the artistic results in general are not very good. What can we do to oppose this?*

AK: You are obviously doing your part because, in your criticism, you point out the films that are made with smaller budgets—the films that are small in name only. It's not possible to change this situation dramatically because the wheel of film is being turned by industry, by business. Many people work within that film industry, and a lot of people go to see films just to be entertained. That sort of film exists and that is as it should be. And that is the cinema which allows our films to be made, because otherwise there would be no reason to show our films. What you do, pointing a finger at the films that are different, is all that can be done.

BC: *Can you envision artists' organizing some kind of alternative production and distribution structures as well?*

AK: I think it is going to happen little by little. There is no choice for cinema other than to become a little bit more internalized, more intimate, more profound. To begin with, the technique and the facilities created by the commercial film industry are going to self-destruct eventually. The bombastic film will destroy itself, because it is so full of itself; it will become so full that it will implode. So there will be a return to, or revisiting of, a past cinema at that point.

I was channel surfing last night with the remote control in my hotel room, and the two times I paused anywhere and focused, I was looking at black-and-white films. And that was not even a conscious choice. One was a *Tarzan* picture with Johnny Weissmuller. It was at least watchable, and even though it was just entertainment, it felt like a healthier thing. The other, newer, color films I couldn't even watch, because there was so much going on and they were moving so fast that it just disturbed my vision; it disturbed *me*. Therefore I believe that even the eyes of the commercial viewership are going to need some serenity, some calm, soon. This itself will increase the opportunities for independent films. And, of course, your relentless finger-pointing at mindless action films will do this as well.

BC: *It seems difficult for many artists today to treat individual psychological truth, sociopolitical reality, and artistic form with equal seriousness, with equal commitment. Is that a reasonable statement?*

AK: I completely agree. As I have implied, moviemakers are always being pushed to focus on the excitation and manipulation of the audience. The question to which I don't know the answer is whether or not the viewer wants to be manipulated. I don't know anyone who says, "Instead of letting me see reality, manipulate me. I would prefer it." This is an illness that comes from somewhere in society—maybe from escapist movies themselves.

BC: *You yourself are choosing to make films about ordinary people, poor people. That itself is quite rare today.*

AK: I get my material from all around me. When I leave my house in the morning, those ordinary people are the ones I come into contact with. In my entire life I have never met a star—somebody I have seen on the screen. And I believe that any artist finds his material in what's around him. Human beings and their problems are the most important raw material for any film.

BC: *How can film art in general contribute to the lives of ordinary people?*

AK: The biggest impact of cinema on the viewer is that it allows his imagination to take flight. There are two possible results of this. Perhaps it will make his ordinary, day-to-day life more bearable. On the other hand, it may result in his day-to-day life seeming so bad to him that, as a result of his newfound awareness, he may decide to change his life.

BC: *A related question. Humanity has suffered a great deal in the past and continues to suffer. How do artists treat such a situation honestly without surrendering to fatalism or pessimism?*

AK: It's a difficult question and I cannot answer precisely *how* artists do that, but the ones who *do* are the artists, the ones who accomplish the task of turning that painful experience of humanity into art. Without becoming cynical. Making it possible for everyone to get some pleasure out of pain, making beauty out of ugliness or desolation. And the painful experience of humanity, be it in Iran, Africa, or the United States, isn't going to change any time soon. In my relatively short lifetime, I haven't experienced a reduction of injustice anywhere, let alone in my own country. And never mind a solution to the problem of injustice. People keep referring to the "global village," but in Africa, in Uganda, I watched as parents put the corpses of their children in boxes, tied them to the backs of bicycles, and pedaled away—barefoot. I'm quoting an author I don't know who said that, by the twenty-first century, humanity will only be four years old. I think that applies. Humanity today, in 2005, is just about at the stage of a four-year-old. So we'll have to wait a long time before humanity even reaches the maturity of an adolescent.

BC: *Doesn't the future of cinema also depend on an improvement in the social and political atmosphere?*

AK: I don't think so. I actually sometimes think that, at least in my country, art has grown the most when the social situation has been the worst. It seems to me that artists are a compensatory mechanism, a defense mechanism in those kinds of unfavorable circumstances.

BC: *There is an idea in many of the Iranian films that I've seen that art is for everyone, and I think that's entirely healthy and democratic. But sometimes some directors, in my opinion, present the artistic problem too simply, as though art were an automatic reflection of life.*

AK: Yes, the exact imitation of life is not art. There is a comment by Godard that life is a film that is not well made. When you make a film you have to make it well, you have to edit it, you have to choose, you have to eliminate. You have to create its essential truth, not merely render what exists in reality.

BC: *Western culture is so accustomed to background music, and there is an absence of such music in your films. Could you say something about that?*

AK: Music is a perfect art by itself. It's very powerful and impressive. I dare not try to compete with music in my films. I can't engage in that kind of activity, as the use of music has a great deal of emotional charge, and I do not want to place such an aesthetic burden on my spectator. Music plays on the spectators' emotions, makes them excited or sad, and takes them through a veritable emotional roller-coaster ride with its ups and downs; and I respect my spectator too much to do that to him.

BC: *Given, for example, your attitude toward background music as opposed to that of Western moviemakers in general, is it still appropriate to speak of national cinemas today, or has film become too internationalized for that kind of labeling?*

AK: The answer to your question is yes and no. Each movie has a national ID or birth certificate of its own. Yet a movie in the end is about human beings, about humanity. All the different nations in the world, despite their differences of appearance and religion and language and way of life, still have one common thing, and that is what's inside all of us. If we X-rayed the insides of different human beings, we wouldn't be able to tell from those X-rays what the person's language or background or race was. Our blood circulates exactly the same way, our nervous system and our eyes work the same way, we laugh and cry the same way, we feel pain the same way. The teeth we have in our mouths—no matter what our nationality or background is—ache in exactly the same way. If we want to divide cinema and the subjects of cinema, the way to do it, finally, is to talk about pain and about happiness. These are common among all countries.

BC: *Let's talk for a minute about* Close-Up's *national "ID" or "birth certificate." The film was made under particular social circumstances in which Iran and Iranians seemed to be going through an identity crisis. A radical change with great political and social consequences forced people to begin asking questions about who they really were.* Close-Up *poses some of those questions about the collective identity of a nation.*

AK: This can be an appropriate interpretation by an intelligent viewer or a film critic. But this could not have been something I was thinking about as I was shooting the film. And actually, I was not. But now that we are revisiting the film, I tend to agree that it can be seen in a different way, one of them being from the angle of identity. And if not identity, then the state of collective depression after a big revolution, in which someone like Sabzian—the obsessive cinephile who got caught impersonating the filmmaker Mohsen Makhmalbaf—did not find a thing he was looking for, and people like the Ahankhah family lost some things they had. But these people have somehow come together. This was pointed out to me once by a non-Iranian viewer, and I found it to be so true. This viewer thought these were people from opposite ends who come together under particular circumstances similar to those of an earthquake or an apocalypse of some kind. A common problem brought these people closer together.

BC: *Most of your characters seem to be living in a no-man's-land between reality and illusion. That may explain why the goals they set for themselves are out of their reach: Hossein Sabzian in* Close-Up, *the boy in* The Traveller, *Mr. Firooz Koohi in* The Report, *Hossein in* Through the Olive Trees, *Hossein in* The Experience, *the boys in* The Wedding Suit.

AK: Someone once told me the reason I was drawn to these characters was that they were all abnormal. And I think the abnormal people who go to great lengths and break the boundaries and cross the lines do us a service, in a sense, by telling us, "The limits you have set for us are too confining and we need more space." We should look at abnormal people, that is, from an artist's point of view. We should not act like a court and put them on trial. We should never want to display their shortcomings. We should show them as examples of people who didn't receive proper and timely care. Despite all the laws designed for the protection of deprived people, they were somehow left uncared for and started using their imaginations at a point where there was no room left for using one's imagination—which then will inevitably turn in on itself.

BC: *So you're defining the children in your films as "abnormal," too.*

AK: Yes, they are the products of the same type of education and society as the thirty-something Hossein Sabzian in *Close-Up*. I remind you of what the actor Hossein says in the film. He says, "I am the child from the film *Traveller* who's left behind." And I would say the child from *The Traveller* is somewhat like the kids from *Homework*. Those kids themselves are all like the kids from *Where Is the Friend's House?* I think these kids are somewhat alike, and they just grow up—or don't.

BC: *Let me conclude by remarking on how curious it is that truly talented people, like you, never create difficulties during interviews; it is only those of dubious ability or talent who put up barriers. Thank you so much.*

AK: We have a proverb in Iran that captures perfectly what you just said: "The fruitful tree bends." Thank you.

Abbas Kiarostami Filmography

Bread and Alley (short, 1970)
Breaktime (a.k.a. *Recess*, short, 1972)
The Experience (short, 1973)
The Traveller (1974)
So Can I (short, 1975)
Two Solutions for One Problem (short, 1975)
Colors (short, 1976)
The Wedding Suit (1976)
How to Make Use of Leisure Time: Painting (short, 1977)
The Report (1977)
Tribute to the Teachers (short, 1977)
Jahan-Nama Palace (short, 1978)
Case No. 1, Case No. 2 (short, 1979)
Dental Hygiene (short, 1980)
Regular or Irregular (short, 1981)
The Chorus (short, 1982)
Fellow Citizen (documentary short, 1983)
Toothache (short, 1983)
First Graders (documentary, 1984)
Where Is the Friend's House? (1987)
Homework (1989)
Close-Up (1990)
Life and Nothing More . . . (a.k.a. *And Life Goes On . . .* , 1991)
Through the Olive Trees (1994)
The Birth of Light (short, 1997)
Taste of Cherry (1997)
The Wind Will Carry Us (1999)
A.B.C. Africa (documentary, 2001)
Ten (2002)
Five (documentary, 2003)
10 on Ten (documentary, 2004)

The Roads of Kiarostami (documentary short, 2005)
Tickets (2005), along with Ermanno Olmi and Ken Loach
Kojast jaye residan (documentary short, 2007)
Certified Copy (2009)

Bibliography

Dabashi, Hamid. *Close Up: Iranian Cinema, Past, Present, and Future*. London: Verso, 2001.

———. *Masters and Masterpieces of Iranian Cinema*. Washington, D.C.: Mage, 2007.

Elena, Alberto. *The Cinema of Abbas Kiarostami*. London: Saqi, in association with the Iran Heritage Foundation, 2005.

Issari, Mohammad Ali. *Cinema in Iran, 1900–1979*. Metuchen, N.J.: Scarecrow Press, 1989.

Mirbakhtyar, Shahla. *Iranian Cinema and the Islamic Revolution*. Jefferson, N.C.: McFarland, 2006.

Najafi, Behrad. *Film in Iran, 1900 to 1979: A Political and Cultural Analysis*. Stockholm: Universitet Stockholms, Dept. of Theatre and Cinema Arts, 1986.

Sadr, Hamid Reza. *Iranian Cinema: A Political History*. London: I. B. Tauris, 2006.

Saeed-Vafa, Mehrnaz. *Abbas Kiarostami*. Urbana: University of Illinois Press, 2003.

Tapper, Richard, ed. *The New Iranian Cinema: Politics, Representation, and Identity*. London: I. B. Tauris, 2002.

Zanganeh, Lila Azam, ed. *My Sister, Guard Your Veil; My Brother, Guard Your Eyes: Uncensored Iranian Voices*. Boston, Mass.: Beacon, 2006.

~

Beyond the Fifth Generation

An Interview with Zhang Yimou

Zhang Yimou (born 1950) is an internationally acclaimed Chinese filmmaker and former cinematographer (on Chen Kaige's *The Yellow Earth* [1983], for example), and one of the best known of the Fifth Generation of Chinese film directors. He made his directorial début in 1987 with the film *Red Sorghum*. One of Zhang's recurrent subjects is the resilience, even the stubbornness, of Chinese people in the face of hardship and adversity, a subject that he has treated in films from *To Live* (1994) through to *Not One Less* (1999). His works are particularly noted for their use of color, as can be seen in his early trilogy (which includes *Ju Dou* [1990] and *Raise the Red Lantern* [1991] in addition to *Red Sorghum*) or in such martial-arts pictures of Zhang's as *Hero* (2002) and *House of Flying Daggers*.

The following interview took place in Hong Kong in late March 2007, during the Hong Kong International Film Festival.

Bert Cardullo: *Much of your adolescence and young adulthood was spent during the Cultural Revolution. How much has that influenced your adult life?*

Zhang Yimou: I think my experience represents a wealth of assets for my life and my work. During the ten years of the Cultural Revolution, I went from age sixteen to age twenty-six. I experienced a lot of chaotic situations, and I saw a lot of terrible, tragic things happening around me. From all that I got a deep understanding of human life, of the human heart or spirit—of human society, really—and I think that it benefits me today: in my work, in my thinking, and even in how I deal with personal problems.

The Cultural Revolution was a very special period of Chinese history, unique in the world. For many years, I wanted to make movies about that period—to discuss the suffering and to talk about fate and human relationships in a world that people couldn't control and which was very hostile. In today's political climate, such a project is impossible—as *To Live* has proved, at least in my native country—so I'll just have to wait.

BC: *You were born into a family that was affiliated with the Kuomintang. How much of a problem was that?*

ZY: We were the children of what was called the "Black Five Categories" of family backgrounds. That was a special name given to us during the Cultural Revolution to indicate that we were not from mainstream families, but rather from a bad background—from low-end families. We were severely discriminated against at that time in so many areas. China was very political—far more than now—so whenever you wanted to do something, like apply for a job or enter university, you had to fill in a form and on that form you had to specify your family background. And then, based on what you put on the form, the administrative people would classify you into different categories. If you belonged to a certain category, you were only allowed to do certain things and not allowed to do other things. It was hard, indeed very severe; your position in society really was determined by your birth.

BC: *Just speaking with you, I can feel your passion—not only for your work and your movies but also for China. Yet you have this love-hate relationship with the Chinese government and still, despite it all, you live in China. Why?*

ZY: Actually, I don't see it as a relationship between myself and the Chinese government. Rather, it's a relationship between me and the Chinese soil, the country of China and the Chinese people. This land of China is where I was born, where I grew up, so you can never sever the ties between us. No matter what this country or this land has done to me, how badly it may have treated me, I will always see myself as a son of this land. And I would never betray my land, my country, and my people. I will be loyal forever to the land, like a son to his mother. So this is the main reason why I always want to stay in China. It's not about the relationship between me and the government; it's more about blood ties between me and the Chinese land, the nation itself. I'm always proud that I'm a director from China, and I'd like to come up with the best possible works to give back to my land and my people.

BC: *When I was young, boys often asked their fathers, "What did you do during the war, Daddy?" So let me follow up with the appropriate question for a Chinese of your generation. What exactly did you do during the Cultural Revolution?*

ZY: In the ten years of the Cultural Revolution, I spent three years working as a farmer and seven as a worker in a factory. When the Cultural Revolution came to an end, I was still at the factory and I really did not want to work there any longer on the night shifts. It was a very tiring and difficult life, and I wanted to get out of that environment. The best solution at the time seemed to be to go to university. Even today that is true for most ordinary Chinese families—if their children can go to university, it could change their lives or their fate for the better. For there would then be a chance of a higher standard of living.

BC: *But you almost didn't get into university, correct? You were too old, twenty-seven?*

ZY: Yes, I was five years older than a student should be to qualify for university. I had to write a letter to the Minister of Culture, who was in charge of all the arts-and-cinema colleges in China. I wasn't even sure myself if my application would be successful. But the Minister personally approved the letter and made a very unusual exception for me. Until then, I myself did not know what my future would look like. I think even the school thought I would be just an informal student who had no intention of completing a degree!

BC: *How did you get interested in film?*

ZY: That happened right at this time: after I was admitted to the Beijing Film Academy in 1978. Before that, I was just an amateur photographer. I was admitted to the Cinematography Department on the basis of a portfolio of my photographs, and there I was exposed to many classics of world film. That sparked my fascination with the cinema.

BC: *There is a famous story about how you bought your first camera. Is it true? How did you buy that first camera?*

ZY: Back then, I didn't have much money. I could save only five yuan every month, after putting aside money for eating and basic living expenses. I really liked taking pictures, and wanted to own my own camera. But to buy a camera at that time, you needed to have at least 188 yuan, or more than twenty U.S. dollars—a lot of money for me back then! I knew it would take me two to three years to save enough money to buy one. I had already saved for more than a year but it was far from enough. During that period, however, it was also possible for people to donate their blood for money. So I decided to do that! I donated my blood to augment my savings. It took many months but I finally had enough money to afford my first-ever camera. That was in November or December of 1974, I still remember. With that new camera I began shooting photographs. So I guess you could say that was my first contact with the movie industry!

BC: *So you actually bought that camera with your own blood?*

ZY: Yes, you could say that.

BC: *What kinds of films did you want to make when you graduated from the Academy?*

ZY: Films that were completely different from traditional Chinese films, of course. My friends and I were absolutely determined to make films that would get a powerful response, so we went against tradition with our first film, *The One and the Eight*. The costumes were in grays, whites, and blacks, and in both the location shots and the interior ones we carefully avoided bright colors, so that every shot was in the end a large black-and-white composition. We also composed boldly asymmetrical images. Natural light was used throughout, and most of the shots were very static.

When we made *Yellow Earth*, I developed the same style further, with yellow, red, black, and white as the dominant colors in striking, simple blocks. The lighting was soft. I tried to keep the compositions uncluttered and direct, with as little camera movement as possible, so as to provoke powerful, deep emotion. In both films, at the same time as we were trying to create a new style, we were also trying quite deliberately to suggest deep meanings or to make strong implications. Of course, if we were making those films again today, we would pay more attention to character and we might be a bit more assured. But that was the best we could do in 1983.

BC: *I understand that you already wanted to take up directing after you shot* Yellow Earth *for Chen Kaige. Do you think this was the result of Chen's influence on you?*

ZY: We worked very well together. Back then, we all shared a common vision, and we all influenced each other a great deal. But as for wanting to be a director, that developed while I was still at the Academy. You could say it was a long-cherished wish of mine, because it was the best way to develop my individual creativity. All artists want to express themselves and get a response. Being a director is one of the best ways to do that. I'm obsessed with film, and I hope to express my artistic ambitions through the films I direct.

BC: *In a number of films that you've worked on since* Yellow Earth, *you've been a cinematographer (sometimes uncredited) and a director. Which role do you feel suits you best?*

ZY: Director, of course, because it's the natural extension of being a cinematographer. And, as far as my acting is concerned, I became an actor only by chance. I'm not trained as an actor; from an actor's point of view, I don't really understand acting. I do have a special fondness for my own performances in *Old Well* and *Terracotta Warrior*, but directing is my true vocation. Although it is very stressful, it holds my interest the most powerfully.

BC: *Are visuals more important to you than plot?*

ZY: Actually, both complement each other, so we should not exaggerate the importance of one over the other. You know this—you are a film critic! Chinese moviegoers themselves appreciate a good balance, so we should try to achieve a perfect combination of thematic content and visual style; those would be the best works. Having said that, I know that highly visual movies can have an extraordinarily strong impact, so I do believe that visuals deserve a lot of attention as well.

BC: *Let's talk about the colors that you use in your movies.*

ZY: Ever since I made my first movie, I have tended to use very rich colors and visuals. And this hasn't changed. Maybe it's because I'm Northern Chinese. I was born and grew up in the northern part of China, and I was heavily influenced by the local folk art and the regional environment there. So I guess my attraction to color could just be a matter of where I'm from!

BC: *Can you walk me through the process of choosing or writing a script and then putting it onto a storyboard? What goes through your mind at this time? How do you proceed?*

ZY: The first step is to find an interesting screenplay, and that's like shopping in a store. When you're first walking around in a shop, browsing, you don't necessarily know what you want or what you're going to buy. Not until something really catches your eye, like a special item or certain clothes. Then you consider whether you have enough money to pay for it. If you do, you get it, and you get it because it interests you; it doesn't matter if you already have a similar item.

Now once you have the screenplay, then you do research—perhaps you spend a lot of time trying to make the screenplay feel right, while at the same time keeping it historically accurate and as interesting as possible. Sometimes it takes me as many as three or four years just to finish fixing or rewriting a screenplay to my satisfaction. But once that's done, you can look for investors, trying to convince them why you want to make that movie and why you think it's a good idea for them to finance it. And this is a lot easier to do if you have a very good screenplay.

BC: *Where do you get your ideas? Do you get them just by walking down the street or even by watching movies?*

ZY: It's hard to tell where inspiration comes from. Very often, it comes when you least expect it. Perhaps you get a tiny detail or a specific image in your mind and you find that image beautiful. Or, sometimes, inspiration comes from another person: something that another person says or does moves you. You find yourself touched and your feelings give you an idea that you can use and develop.

And sometimes the ideas come from watching other people's movies, because I really love to go to the movies myself. Whenever I see a very beautiful movie I become sleepless at night. I'll be lying there thinking that the person who made the movie did such an excellent job—why can't I do that, too? Can I do something as good? So then I try to learn from other directors, learn from their different approaches to angles and perspective and adapt them to my own work. So that's another place where I get my ideas.

BC: *As a director, what do you feel that you've accomplished thus far in the Chinese cinema?*

ZY: The filmmakers who started making movies in China in the 1980s, including me, are known as the Fifth Generation, and it's said that we have made a contribution to the development of Asian cinema. Of course it's nice to hear that sort of thing, but all I did as a film director was to shoot my own movies. However, I think it's clear that the Fifth Generation did manage to extend the influence of the Chinese film industry throughout the world. The reasons it was able to do so are rooted in the special conditions that existed in China at the time. The Fifth Generation did not have to worry about a movie's financial potential; they could follow their artistic impulses and create a movie they liked. That's because in those days the government paid for production costs.

Nowadays, film directors—myself included—have to go out and collect the capital they need for their movies by themselves. If you don't think about a movie's financial potential before making it, you won't be able to cover your costs and no one will fund your next movie. So the economic environment surrounding Chinese cinema has changed.

BC: *Has the Chinese people's perception of movies changed as well?*

ZY: China is very rapidly progressing in its economic development, and along with this the Chinese people's perception of movies has also changed, so that entertainment movies are increasingly in demand. I believe there's a strong relationship between the development of commercial cinema and the strength of the native economy. When a country's economy is stagnant, its popular culture becomes stagnant as well. The overwhelming strength of the American movie industry, for example, is directly related to the United States's economic power and influence.

Every country, of course, has movies that exist as works of art. But I believe that movies are both works of art and mediums of entertainment. In today's world, the main trend in movies is to make them highly commercial entertainment vehicles. And right now, no country's movies can resist the power of Hollywood's entertainment-oriented industry. Therefore, our major challenge today is to discover how each country can protect its own movie industry.

BC: *If you do think about the audience's tastes, which audience do you think about more? The Chinese audience or the Western one?*

ZY: I don't understand foreign audiences because I cannot speak a single word of English; without a translator here beside me, we ourselves would not be conversing. So, I really don't know what Western audiences like to watch. But of course I am delighted if Western audiences are able to see my films and understand them.

In China itself, people sometimes say of me that I'm a director who makes movies for non-Chinese; but when I have the chance, I tell these people, "Since I can't speak English, I make movies for the people of China." Moreover, from my first movie *Red Sorghum* to my most recent work, my films have made money not only abroad but in China as well.

BC: *Hero was certainly a huge commercial success both in China and around the world. Did you set out to make it as big a hit as possible?*

ZY: I never expected that it would be so popular internationally. I am more in the habit of judging the tastes of Chinese audiences. I couldn't have predicted that so many foreigners would like it, and I have been thinking about this a lot since completing the movie.

BC: *In China, though a lot of people went to see* Hero, *there was some negative response, wasn't there?*

ZY: Yes. The Chinese often look beyond the literal content of a film, to the ideology represented by it. Chinese education prioritizes content over style: so if the filmgoers disagree with a film's ideas, the style must be poor, too, according to their thinking. I don't see it like that; and I think they are missing the point. The form and style of *Hero* are really special, and this is what attracts international audiences, who have no idea about any critique of Emperor Qin that may be found in the film—they are attracted by the form, the style, and the tone of the movie.

BC: *To what extent did you try to make this film appeal to a Western audience and their idea of China as an exotic place?*

ZY: You can't really proceed in that way. One's appreciation of a good film is something universal. It is about feelings, characters, stories, colors, scenery, beauty—all of which are common to every human being, especially feelings. As long as the film appeals to human emotions, all audiences will enjoy it.

Specifically to address your question about my making *Hero* to appeal to a Western audience, I have to say that since I was very young I'd always liked reading martial-arts novels, but in the early years of the Fifth Generation, no one wanted to make these kinds of movies; everyone considered them as mere entertainment, too low-brow, and as lacking in any artistic value. So even though I liked them, I'd never dared to think of making one.

Let me add that *Hero*, as a martial-arts film, conveys my idea for this genre. Personally, I think China's martial-arts films are different from Western action films. The most important difference is that China's martial-arts films place a lot of importance on aesthetics, even poetry—the beauty of the whole story, you could say. I think that this really distinguishes martial-arts films from mere action movies. I must tell you that ever since I was little, year after year, I have watched martial-arts competitions. And the aesthetics of the actions of these masters was really a big component in their final scores. So when I make martial-arts films, I try to differentiate them from the West's action films by placing lots of emphasis on aesthetic appeal to the eye. This is what I feel will be my signature mark on the martial-arts genre.

BC: *How do you think Hollywood has influenced the film industry in China?*

ZY: In mainland China, almost every year we're seeing around twenty Hollywood films, so there's a big impact on the younger generation and on young filmmakers in China. I think the best part about Hollywood films is that they've always had really good publicity and marketing, and they also usually have a good and touching story. But for Chinese films, we need to invent and retain the nationality and flavor of the Eastern.

I think it would be good for a Chinese marketing system to be able to compete with Hollywood, but this is really difficult to do. Not only Asian films want to fight Hollywood, the whole film world wants to fight Hollywood. When you go around the world and talk with film practitioners, this is always the topic that comes up—how to fight the invasion of Hollywood's commercial films and how to protect your own national films. Both artists and governments are talking about the same thing. But Hollywood will not easily give up the market it has seized. Hollywood is really smart and has gotten many good directors from all over the world. It has got some of the best directors in China, including martial-arts instructors from Hong Kong, to help them. So much so that we can't even find qualified people to work on our films because Hollywood is paying them more money. They are employed in Hollywood permanently, designing martial-arts postures! So Hollywood is really digging up talent all over the world, and it attracts these talents with lucrative salaries. It has also continuously changed its tactics and tastes over time to make money from all over the world. This trend has a strong momentum and one can't really reverse it. Hollywood, as everyone knows, has been built up over many years. No one can fight the Americans in the area of pooling resources and money.

A more serious problem is that Hollywood has cultivated its own new generation of international audiences for its commercial films. In China, young people like only Hollywood hits. They can easily name all the Hollywood stars. If you ask American young people, "Who among you can name Chinese movie stars?"—well, no one can do it. How many Chinese films, after all, do you see every year in the American market? There is just a handful. We can see from China that Hollywood unquestionably has a young generation of followers from all over the world. We feel as a result that our national film industry is under pressure, because we know that the most important audiences for films are young people. This really presents us with a challenge, and we have always taken it to be our responsibility to make good Chinese films and do our part to attract the Chinese audience. For instance, we show them *Hero*—whether they like it or not!—and we present it to them in Chinese color, with a Chinese cast playing Chinese characters.

BC: *What do you think of the Oscars?*

ZY: I've been to the Oscars twice. And sitting there during the awards ceremony, I felt as if it were a purely American game. It really didn't have a lot to do with American film style and standards—just American economics, American business. I can understand why European directors say Hollywood is poison. And it's sobering for me to sit in the Third World, watching the Old and New Worlds argue about how European movies have no values while American movies have no culture.

BC: *What are your favorite American movies? And what do you think of Asian Americans in Hollywood?*

ZY: Given that there are many American film genres, I spend most of my film time watching American films; besides, American films take up a large part of the world market, as we all know only too well. Wherever you go to movie theaters around the world, what you see are mostly American films, especially American commercial films. There are many American directors and actors that I like a lot. But, of course, there are good ones and not-so-good ones. I am not against Hollywood's commercial films, as I hope I have made clear; I watch them very often and often find good ones among them. One can't really make a generalization about Hollywood. I am not like the French and the Italians who are hostile to Hollywood, calling it all junk. I have varied taste, and I watch a lot—whatever catches my attention. The most recent American picture I saw was here in Hong Kong. It was a sci-fi film, mixing ghosts, vampires, and the like all into one big stew. I don't remember the name of the film because it was translated into Chinese. But I really liked the computer animations and special effects.

There are many foreign directors who are seeking to further their careers in Hollywood. It is true in many countries that directors, once they make their names known in their own country, are immediately brought over, or drafted, by Hollywood. I think these are all personal choices on the part of the directors themselves. The large market that Hollywood can provide constitutes a great temptation to many filmmakers. An audience of two million is very different from an audience of 20,000. It's natural, therefore, that lots of directors want to develop their talents in Hollywood, where they will have more space, so to speak, and a larger audience.

Ang Lee and John Woo are examples of Asian American directors—and successful examples, too. I think they made the right choice in going to Hollywood. But often, I myself have been asked whether I wanted to go to Hollywood. My answer is that I am not suitable for Hollywood. First, I don't know the language. Second, the films I make are all based in China. If I go to the United States, I can't really make the films I want. So I know myself, and know that I can't really be separated from the land where I grew up. I can only stay in China and make movies there.

BC: *Do you feel that Chinese films are having an influence on Hollywood?*

ZY: I used to think many Hollywood action movies were pretty stupid, but now those movies are becoming much better visually. Like John Woo's—his martial-arts pictures are quite poetic. Many big American movies are beginning to have Chinese Kung-Fu scenes—*The Matrix*, for example. The action sequences in these films are now more beautiful, more rhythmic, and I think that this is because of Chinese influence. It's great to see Chinese aesthetics affecting Hollywood in a positive way. Kung Fu can influence people all over the world; it inspires hope, and it can help people learn about traditional Chinese art. Any Chinese person would be proud of that.

BC: *Which do you feel has had the greater influence on you, Western cinema or Chinese culture?*

ZY: Western film has probably only influenced me with regard to cinematic form and technical matters, but the influence of Chinese culture—the Chinese spirit and Chinese emotions—is absolutely basic to me. That's because I'm one hundred percent Chinese, and so are my films.

BC: *What should Asian movies be?*

ZY: South Korea is doing the most interesting work in Asian cinema right now. I watch almost every South Korean movie that comes out, and there are a lot of movies from South Korea that I like. Even if they don't succeed on the same level as Hollywood, in recent years what I think has made South Korean movies a success is that, while presenting political and other issues of great interest to the general public, they produce entertaining pictures that find a place in the market. And you can't forget that they express something uniquely Korean as well.

The young Chinese directors of the Sixth Generation need to do like the South Koreans and spend more time thinking about the needs of their era and their viewers. Young Chinese directors don't go much beyond trying to express their own individuality. Individuality is also important, of course; but because movies are a mass art, you can't use them simply to reveal your native individuality or special ego. If a lot of people don't go to see your movies, you'll never find anyone to fund your second or third movie.

I think the South Koreans succeeded by capturing the audience of their own country. China's young directors could learn a lot from South Korean directors—and I could as well. I *am* learning from them.

BC: *As you know,* House of Flying Daggers *and* Hero *have been read in certain quarters as political allegories about contemporary China. The latter was even interpreted by some as an apology for modern Chinese imperialism.* Hero *portrayed the King of Qin [China's first emperor, and the man behind the building of the Great Wall] as a wise, temperate ruler who has a capacity for humility and forgiveness, even if he did sometimes kill his subjects in the name of progress. Conversely,* House of Flying Daggers *is far less sympathetic toward its emperor. We never see him, but we learn he is incompetent, that his soldiers are brutal, and that his government is riddled with corruption. The film may be set in 859 A.D., but with its depiction of an imperial army ruthlessly tracking down a shadowy terrorist organization, it, too, seems to have a contemporary resonance.*

ZY: I am surprised that you see political references in these films. The objective of any form of art cannot be political. I had no political intentions in making these two movies. I am not interested in politics.

BC: *But at the start of our conversation, you declared your great ambition was to complete a series of movies set during the Cultural Revolution.*

ZY: It's not that I want to make political films about the Cultural Revolution, but instead, with the Cultural Revolution as the background, I want to show the fate of people, their love and hate, their happiness and sadness, and the most valuable things in human nature that survived this recent period of Chinese history. I really like stories that reveal the way people lived, not how or what they believed; and I think that *To Live* achieved this aim.

BC: *What are the difficulties involved in making movies in China?*

ZY: Censorship is one of them, of course. Critics say, for example, that I'm not being sharp enough or not cutting deeply enough in my films. But every director in China knows in his heart how far he can go and how much he can say. If anyone tells you that he always says what he wants to say or films what he wants to film, he is lying. Even underground movies have a limit past which they cannot go. I hope in the future we have more freedom and artists are given more space. But the question now isn't whether you're good at balancing things: you *have* to balance what you say against what you cannot say. This is a reality directors have to face.

Over the years many people have talked about the difficulty of making movies in China, but each person has his own story to tell. In my case, my movie *To Live* has yet to be shown in China. I'm not sure of the exact reason, but it may be because the film deals with forty years of Chinese history, including the Cultural Revolution—whether as background or not.

BC: *Could you tell me something about the evolution of your movies?*

ZY: My early movies laid stress on beauty of form and concept, but I then moved on to deliberately focusing on human emotions, particularly human warmth. And the reason I deal so much with Chinese peasants is that China is an agricultural country. Personally, I love the simple emotions of farmers. If you investigate everyday life in China, you'll see that the heart of China is in its agricultural villages.

Also, because my movies frequently have the theme of "searching," I've made a lot of pictures where the heroine in particular searches for or pursues something in society or in the wider world. As for *Hero*, which explores the theme of heroism, some people may wonder if I was copying Ang Lee's *Crouching Tiger, Hidden Dragon*, but I had started *Hero* long before Lee's picture came out. Unlike my previous films, *Hero* marks a change for me, because it is a grand-scale entertainment movie with beautiful sound, visuals, and costumes, and it depicts a rich tapestry of romantic and tragic relationships. My hope in this film, as I have tried to make clear, was to help give Chinese cinema greater international influence in the realm of big-budget entertainment movies—the main trend in the movie industry right now.

BC: *Well, it seems to me you have always emphasized the spectacular aspect of cinema, even in your smaller-budgeted films (let us call them!). Or, to put it another way, ever since your début with* Red Sorghum, *you have quite consciously sought to make your films look good. That itself seems to indicate a special concern for the audience.*

ZY: That's true. I always insist on visually striking films. A film must look good, and you have to work out what "looking good" means. You cannot afford to get self-indulgent or too isolated and self-involved. But I must emphasize that the "looking good" I'm talking about is not at all the same as the kind you find in Hollywood commercial filmmaking. What I make are still works of art, of visual art.

Gong Li as Songlian in Zhang's *Raise the Red Lantern*.

BC: *A film like* Curse of the Golden Flower, *though, is nothing like* Ju Dou *or* Raise the Red Lantern, *those intimate, Oscar-nominated period dramas that brought you to the attention of Western audiences during the early 1990s. Today, some of your longtime devotees are scratching their heads over your newfound affinity for martial-arts flicks, big budgets, and computer effects.* Curse *cost $45 million to make, a huge sum in China, so I have to ask, are you just chasing the money now?*

ZY: Well, you can't duplicate the success of *Crouching Tiger, Hidden Dragon.* That kind of phenomenon can happen only once. This film genre actually has a long-standing tradition in China, beginning with Bruce Lee. It's popular among Chinese audiences, especially the youth. That's why Bruce Lee, Jackie Chan, and Jet Li are such movie icons. And this is the reason so many Chinese directors want to make movies of this type. It's our one fighting chance at competing with Hollywood. You know, Hollywood is not just *big* in China: in fact it has eaten up 95 percent of the Chinese market, and our native industry has gone through some serious soul-searching as a result. Nearly all of my fellow Fifth-Generation directors, who began working in the 1980s, have now expanded their repertoires to fit the increasingly international and commercialized film climate. But my own feeling is that there's no need to impose artistic limits, or commercial restrictions, on Fifth-Generation directors. Nowadays, it's increasingly difficult to differentiate between art and commerce, anyway. The direction in which we're heading is probably to make artistic films that also attract a wider audience. We *have* to compete with Hollywood films; we can't simply indulge our artistic impulses and neglect the audience. Making commercial films is a good exercise for Fifth-Generation directors. Once you are adept at the mainstream approach, you can rejuvenate your artistic spirit by doing something else. Otherwise, you'd just be making films that earn awards, but that no one would go to see. And you have to remember, or I have to reiterate, a filmmaker must make sure that his investors break even: this is also a director's responsibility. I have a pretty good record in that regard, therefore I have never had to worry about money.

BC: *What is the difference for you between making a big-budget film and a small-scale one?*

ZY: Shooting a big-budget film gives the director a huge sense of responsibility. You can't experiment too much with things that are very personal, things that other people wouldn't understand—you just can't do too much of that. But if I am shooting a small-scale or intimate movie, I can try something that is very personal, artistic, and unique in style, without considering whether or not it will be accepted by the masses.

It's always been challenging for me to direct different kinds of films: before, I was doing films on a small scale, with a small budget, treating ordinary people's lives; but *Hero* and *House of Flying Daggers* are huge-scale films that are as different from *Red Sorghum* and *Raise the Red Lantern* as heaven and earth. For me, it's always great to face such different challenges. That makes me grow as an artist, and it forces me to develop and learn and enhance my filmmaking skills. I agree with what the Japanese director Akira Kurosawa said upon accepting the Oscar in 1990 for lifetime achievement: he said more or less that he was still learning how to make films, and that he had to continue working if he was ever going to be able fully to comprehend the art of cinema.

BC: *Many of your films are set in the past at some distance from contemporary, everyday life. Why is that?*

ZY: It probably has something to do with the novels I have picked. A number of my films are such adaptations, and it so happens that most of the novels I have read are set in the past. For example, *Ju Dou* and *Raise the Red Lantern* were adapted separately from novels by different authors that I like very much, but I guess this has given people the impression that I specialize in historical films. Actually, I'm always looking for different material. *The Story of Qiu Ju* is about the life of farming people today, for instance, and I have also done two films about contemporary city life. Artistically speaking, I just want to keep moving on.

BC: *Yes, but what is it that interests you so much in making period pieces?*

ZY: Most of my films are in fact historical in nature, so this is a good question. Since the very first film I made, *Red Sorghum*, I have really liked historical stories. But at the time I made this film, the main reason I decided on such a time period was that China had very strict censorship. When you make a film, especially about a tragic story, you have to put the characters under a certain pressure from society, and then you have to show that the characters fight their fate and resist their social as well as personal tragedy. But what kind of pressure are you going to put them under? Obviously, there would be a political problem involved in depicting such outside pressure in contemporary Chinese society. Such films would not gain easy approval from the censors. So I decided to set *Red Sorghum* at a time in the past, when China was under feudalism. This way the subject became easier to deal with. My original idea wasn't really to make a political statement, but the story does require strong external pressure so that the fate of the characters can be realized. And that pressure had to come from a societal or social background.

Today, a number of Chinese directors resort to this method when they have a story to tell. They simply trace time backwards and place the story in a safe period where it will be easier to make the film—because then it will not cause them any political trouble. In doing things this way, it is not necessarily that we have a special or sentimental attachment to a certain time period. Sometimes, as I have indicated, we pick such a time period solely for the purpose of implementing a "political" plan. That was what happened to me at the beginning of my career, and so I made several historical films. After some time, you just get used to it, and actually I find historical stories more interesting. With them, one simply has a larger space in which to give free rein to one's imagination.

BC: Curse of the Golden Flower, *your third action film, takes place in the Later Tang Dynasty, more than 1,000 years ago. Yet the film is based on a modern Chinese drama, isn't it?*

ZY: Yes, indeed, it's based on a modern drama called *Thunderstorm*, which is one of the most famous works from the canon of contemporary Chinese literature. It was written by Cao Yu and set in the 1920s and '30s. It's so important, in fact, that students of dramatic art in China are actually trained by using this text. It's part of their basic repertoire, and they must all perform *Thunderstorm* during their student days. So this is a work with which I've long been familiar, and it's so popular it's performed virtually every day in China. If you picked a random day, like today, in some city in China you would find a production of *Thunderstorm*.

And it's a story about the way that people are twisted and pushed as they struggle to survive under the feudal system in China. It has strong characterization—very powerful characters are featured here—and I thought it would be interesting to take this modern play and transpose it to pre-modern China, to the Tang Dynasty. Not just any dynasty, mind you, but the most glorious, vibrant, and colorful of dynasties, where all the external beauty would be heightened because it is juxtaposed against the dark portrait of humanity that the play is offering up.

BC: *What is the relationship between this film and a film of yours like* Hero?

ZY: I think the major difference between this film and *Hero*, as well as between *Curse* and *House of Flying Daggers*, is that the earlier two are really very much in the tradition of conventional martial-arts films. *Curse of the Golden Flower*, however, is quite different because it's more of an amalgamation of a melodrama and an action film, and that's something I quite consciously endeavored to achieve. The plot and the characterization, as I've said, both come from the original play, Cao Yu's *Thunderstorm*; it's the setting, the period, that I have changed.

BC: *Have you found that the final film product you end up with is often very different from the idea you started out with?*

ZY: There are some differences from what I imagined by the time I complete a project, but the basic idea doesn't change. There are all kinds of reasons why you have to make adjustments—everything from the actors to the lighting, the sound, and the cinematography. In the case of *Raise the Red Lantern* and *The Story of Qiu Ju*, it was only when the shooting started that I got an overall sense of each film, but with *To Live* and *Red Sorghum*, I knew from the very outset where I was headed. Every film is different and requires a different response.

BC: *With* Shanghai Triad, *you were looking for something exceptional from the start.*

ZY: Yes, I wanted the unusual, the unconventional, the uncommon, something individual and special. But sometimes even I want the familiar. In *To Live*, for instance, I used a traditional popular narrative, deliberately aiming for the familiar.

BC: *You seem to be particularly indulgent towards actors. How do you normally work with them?*

ZY: I understand what you're getting at. You're thinking of the way in which so many of my shots work on account of the acting. You can put all sorts of demands on actors, but it only works if they are able to accept those demands. So I feel it's vital to respect the actors as individuals from the outset, and to make sure that they understand the way I think and work. I don't believe any actor anywhere in the world can do everything. Actors bring their own temperament, character, experiences, and acting habits to bear on every performance. They need your respect, and sometimes they also need your guidance. I often find that what the actors are able to give me on the set far exceeds my own imagination, but at other times what they give me doesn't fulfill what I had hoped for, or is even completely different from the way I had imagined their performance would be. At those times, the director has to develop the best aspects of the performance or change plans according to what the actor is able to deliver. When you're making a film, it is relatively easy to control things like the costumes, props, sets, lighting, colors, and camera movements, but the main thing is the actors, because they're giving life to what had only existed before in your imagination.

BC: *You worked with Gong Li for over eight years, producing a string of films that fascinated the world. Your personal relationship with her has now ended, but will your working relationship continue?*

ZY: Of course it will—and it has continued recently in *Curse of the Golden Flower*—because I still feel she is a very special, very rare actress. She has excellent instincts and is very talented technically. As long as the right scripts and the right roles come along, we will go on working together.

BC: *Lots of people keep advising you to learn English, and then go overseas to make movies. Do you think you might follow their advice?*

ZY: I've never wanted to go to the West to make movies. Let me say this once again: my roots are in China, and I can only make Chinese films in Chinese. That's one thing that will never change. My sole ambition, as I've indicated, is to make different films in different styles. And I also hope that they will reach even larger audiences all around the world.

BC: *Let's talk for a moment about* Happy Times, *which itself is different in so many ways from your previous work, despite the fact that it's your second film set in a modern city. How did you first get involved in this project?*

ZY: It's adapted from a short novel. I loved the story, which is about dreams, how to fulfill a little girl's dream. In adapting the novel I saw an opportunity to make a different film, and not simply to repeat what I had done before. In the novel, the material world is fake but the spirit is very real, and it was this premise that attracted me. I used a very different method to shoot this film, and many people have told me that it looks as if it had been shot by a first-time director. I wanted to keep everything as simple as possible. I didn't want to use any "sexy" camera movements or to define anything visually in a deliberate way, which is very different from what I've done in the past— which is to try to shoot from the most beautiful angles. The shooting-time for *Happy Times* was much shorter than usual; it took only about forty days to finish the film. I think that's one of the reasons it looks as if it were made by a first-time director.

BC: *What were you most concerned about before shooting the film, considering the fact that it is visually less complicated than your earlier work?*

ZY: I spent most of my efforts training the young actress who portrayed the blind girl. I had never shot or portrayed any blind characters in my films, so we spent a lot of time training the actor. I also visited several schools for the blind to understand how they function. And we were able to find a nineteen-year-old blind girl, who, just as the film depicts, went blind when she was ten. We got this blind girl's family to agree to let her live with Dong Jie throughout the production in order to have the actress learn to play the blind character. I was giving homework to Dong Jie every evening. I would tell her, "I'm going to shoot you looking for things for five days." So you have to ask the real blind girl how to look for things, and then in between I would give Dong Jie a quiz. I asked the assistant director to shoot her looking for things with a video camera, just to see if she was getting everything right.

BC: *I know in the past you've cited certain filmmakers as influences on your work. One person I know you have mentioned is Abbas Kiarostami, and also the Italian neorealists of the late 1940s and early 1950s. Were there any specific influences on you when you were making this film, Happy Times?*

ZY: No, but, in the general sense, there are many directors who have influenced me. I'm a real film buff, as I've already said. Going to the movies is my only habit. So when I see any great work, that great work will become my new model. I don't believe anybody is a born filmmaker; we all learn from the past, from past masters. As for Italian neorealism, we watched a lot of films from this movement when we were at the Beijing Academy. Obviously, it interests me a great deal.

BC: *As I implied earlier, while your films rarely have overtly political content, they can always be read as political. At least that's what I think. Do you think Happy Times can be read from a political point of view?*

ZY: Because China is a very political society, you can read the political situation into any Chinese story if you want to. But *Happy Times* is not a political story; rather, it is a story about life. However, there are many details in the film that reflect today's society, such as everybody trying to make money. Money is very important in Chinese life today. For example, in the film the mother only sees money, not people: whoever has money can be her boyfriend. This kind of satire can be read politically as well, I grant you that.

BC: Happy Times *is generically described as a comedy, even though there is a lot more than just comedy in it. Do you think that you are going to return to comedy in the future?*

ZY: No, not really. I personally prefer tragedy. And, like you, I think *Happy Times* in the end still has serious or even tragic elements in it: you could call it a bittersweet comedy. I guess I probably reflect Chinese sentiments better through tragedy.

BC: *Could you talk a bit about the role of women in Chinese society, since you always have strong female leads?*

ZY: Asking about the position of women in Chinese society requires a large answer, because there are millions and millions of Chinese women out there; but let me just talk about the role of women in the context of big cities. In the big cities, the male and the female are equal, but there are still lots of problems in the countryside. Men still look down on women there and women face a lot of pressure because of tradition; and we need to protect women's position and their rights in the countryside, as well as in the big cities. In the films I've been making, it wasn't my intention to make female-themed movies, but people have drawn that conclusion; and, looking back, yes, maybe they are right and maybe that's why people have called me a women's director. I'm always interested in female stories, but, dramatically speaking, maybe it's easier for me to capture the female as she fights back against society and adversity. In any event, a number of my films deal with this feminine theme—what can even be called an anti-patriarchal and anti-feudalistic one.

BC: *I'd like you to compare your start in filmmaking with that of the Sixth Generation of Chinese filmmakers, because I want you to expand a bit on the negative comments you made earlier about this new generation of directors.*

ZY: Looking back now at films like *Yellow Earth* and *Red Sorghum*, I can tell you that they both have warm blood and intense life, which are missing from the works of the Sixth Generation. I think this is because the Sixth Generation was subject to too many practical considerations. They cannot be resisted these days: the need for money, the dilemma caused by censorship, the awards offered at international film festivals. At a very early age, therefore, the young artists of the Sixth Generation knew much more and saw things more clearly than we did. And I think that this is bad at a time when you are just getting started in film. It is not that Sixth-Generation filmmakers are not talented. Judging by their works, I should say that they are quite talented. What they lack is will. In the last analysis, our first films—those of the Fifth Generation—were not necessarily the result of talent. I now firmly believe that, no matter what you pursue, *will* is needed in addition to talent—a strength from the bottom of your heart. Deliberate calculation is no good. Some Sixth-Generation directors I know are too smart. They understand too many things; they are so well informed about the outside world and so familiar with the path to success that, as a result, their filmmaking becomes an unemotional process.

When Chen Kaige and I were making *Yellow Earth*, he knew little about the outside world, but he had an urge to talk about culture and history. At that time I knew this picture would be outstanding. People say it was because of my cinematography, but no matter: the director's intention was expressed, and a very ardent intention it was. His *emotions* were expressed in a work that was otherwise supposed to be concerned with contemporary politics. That to me is the most crucial. Now I judge a film not by how much philosophy or thought it contains; in fact, the more philosophy it contains, the more I dislike it. I revert to the most basic elements in watching a film. I don't just watch how skillfully the story is told or whether the actors perform well; I look for the director's inner world, whether his emotions are strong, and only then do I look for what he is trying to say. If his emotions are strong, whether they are expressed in a tragedy or a comedy, he will move the audience. That is what I mean by strength or willpower.

BC: *What is it that you want people to remember most about your films?*

ZY: The visual spectacle. I've tried using realism—the spareness of realistic style—before in my movies, in the cinematography. But I am most in love with the Chinese style of visual presentation. If in twenty years, after I've made a lot more films, they write one sentence about me in a textbook, I'd be satisfied if they said: "Zhang Yimou's cinematic style is strongly visual in a distinctly Chinese fashion."

BC: *For you, what is the most important thing to keep in mind in the creation of film art—of any art?*

ZY: To create art, one must always remember that the subject of people in misery has the deepest meaning, the deepest resonance. Human beings in misery constitute the most important subject of art, be it film art or any other kind. That's because strength is born from such suffering—like the strength of the Chinese people.

Zhang Yimou Filmography

Red Sorghum (1987)
Codename Cougar (a.k.a. *The Puma Action*, 1989)
Ju Dou (1990)
Raise the Red Lantern (1991)
The Story of Qiu Ju (1992)
To Live (1994)
Shanghai Triad (1995)
Keep Cool (1997)
Not One Less (1999)
Turandot (1999)
The Road Home (2000)
Happy Times (2002)
Hero (2003)
House of Flying Daggers (2004)
Riding Alone for Thousands of Miles (2005)
Curse of the Golden Flower (2006)
The First Gun (a.k.a. *A Woman, a Gun, and a Noodle Shop*, 2009)

Bibliography

Berry, Chris. *China on Screen: Cinema and Nation*. New York: Columbia University Press, 2006.

———. *Postsocialist Cinema in Post-Mao China: The Cultural Revolution after the Cultural Revolution*. New York: Routledge, 2004.

Browne, Nick, et al., ed. *New Chinese Cinemas: Forms, Identities, Politics*. New York: Cambridge University Press, 1994.

Chow, Rey. *Primitive Passions: Visuality, Sexuality, Ethnography, and Contemporary Chinese Cinema*. New York: Columbia University Press, 1995.

Clark, Paul. *Reinventing China: A Generation and Its Films*. Hong Kong: Chinese University Press, 2005.

Cornelius, Sheila. *New Chinese Cinema: Challenging Representations*. London: Wallflower, 2002.

Fu, Poshek. *Between Shanghai and Hong Kong: The Politics of Chinese Cinemas*. Stanford, Calif.: Stanford University Press, 2003.

Gateward, Frances, ed. *Zhang Yimou: Interviews*. Jackson: University Press of Mississippi, 2001.

Kuoshu, Harry H. *Celluloid China: Cinematic Encounters with Culture and Society*. Carbondale: Southern Illinois University Press, 2002.

Lu, Sheldon H., and Emilie Yueh-yu Yeh, ed. *Chinese-Language Film: Historiography, Poetics, Politics*. Honolulu: University of Hawaii Press, 2005.

Lu, Tonglin. *Confronting Modernity in the Cinemas of Taiwan and Mainland China*. New York: Cambridge University Press, 2002.

Ni, Chen. *Memoirs from the Beijing Film Academy: The Genesis of China's Fifth Generation*. Trans. Chris Berry. Durham, N.C.: Duke University Press, 2002.

Semsel, George Stephen. *Chinese Film: The State of the Art in the People's Republic*. New York: Praeger, 1987.

⸺ et al., ed. *Chinese Film Theory: A Guide to the New Era*. New York: Praeger, 1990.

⸺ et al., ed. *Film in Contemporary China: Critical Debates, 1979–1989*. Westport, Conn.: Praeger, 1993.

Silbergeld, Jerome. *China into Film: Frames of Reference in Contemporary Chinese Cinema*. London: Reaktion, 1999.

Tam, Kwok-kan, and Wimal Dissanayake. *New Chinese Cinema*. New York: Oxford University Press, 1998.

Zhang, Yingjin. *Chinese National Cinema*. New York: Routledge, 2004.

Zhu, Ying. *Chinese Cinema during the Era of Reform: The Ingenuity of the System*. Westport, Conn.: Praeger, 2003.

TALKING ENGLISH

"I Call My Films Subversive"
A Conversation with Mike Leigh

Born in 1943 in Lancashire, Mike Leigh began his career as an actor, theater director, and playwright before moving into television and, eventually, film. After more than a decade of writing and directing for British television, he became known to a wide international audience with *Life Is Sweet* (1990). Now, after more than three decades and over twenty films, Leigh has earned himself an international reputation for his bracing, bittersweet dramas about quotidian British life. In a generally bleak artistic landscape, he stands out importantly as someone who has attempted to make complicated and sensitive—and socially engaged—films about middle- and working-class England. Moreover, despite their perpetually gray English skies, pasty-skinned protagonists, and often minimalist plotlines, his movies appeal to a broad audience. What makes Leigh's films unique, even in Britain, is his gift for constructing an often humorously bleak and desperate world filled with characters whose comic behavior springs from their essence as human beings. The comedy connects to their genuine agony as well as joy, and therefore the films almost never contain scenes designed to just to get easy laughs. Indeed, Leigh's trademark could be said to be his almost preternatural gift for capturing, with emotional honesty, complex human behavior.

Leigh's greatest box office success to date has been *Secrets & Lies* (1996), the story of a white woman who comes face-to-face with the half-black daughter she gave up for adoption years earlier. *Naked* (1993) exposes the destitute and painful realities of urban life with its tale about a mixed-up drifter's misadventures in London, while the early *Bleak Moments* (1971) concerns the financial struggles of—and awkward relationships among—a group of young, socially isolated city-dwellers. In *Topsy-Turvy* (1999), the filmmaker examined the artistic-theatrical process in a work about the Victorian lyricist-composer team of Gilbert and Sullivan. In *Vera Drake* (2004), he treated the problem of illegal abortions in the 1950s. And one of Leigh's most recent films is the perennially optimistic *Happy-Go-Lucky* (2008), about a woman who sees the bright side of life even when presented with darkness.

Instead of coming to rehearse and shoot a film with a prewritten script, Leigh works closely and intensively with all his actors—from the main roles to bit parts—developing characters, scenarios, and dialogue over months of solo and group improvisations to build a finalized screenplay. Actors seem to love the director's way of involving them so integrally in the process. His process has been the constant approach that has allowed Leigh to craft some of the most extraordinary and seminal films of British cinema. A vociferous supporter of the British film industry, the director, unlike many of his British filmmaking colleagues, hasn't been lured to Hollywood. In recent years, he has even started writing for the English stage again. *Two Thousand Years* (2005), a play exploring Leigh's Jewish roots, received its world première at London's National Theatre.

As Leigh likes to note, he is anything but a naturalist. He refers to his love of circus, vaudeville, and the music hall. His films do not imitate everyday human activity, nor do his characters repeat ordinary conversation. The events and dialogue are deliberately heightened, as part of an effort to get behind the reality of day-to-day life. The exaggerated, sometimes grotesquely exaggerated, goings-on take their place in a certain British tradition, however. André Breton once said something to the effect that there was no need for a surrealist movement in England because life and art there were already surreal enough. Just so, one of Leigh's most interesting features as a film writer and director has been his willingness to bite into reality at a somewhat different angle from both the British "neorealists" of the early 1960s and the director Ken Loach, with his working-class portrayals along the lines of "docudrama" and the "kitchen sink" school.

That Leigh's film career has had its share of ups and downs, veering occasionally toward sentimentality and occasionally toward condescension, owes much to the unfavorable climate in which he has had to work. The Thatcherite counteroffensive against the working class and the protracted rightward lurch of the Labour Party, as well as the British trade unions, have framed the past several decades. The systematic dismantling of the welfare state, the destruction of entire industries and even communities, the attempt to eradicate social solidarity in favor of ruthless individualism—all of these have made their impact felt. And in a traditional society such as Britain's, the traumatizing consequences have been particularly severe. More than he perhaps suspects or has intended, Leigh—a socialist and a proponent of social equality— has registered and often critiqued these developments.

The following interview took place at Leigh's Soho office in London in June of 2009.

Bert Cardullo: *When did you begin to get interested in the cinema?*

Mike Leigh: I was seventeen in 1960 and it was then that I left Manchester and came to London. Prior to that moment, I had almost never seen a film that wasn't in English. You didn't see world cinema in those days; you saw Hollywood movies and British movies. About the first foreign film I recall having seen was *Le Ballon rouge* [1956], the sentimental French film. However, when I hit London as a student, that was exactly the time of Jean-Luc Godard's *À bout de souffle* [1960] and the French New Wave, plus I discovered the rest of world cinema. What were my feelings about all that? I was completely blown away by everything. This was also the time of the parallel British "New Wave."

BC: *That was what I was going to ask about next: the films of Tony Richardson, Karel Reisz, Lindsay Anderson, and others.*

ML: I personally felt that the purest, most important, and most organic of those British films wasn't actually made till the late 1960s, and that was Anderson's *If . . .* [1968]. And it was not a film about working-class life, like a number of the British social-realist pictures—that was Lindsay digging into his own upper-middle-class, public-school experience. About the so-called British New Wave films, good as many of them were and inspirational, because they were looking at working-class life, the fact is that none of them, without exception, was an original movie: every single one was an adaptation of a play or a novel. And although it's true that François Truffaut's wonderful *Jules et Jim* [1962] was also an adaptation of a novel, nevertheless, the inspiration for me was that À *bout de souffle*, Godard's *Vivre sa vie* [1962], and Truffaut's *Les Quatre cents coups* [1959] were original films that actually used film, as painting uses painting, to investigate something in a direct and original way.

BC: *There's no question that there is something to those British films of the early 1960s, but there are also problems.*

ML: They're script bound, as I've just suggested. The truth of it is, though, that there was great integrity to this cinema. Karel Reisz's *Saturday Night and Sunday Morning* [1960], Tony Richardson's *A Taste of Honey* [1961], Lindsay Anderson's *This Sporting Life* [1963]: these were serious works of art, that's not in question.

Curiously and importantly, the first film that did what those films did was really outside the fold; it was *Room at the Top* [1959], directed by Jack Clayton. The real revolution, in a way—which I didn't pick up at the time, because I didn't watch television—was what producer Tony Garnett and director Ken Loach did, which was to say, "Why don't we get away from this terrible studio-bound convention of doing what amounts to plays? Let's get out on the streets with lightweight cameras and newsreel equipment," as the French were doing. That was the revolution, and, a few years after it started, Tony Garnett himself got me into the BBC.

BC: *There was a certain occupational hazard, so to speak, in the British cinema at the time. To work in a country with such an immense literary tradition, including Shakespeare and Dickens—it must have been like having a very powerful father, and a certain parochialism and insularity seem to have resulted, in the theater as well as the cinema. I am thinking of the provinciality of so much kitchen-sink drama.*

ML: Yes, I agree, but let's not throw out the baby with the bathwater. For me, the natural influence, the early influence, was not so much British literature but the theater, vaudeville, circus, and pantomime, together with the British "New Wave" films; the Marx Brothers, Laurel and Hardy, Chaplin, and Keaton. This is one of the things that make me different from Ken Loach. There's also no question that a major influence is the time I spent as a youth in a socialist-Zionist movement. But the fact of the matter is that the heightened, theatrical, almost vaudevillian aspect of what goes on in my films is as important as my hard, socially realistic way of looking at the world. Those two elements are absolutely and mutually inseparable.

BC: *Let's talk now about practice as opposed to influence. Can you elaborate on the process of improvising with actors?*

ML: First, the final script has to work for me dramatically and from a literary point of view, but it also has to work from each actor's point of view of the character. I would never say to an actor, "You have to say that whether you feel it's right or not, and I don't care if you think he or she would say that— just do it." That's never happened, ever, and I wouldn't do that. Because by the time I get to that stage, I've been on this long journey with each actor such that I really understand the actor and the character and the actor understands his or her character totally. On the journey, one of the many jobs we do is to decide, and to work on, how the character talks and thinks; we determine the kind of language the character uses, the sort of ideas in the person's head, etc. It's a very precise process but also very much a harmonious collaboration. It is quite precise, indeed, down to whether there's a full stop or a semicolon at the end of a main clause!

BC: *O.K., so your process is very different from that of most other directors: you ask actors to go along with you on an intense journey during which they will spend months doing improvisations to develop their characters before anything gets set in stone. Because you arrive at defining the characters and storyline only after months of workshops with the actors, you are unable to tell them much about the roles they'll be playing at the start of the process. So how do your actors learn to trust you at the very start?*

ML: In the first place, I'm pretty careful about whom I choose. I instinctively look for the kind of actor who *is* going to be trusting. There are all kinds of insecure people out there called actors; and some deeply untrusting actors— the kind that need to know exactly what's what at all times—might be quite good within the parameters of a certain sort of acting. But I can't work with such people. On the whole, I get people for whom not always knowing what's what isn't a problem.

BC: *How do you find out that this isn't going to be a problem?*

ML: It's an instinctual thing on my part: I have a feeling about an actor when I meet him or her for the first time during our initial interview.

BC: *Is the interview a "twenty-minute get-to-know-you" chat?*

ML: Yes, precisely. We're sitting in a room and there's nobody else there but the actor and me. We talk about the actor's life. Then if I feel the relationship's going to move forward, I call that person back in and we do some work for a while. At this point I'm just trying to get a sense of the person and the performer. The actors with whom I collaborate tend to be confident in the best sense of the word: relaxed, cool, together, focused, open, intelligent, and they have a sense of humor.

My job, apart from anything else, is to build an ensemble composed of actors who all come from such a secure place that they can work together to make a film—my film. So on the whole, frankly, trust is not much of an issue. What I don't do is throw actors instantly into a dangerous situation. The actors I select for my projects sit and chew the fat with me for ages before we gradually get the characters going. And by the time they get to the bit that's dangerous, they've spent a lot of time sorting things out without any pressure. We're careful and slow. The reason my films work is that every actor on set is very secure; that makes them able to fly.

BC: *But there's still a sense of danger in your films. I'm thinking of the rape scene in* Naked, *or the scene in* Life Is Sweet *where a young Jane Horrocks has her body smeared in chocolate.*

ML: Sure. But it takes work to arrive at the stage where you can tackle those things on screen. Here's a bit of truth: very, very occasionally I hire an actor and get it wrong. The actor just doesn't trust the process or me as fully as I thought he would. But such a lack of trust has nothing to do with me or the process: it has to do with the actor himself.

BC: *In the United States, the actors I've seen seem to fall into two camps: you get the ones that work very much with their heads, or in their heads; they tend to be very literate and extremely intelligent. And then there's the other sort—the emotional, feeling actor who doesn't really read anything and has little idea of what's going on in the world, but nevertheless creates a performance from some apparently deeper or more instinctual place. When I watch your films, I feel that there's cohesion between these two different approaches.*

ML: I couldn't agree more. I'm very familiar with both these sorts of American actors; I know exactly what you mean. The second category of actor you mention comes as a result of the so-called Method. The notion that acting is simply about intuitively responding to situations in the way you "feel" them couldn't be farther away from how I ask actors to work. On the other hand, the kind of acting that's wholly literary or cerebral is also wrong. It's useless for me to have actors so much in their heads that they can't be organic or whole.

What it all comes down to, really, is having actors who are totally able to think deeply about their characters while at the same time—once we have developed those characters—they can respond emotionally, and organically, to anything that comes their way. For actors to be able to differentiate between themselves and the characters they're playing while simultaneously remaining in character and spontaneous requires a sophisticated combination of skills and spirit. The bottom line is this: for those that can do it, it's a natural combination and they don't think twice about it. For those who can't do it, they can bang their heads against a brick wall from now till kingdom come and they still won't get there.

BC: *Do you think that the English actor-training system prepares actors to be people with whom you'd want to work? Or does the kind of actor you're looking for flourish in any kind of educational or cultural environment?*

ML: There's a wider issue at stake here. It would be wrong to overlook the fact that I make films within an English context with actors who come from the same social environment as I do. There's something about the whole environment in which we all come together that makes my projects work. The success is further bound up with being committed, caring, and emotionally connected to the project while at the same time being detached from it and even humorous about it. This is what makes my work idiosyncratic and something that no one else does. But that's a whole other discussion. As to the training, I myself was trained as an actor. I trained at the Royal Academy of Dramatic Art [RADA] in London and began my career with the Royal Shakespeare Company [RSC]. But the training, I have to say, was very old-fashioned and prescriptive.

BC: *What, just Shakespearean monologues?*

ML: We didn't just do Shakespearean monologues, but the approach to acting in general was very mechanical. You learned the lines and the moves; you didn't discuss the play or improvise. Since then, the culture of drama schools has completely changed. Improvisation—the cornerstone of my process as a director—is now a standard part of actor training. Once upon a time when I was auditioning actors, a large proportion would come in and say, "I've never improvised. What do you mean there's no script?" Today, that's no longer the case. If I'm meeting actors under the age of forty, very rarely will I encounter this attitude; they all take improvising for granted. This is great for me because I wind up getting actors who are ready to hit the ground running. Then again, the way an actor is trained in the end doesn't ultimately have much bearing on my work. I'm interested in the actor as artist.

BC: *In the commentary for the DVD of* Naked, *one of those artists, David Thewlis, talked about rehearsing a scene between his character—the protagonist in the film, Johnny—and the young Scottish homeless character, Archie, played by Ewen Bremner. Thewlis talked about how the actors were so immersed in their roles that their characters got into a fight during an extended improvisational sequence and the police had to be called. Thewlis said that you had to intervene, imploring him and Bremner to step out of character in order to keep them from being arrested. Comically enough, Thewlis then said that he kind of wished he and Bremner had been arrested because the court would have been faced with trying a couple of fictional characters. You're so clear about the actor's being separate from the character, and yet this incredible visceral reality you create makes it hard, especially for the actors, to accept that it's all just fiction. What are your thoughts about this tension between performer and role?*

ML: The delineation between the actor and his part is a practical matter. When the camera runs, you want the actor to *be* the character. But from a practical point of view—and this relates back to the second category of American actor that we discussed earlier—I can't negotiate and collaborate with a *character* in the creating of a distilled dramatic investigation of the raw material. I need to work with an *actor*. That stuff about actors who stay in character all the time is nonsense. It's bad for them. The thing is that when you work on a character over time, it gets to you; after all, you spend day in, day out, week in, week out with the character. I'm just pretty strict about making sure that when an actor goes into character, he or she comes out of character eventually, too. I like to be objective about what happens. For example, I never allow actors to talk about their character in the first person, as "I." This helps us remember the fact that we really are creating a fictitious person and that the actor is—and always will be—the actor.

BC: *Does asking the actor to be a key collaborator in defining the character sometimes cause problems? For example, I've heard that actors sometimes come back at*

*you and say things like, "My character wouldn't rape this other character." How
do you deal with that?*

ML: That's true. It happened with *Vera Drake*. Understandably, this kind of
issue has to be gently negotiated. I knew that the character in question could
perfectly well be a rapist. And so did the actor, when it came right down to it.

BC: *But he was in denial for a bit?*

ML: Yes, in some way he was, and fair enough. In that particular case—unusual, for one of my projects—the rape was a prerequisite. Normally I don't
set plot points in stone. Another instance:There was a moment during the
making of *Secrets & Lies* where Claire Rushbrook, who plays Roxanne, just
buggered off in the middle of a massive improvisation. She disappeared and
we had to go and find her. She left at a point that was effectively in the structure of the sequence I'd put together, but the final proof hadn't come out. I
knew there was more to flesh out. But after I located Rushbrook, the actress
said, "There's no way that Roxanne would go back." She knew that I wanted
her to go back, but I can't just say to an actor, "Let's go back," because the
action has to be organic and motivated. Then we discovered that if her boyfriend, as he does in the finished movie, says, "Actually, I think you should
go back," she would do as he says, because she's getting fed up with his being
a wimp and wants to validate any assertiveness he shows.

So these things have to be thought through and gently negotiated. Sometimes I have to say to an actor, "Is it plausible or impossible for the character
to do this?" I do this because my job—and this is what all artists do whatever
the medium, since all art is based on improvisation *and* order—is to start
something that grows all over the place and then figure out how to shape it
into something that's coherent.

BC: *Considering that this monologue is going on in your head all the time, when
do you get to step out of character? Do you ever get to switch off? Do you sleep?*

ML: What, while the film is happening? No. What do you want me to do? Go
to Bermuda? It's a privilege to get to work on something that's so completely
absorbing. It's terrifying, too. I have to get out of bed every day to make something happen. I wonder if I would have been capable of producing anything
had I worked in a more conventional way with a prewritten script, because I'm
of the procrastinator class. I could see myself waking up and saying things like,

"Today I'll just have a reading day, tomorrow I can write," "I think I need to see a movie today," "I'll do the shopping first," or "I'll just make another cup of coffee." But because of the way I work, once the film goes into rehearsal, I have to be out of bed and on site by nine o'clock every single day—there's no point in hanging around, because the writing won't get done at home. When the project does take off, it becomes immensely stimulating. The whole thing is a powerful, gregarious, collaborative process. And I'm the one who has to make it all work for the actor.

BC: *You put actors at the center of your process, I gather.*

ML: I'm asking actors to be creative collaborators.

BC: *For the uninitiated, how would you differentiate between improvisation and collaboration?*

ML: What you're really asking me has to do with the general assumption that in a Mike Leigh film, we are looking at actors improvising on camera. Which we're not: that's not how they collaborate with me. We spend a great deal of time, six months or so, bringing the world of the characters into existence: that's the collaboration, which also involves improvisation. So that

Imelda Staunton (center) as Vera in Leigh's *Vera Drake.*

when it comes time to shoot, everything has been worked on, scene by scene and location by location; it's all been made very precise, before it's been shot. That's because the dialogue and the action have come organically: the actors have worked with me to create them from the ground up. What you don't get on my set is the sort of random line reading you get from take to take on a film where the dialogue is just thought of as lines on a page. It's never lines on a page in my films; my actors never see a script.

BC: *Who ultimately is responsible for the script?*

ML: It's a complicated process, as we explore the situations that are going to be the actual scenes in the film, then gradually deconstruct relations and reconstruct them, experiment with them, pin them down, fix dialogue, change things around here and there, cut and paste, until we arrive at something coherent and pithy that works. As soon as I can, I share with the cinematographer what the general spirit of the film is. The production designer and the costume designer then tune in to what's going on and start to find out about the characters, and work with the actors so that everyone's on the case. I have constant conversations with the production designer in particular about possible images and locations and the reason behind things. So we gradually talk the thing into existence, making the film up as we go along. I do set down a kind of structure before we start shooting, but there are always elements that creep in; indeed, I very often don't know what the end is going to be.

BC: *Does the process of discovering a film get any easier for you?*

ML: I can only say what any artist would say, and that is that some things come easy and some things are tough, depending on a whole variety of factors.

BC: *Do you watch your films?*

ML: I do, and I like them. I mean, I'm not Gloria Swanson in *Sunset Boulevard*, sitting there every night watching my own movies. But I do watch them, and I particularly love watching them with audiences. Some filmmakers say, "I can't watch my films; I can't stand them." My feeling, rather piously, is that if *you* don't like your films, how the hell can you expect anybody else to like them?

BC: *Would you rank* Naked *among your better works? It's one of my favorites.*

ML: Well, it's very hard to talk about better or worse. I don't know. I'm very close to these films. There are filmmakers who, very legitimately, have relationships for better or worse with their films depending on, say, whether the picture is too close to the book it's adapted from or taken from an original screenplay, whether they were hired into a project that already existed or were part of the project from day one, etc. None of those things apply to me. I'm as close to all of my films, each and every one of them.

BC: *Until recently, your films could be quite negative or dark, I must say.*

ML: That may be, but all my films, in the end, contain a balance between the comic and the pathetic.

BC: *But wouldn't you agree that* Happy-Go-Lucky, *on the whole, has a more festive and sanguine tone?*

ML: Well, maybe you're right, because one reviewer wrote, "Can this be true, Mike Leigh has made a comedy?" Does it surprise me? No, not at all.

BC: *There's a real brightness to this film, isn't there? There are splashes of color in the set design, the costumes, and the very film stock that you used.*

ML: At the point where I got a sense of what the film should be, and I was able to share that with Dick Pope—the cinematographer who's shot all my films since *Life Is Sweet* in 1990—and also my various designers, I immediately began talking about Poppy. I said that this is going to be a vivacious, positive, intelligent, bright woman with a great sense of humor and buzzing with energy, and the film really needs to take its cue from her character: i.e., the film itself should burst with energy and color. At this point, we decided to shoot *Happy-Go-Lucky* in widescreen—it's the first film I've made that's been widescreen. And we set about shooting tests, just to work out what stocks to use, how to treat them, how to find the palette, etc. Curiously, at that precise moment—that week in fact—Fuji announced this new film stock called Vivid, which we used. And it's an absolute delight, which made possible this wonderful, rich, succulent color experience you see in the final film.

BC: *What interests you most as a cinematic subject?*

ML: People relating to each other and the relationships between men and children and work.

BC: *British people, right?*

ML: I have to say that I don't personally see my films as being about London, England, Britain, or English things. Obviously, the milieu, the territory, or the landscape is that, but I am more concerned with the emotional landscape, as I have always been when the chips are down. Although it may sound pretentious to say so, I guess I think my work is about something more universal than just the U.K. I don't really see it as so nation based.

BC: *What are your views about filmmaking in the United States, and about Americans' views of your films?*

ML: First of all, most of us, myself not least, grew up on Hollywood movies, as I suggested at the start of our conversation—specifically, the great Hollywood movies of the Golden Age. Some of my favorite movies are Hollywood movies; Hollywood is obviously a large part of the cinematic spectrum. I nurture a healthy love-hate relationship toward the place. Of course, there's been a bit of American money in some of my films—*Topsy-Turvy*, for example—though not a lot. The important thing is for the funding to come without classic Hollywood-style interference.

BC: *Yes, because you don't create "packages," and everything in Hollywood has to be "packaged."*

ML: The main problem is that the Hollywood system has already made the film before the director shoots a single frame. But to get back to what I think was the subtext of your original question: in the seventeen or so years between *Bleak Moments* and *High Hopes*, I talked to people in Hollywood who might have backed my films on a number of occasions. And one of the things I always heard was, "The trouble with your films is that they will never work in the States. People won't get them." At the time, I thought there might be some truth to this. Then, when I came to the United States in 1986, for the first time—the San Francisco International Film Festival brought me out to the West Coast and screened all six of my films to date—audiences over there started to know about me and it turned out that the prediction about how American audiences would receive my films was wrong. The American audience, or a part of the American audience, really likes my films. On the one hand, I am very happy to be part of European and world cinema as a British filmmaker. But on the other, it's also very stimulating and rewarding to come to the San Francisco International Film Festival or the Oscars (which I've done three times) with these low-budget, foreign, offbeat, quirky, real-life, uncompromising films and be a bit of a Trojan horse. I enjoy the subversion of it all. Curiously enough, I've done industry screenings in Los Angeles with huge audiences and industry insiders. They say things like, "Wow, this is fantastic. Why can't we do this here?" And I think, "Well, actually, with all the resources you've got kicking around here, you could do anything you wanted."

BC: *But the Hollywood system stymies them.*

ML: Yes. But the other thing I want to say is that there is a great tradition of independent filmmaking in the United States that I absolutely respect. There's some wonderful stuff that comes out of America against all the odds, like Steve Buscemi's *Trees Lounge* [1996]. Independent American filmmaking has always been there and it's not to be forgotten. Also, it would be ludicrous to suggest that nothing good comes out of Hollywood, because that's not the case. Sometimes really truthful, organic stuff surfaces by those who managed to stick it to the man and just got on, and away, with it.

BC: *There's been quite a migration of directors from the U.K. to Hollywood, from Sam Mendes to Phyllida Lloyd.*

ML: There always has been. What about Hitchcock? The Brits have always drifted over and that's fine. It's a complex issue. One of the reasons that I'm resistant to making films in the United States has nothing to do with *not* doing a film in Hollywood, but rather to do with what I'm committed to doing in the U.K. I feel very committed to the British film industry and its infrastructure.

BC: *How would you describe the film industry in the U.K. right now? Some people are very critical of it.*

ML: The problem with the British film industry is its nervousness or insecurity about—and genuflection toward—Los Angeles. All those Hollywood grandfathers like Irving Thalberg and Louis B. Mayer have got a lot to answer for, because they invented a monster that is a curse to filmmaking: the interfering producer. Such insecurity leads to things within the U.K. film industry like wheeling in an American actor to play a part that should plainly be played by a Brit—Renée Zellweger playing Bridget Jones, for one stellar example.

BC: *How much does commercial success matter at this point in your career, anyway? You've now got a body of work that speaks for itself, so does commerce matter as much as it might have done in the past?*

ML: That's always mattered. First of all, I make these films to be seen. There's no virtue in a film that nobody sees or very few people see. But unconventional as my films may seem to be, they're perfectly conventional in the sense that they are narrative films; they're movies that tell stories. They're not alternative or experimental films that we shoot for no money at all with a little camera. They're proper movies and they have to be funded, and although the budgets are tight, the money has to come from people who back films. And if you've made films that are not commercially successful, people don't want to hear from you. And they especially don't want to hear from filmmakers such as myself, someone who doesn't have a script, who can't tell the backer what it's going to be about, and who will not enter into any discussion about having Hollywood stars involved. The main thing is, I'm not a Trappist monk up in the mountains. I'm in the movie business, and I want people to see my films. Also, if there's any money made, it simply goes back into things. My most successful film commercially was *Secrets & Lies*, partly because it got the Palme d'Or at Cannes, partly because it was nominated for five Oscars. But as much as anything, it was because at the time of its release, to trace your birth mother—which is what the film is about—was illegal. And it remains illegal today in many countries, including all of South America and many of the Catholic countries in Europe as well as almost all the states in the USA. So there was enormous interest in the film. And because the film was, relatively speaking, commercially successful, it enabled us to raise rather more money than we normally would have done to make *Topsy-Turvy*. So the short answer to your question is that commercial success is very important, indeed.

BC: *Commerce aside for the moment, what is the relationship between theater and film for you?*

ML: I love theater less than I love films, that's for sure; for every film that I've ever walked out on—which is not very many—I have walked out on about a thousand plays. Film always seems so grown-up compared with theater. I love working with actors, I love working with technicians, and I love the family thing that is created on every film. And it really is a family—on my films, the atmosphere is very, very harmonious, always. Because if it weren't, you couldn't do this sort of work. You just couldn't: people really have to commit, on either side of the camera. Aside from that, I love the medium itself. I love the whole idea of what making a film means—you know, taking that little machine out and capturing the world with it. I love to shoot in places, on location. And I love the rhythm of filmmaking, what you can do with time. I even like the actual feel of celluloid. The post-production process itself is great, because that's when you really make the film.

BC: *Do you have a sense of advocacy? Do you feel any sense of advocacy, on behalf of your audience, about how to cope with this world we're all messing up?*

ML: I think there are different ways of advocating, to use your word. I would suggest that some films talk to you emotionally and not necessarily with a clear, rational slogan; they simply leave you with a feeling that may in some way inform the way you look at the world. Whereas other films may work through your emotions and the way you feel about the world, and the way human life is and the way society organizes itself, at the same time that they make a very specific, if implicit statement, about one sociopolitical subject or another. My natural instinct is to see society as a society that works because of the nature of the individuality of its individuals. I can't look at a crowd without seeing a thousand individuals. What's fascinating to me is that each of us is different. So in each of my films, each of the characters, large or small, is properly and organically and thoroughly, in a three-dimensional way, at the center of his or her universe. Such that, even though there may be a clear objective or point that I'm moving toward, you nevertheless get multiple perspectives, because the characters aren't ciphers. They're people, and the details of their humanity are what it's all about in the end.

BC: *As opposed to what you find in overtly political filmmaking, yours are genuinely, spontaneously created human beings. And that's not an easy thing to do.*

ML: No, although in my view, Mike Leigh films are political in the sense that they are concerned with investigating, and reflecting on, how we lead our lives. But I would challenge anybody to say that they've walked out of a film of mine with one single, clear notion as to what I was telling them to think, because that's not what I'm up to. I want you to walk away with things to argue about and ponder over and reflect on and procrastinate about and, you know, supply for yourselves.

BC: *We have been living through difficult times for the past several decades, as a result of the culture of wealth and greed. But the present economic crisis is going to* *put an end to that cult, one way or the other. Can you imagine a resulting, new political environment that would affect your own work?*

ML: I suppose the answer to that question, at a fundamental level—it's a dodgy thing to discuss, because nothing is ever black and white—would have to be no. I think that I make films about how we are, although that's a pompous thing to say in a universal sense. Although my milieu is always specific, the actual things that happen, at a fundamental level, are endemic to what human life is about. You know, I've been to screenings of my work—in particular, *Meantime*—in London and Sydney where people stood up and harangued me for having the tools to make a film about the manning of the barricades . . . and not making it, not dealing with those issues. I accept the criticism because that is not what I'm concerned to do; I'm concerned to do other things. Were a revolution to come, the job for me, in fundamental terms, would still be to take the human temperature, as I always do; to look at people in terms of their needs and emotions, of how men and women function, what it is to be a parent and child, how to survive in the world as we know it. Having said that, I must also say that nothing makes sense to me except a world in which there is real equality. I can't believe, for example, that I live in a country where, after more than a decade of a so-called "socialist" government, we still have a railway system, an educational system, a healthcare system, and a steel industry which are riddled with the curse or disease of privatization.

BC: *We all know that no individual book or film changes the world, yet books and films, as an aggregate, do change the world. Do you have any thoughts about the relationship between art and social change, a long-term, indirect, complex, often subterranean relationship?*

ML: Look, this goes back to something that has already more or less been said during this conversation. If I make films to which people genuinely respond, whatever their response, I feel that I'm justified in thinking that, in some minuscule way, I'm making a contribution to that person's life, or to individual people's ideas. I call my films subversive. I think it's subversive to tell the truth about things—not the obvious political truths, but about how ordinary people get on with their lives. That's what I do.

BC: *Have you ever considered shooting in a foreign country, apart from the United States, with a completely different crew and getting away from all that's familiar?*

ML: It seems natural to work in a context that one understands. I think the most important thing is to work here in England with teams of people on both sides of the camera that are completely in tune with everything you need to make these great films with their very specific roots. The instrument is totally tuned and we can play anything on it, so to speak, within the parameters of the sort of film that I make. To go, for example, and make a film that isn't in English, where English isn't the first language—because specifics are so much a part of what I do, and language is so very important—it would be very difficult under such circumstances to play the instrument properly.

BC: *I don't mean necessarily to use foreign actors, but to be in a foreign place, a different environment, a different context.*

ML: I must admit, I have done it twice. I made a film, the last BBC television film I made, *Four Days in July*, which was set in Belfast, and which took a year to do. This is not a joke, for it was very much a case of making a film in a very "other" place. It was in English, but tapping into a whole different world, in the same language that was at the same time a different language—this was in 1984. Also, at the end of the 1980s, I went to Australia, where I created a play called *Greek Tragedy*, which was actually about Greek Australians and all the actors were from a Greek-Australian background; and that was again a very specific investigation into a world that I didn't actually know very much about. So I've experimented with a "foreign context" to that extent. The only thing I would say in addition to this is that it remains a frustrated aspiration of mine to make a film with a much bigger budget, which would allow us to get out and about more, and such a film might involve what you're talking about. But if I wasn't allowed to take my regular crew along, where we all speak the same language and have a real rapport, I think it would be very difficult. I certainly don't see any inherent virtue in doing what you've posited just for the sake of doing it.

BC: *Larger budgets and foreign contexts aside, do you regret not having explored your Jewishness on film, which you have done in the theater?*

ML: I don't regret it, and should I wish to do it, I will.

BC: *Enough said.*

Mike Leigh Filmography

Bleak Moments (1971)
Hard Labour (1973)

The Permissive Society (1975)
Nuts in May (1976)
Abigail's Party (1977)
Kiss of Death (1977)
Who's Who (1978)
Grown-Ups (1980)
Meantime (1983)
Four Days in July (1985)
The Short and Curlies (short, 1987)
High Hopes (1988)
Life Is Sweet (1990)
Naked (1993)
Secrets & Lies (1996)
Career Girls (1997)
Topsy-Turvy (1999)
All or Nothing (2002)
Vera Drake (2004)
Happy-Go-Lucky (2008)
Another Year (2010)

Bibliography

Carney, Raymond, and Leonard Quart. *The Films of Mike Leigh: Embracing the World.* New York: Cambridge University Press, 2000.

Clements, Paul. *The Improvised Play: The Work of Mike Leigh.* London: Methuen, 1983.

Coveney, Michael. *The World According to Mike Leigh.* New York: HarperCollins, 1996.

Jones, Edward Trostle. *All or Nothing: The Cinema of Mike Leigh.* New York: Peter Lang, 2004.

Movshovitz, Howie, ed. *Mike Leigh: Interviews.* Jackson: University Press of Mississippi, 2000.

Raphael, Amy, ed. *Mike Leigh on Mike Leigh.* London: Faber and Faber, 2008.

Watson, Garry. *The Cinema of Mike Leigh: A Sense of the Real.* London: Wallflower Press, 2004.

Whitehead, Tony. *Mike Leigh.* Manchester, UK: Manchester University Press, 2008.

~

"It's Not Just about Me"

Ken Loach and the Cinema of
Social Conscience—An Interview

Ken Loach (born 1936), unquestionably one of Britain's most important filmmakers, is best known
for his gritty and compassionate
portrayals of working-class life.
Early in his career, a series of socially conscious BBC films established the fact that Loach was
both a skillful artist and a crusad-
ing social critic. *Cathy Come
Home* (1966), an accomplished
blend of fictional and documentary techniques, was one of his
most successful—and controver-
sial—early efforts. Although Loach occasionally returned to television (the
even more controversial *Days of Hope* [1975] was a landmark BBC mini-
series), he subsequently moved on to feature films, most notably *Kes* (1969),
Family Life (1971), and *Ladybird, Ladybird* (1994), which are justly regarded
as milestones of British social realism.

Loach's films can be divided, however roughly, into two broad categories—intimate family dramas that illuminate the politics of everyday life
and more militant films determined to skewer both the forces of reaction
and the reformist wing of the labor movement. The first category is best

personified by the now classic *Kes*, a moving account of how a young boy's alienation from the rigors of school and the demands of a dysfunctional family is temporarily assuaged by his devotion to a pet falcon. *The Big Flame* (1969), a stirring chronicle of a group of dockers whose experiment in workers' self-management is eventually sabotaged by the union bosses, typifies the more didactic strand in Loach's work, which is often labeled Trotskyist but is equally amenable to positions espoused by anti-Leninist Marxists and anarcho-syndicalists. Historically based films by Loach such as *The Big Flame*, *Days of Hope*, and *Hidden Agenda* (1990) were condemned as subversive by conservatives and chided for supposed "ultra-leftism" by orthodox radicals, but they remain some of the few cinematic examples of bona fide anti-Stalinist leftism to reach mainstream audiences.

With his no-frills visual style and lean, sequential narratives, Loach is not out to impress anyone with technique. In fact, it is his bug-like dedication to the task at hand—concentrating on nailing down one moment without glamorizing it, but forgetting this accomplishment as soon as it has been passed—that makes his films so unerringly lifelike and effective. Another defining trait in Loach's oeuvre is that he often casts unknowns and non-professionals for leading roles. Crissy Rock's heart-wrenching turn in *Ladybird, Ladybird*, for instance, about a volatile woman's fight to wrest custody of her children from Social Services, is a quintessential example of Loach's gift for drawing gutsy, memorable performances out of unseasoned players. Throughout his work, Loach immerses us in human problems or conflicts— addiction (*My Name Is Joe* [1998]), mental illness (*Family Life*), poverty and street life (*Cathy Come Home, Poor Cow* [1967]), the travails of labor organizers and immigrants (*Days of Hope, Bread and Roses* [2000]), political struggle (*Carla's Song* [1996], *Land and Freedom* [1995])—that are noticeably from the "real world" and populated with characters who appear to inhabit, with grit and integrity, the same fraught universe as we do.

Ironically enough, the Thatcher-Major era, usually considered the most dismal epoch of the twentieth century by British radicals, engendered Loach's most productive and artistically satisfying period, during which he produced a series of award-winning feature films that firmly established him in the pantheon of great European directors. (His films have always been more popular in mainland Europe than in his native country or the United States.) *Hidden Agenda*, for example—a drama about the conflict in Northern Ireland—won the Special Jury Prize at the 1990 Cannes Film Festival. *Riff-Raff* (1990) won the Felix Award for Best European Film; *Raining Stones* (1993) won the Cannes Special Jury Prize; and *Land and Freedom* won the FIPRESCI International Critics' Prize and the Ecumenical Jury Prize at the

1995 Cannes Film Festival. It was also a substantial box-office hit in Spain, where it sparked intense debate about its subject matter, the Spanish Civil War. *My Name Is Joe* won numerous accolades, including three British Academy Awards and Best Actor at Cannes for star Peter Mullan. Cannes jurors went on to award the Palme d'Or to *The Wind That Shakes the Barley* (2006), Loach's militant, stirring drama of the Anglo-Irish War (1919–1921).

Loach's more recent output has proved uneven, even though *Land and Freedom*, *Carla's Song*, and *My Name Is Joe* are all peppered with vibrant, privileged moments. *Land and Freedom* is probably the closest approximation of the revolutionary fervor of the Spanish Revolution of the 1930s that will ever be committed to film. Before *Carla's Song* becomes bogged down by an unwieldy romance set against the backdrop of the Nicaraguan Revolution, it itself is enlivened by a spirited romp through the streets of Glasgow in which Robert Carlyle shines in the role of an antiauthoritarian bus conductor. The focus of *My Name Is Joe* on drugs and crime frequently recalls genre movies that have mined similar material with more panache, but the plucky hero's humor and perseverance nearly make us forget the film's convoluted, overly schematic plot.

The following interview with Ken Loach took place in July 2009 at his home in Bath, England, shortly after the release of *Looking for Eric*—which may turn out to be his most popular, or accessible, film yet.

Bert Cardullo: *In interviews, sometimes, you express a lot of optimism about the power of cinema to change hearts. At other times, though, you express cynicism about the very same potential of movies to do anything other than reassure and entertain. If that's true, why choose this medium for consciousness raising? You seemed discouraged at the time, for example, by the response to* Cathy Come Home, *since it promoted piecemeal reform rather than radical transformation.*

Ken Loach: That film portrayed an injustice but, of course, homelessness is worse now then when that film was made. With *Cathy Come Home*, we were adopted by people with whom we really didn't feel we had much in common. I think that was influential in pushing our little group to the left; we were social democrats when we made that film and would-be Marxists when we finished it. We realized the inability of social democrats to do anything constructive.

Just to judge in more general terms, if the cinema is any kind of force for social change, then it's a force for the bad, because most films are about one guy with a gun solving a problem. The ideology of the cinema, of mainstream films, is a very right-wing ideology. One hopes to God that such a cinema can have no effect whatsoever, because, if it does, we're all screwed! Of course, maybe my films can have a small sort of impact with one or two people, now and then. That's all I can do, really: make films and hope they have some impact. Some people are writers, some people are poets and paint-ers. Filmmaking is all I can do—I couldn't really do anything else. But also, films are more than wanting to set out to make a political statement. I hope filmmaking is much more than that. It's more about how people live together and what families are about, and all the things that make drama, not just something you can put in a slogan.

We shouldn't have any illusions about what film can do. I mean, it's just a film, and when all is said and done, everybody gets up and walks out of the cinema. So, the best thing you can do is to leave people with a question or to leave people with a sense of disquiet—in the case of *My Name Is Joe*, for example, a sense of solidarity with the characters, a sense of "that's my world, I'm part of it, they're part of me." It's not about some other people, it's about the world I am a part of and a world I am responsible for. And in a way, that knowledge is responsibility, I think. You can't know about that and then walk away from it—at least I hope not. The only old-fashioned word I can think of in this regard is, again, solidarity.

BC: *Still, there is a political conviction embedded in your work. There's a very palpable progressive current running through your oeuvre, from beginning to end, and I wonder if you don't ever feel that it's a sort of Sisyphean task to tell the truth about a historical situation or the way people live.*

KL: Well, I never see my work in such all-embracing terms. Also, I always work with a writer, and there's a producer, and we all put our heads together and try to make the film. It's not just about me. I suppose that, in the end, all you can do is make a little contribution to the general noise in the world and say, look, maybe you should look at things in this way, or did you know what happened here? "Just consider this for a moment," or "Look at these few people"—and hope such a question or exhortation hangs around in your mind a minute or two after you leave the cinema. You can't do more than that, I believe.

BC: *What's the difference, do you think, between making a film which is politically charged and a film that's propaganda?*

KL: I don't know. I suppose what you try to do—I'm not saying you always succeed—is just to be a sympathetic observer. And also you show that the filmic action exists in a context, not in a vacuum, and you just observe it in a kind of cool yet engaged way, without winding up in melodrama. That's the aim, anyway.

BC: *A follow-up question, connected to the debasing of culture as a result of its commercialization in a market economy. At present one can observe a homogenization of culture: cities become more and more alike, people all over the world listen to the same music, watch the same soap operas on television, buy the same brands of consumer goods, etc. It has been argued that this phenomenon is directly related to the liberalization and deregulation of markets and its by-product, i.e., globalization, which in turn has led to the monopolization of the production and distribution networks by American, privately owned conglomerates and to the trivialization and debasement of world cultures. How has globalization affected the cinema and the work of cinema directors? And do you think that this cultural homogenization is reversible within the framework of the internationalized market economy?*

KL: I do not think that cultural homogenization is reversible within the framework of the global market economy, no. The laws of the market are inexorable. They lead to monopoly, a continuous search for profits where new technology has to be constantly harnessed to cut labor costs in order to increase production. We find ourselves in this spiral that is actually actively pursued by politicians who try to increase the growth rate. In doing so, they increase the spiral of exploitation and overproduction, reducing profit margins at the same time as they reduce wages, and so on. I think that if this is the system in which you find yourself, its laws are inexorable. So, I do not think it is possible to reverse it. In the cinema, people can act as artistic eccentricities around the margins but the central thrust in cinema, as in everything else, is driven by economics and investment.

As far as the world of cinema is concerned, the pressure from the United States is unrelenting. They make occasional concessions, or they talk about concessions, to the Europeans and to the rest of the industry. However, they are dominant and they are pushing for more and more free trade, which means more and more access for them to European cinemas. Even the small subsidies that the French are giving to their own cinema are under threat from the United States, especially in its pursuit of the MAI [Multilateral Agreement on Investment] proposal, which, among other things, aims to increase free trade in the film industry. According to this agreement, the subsidies given by the French have to be granted to everybody, such that it would further weaken European cinema. Against that, you have very weak European politicians who engage in a rhetoric of safeguarding European cinema but in practice, apart from the French, do very little. So, the Italian cinema has more or less been wiped out, the Spanish cinema is battling hard, the British cinema for a long time was wiped out and is just now struggling back, but without much help from the state. Although there is a continuous effort from people who care to rescue some kind of cinema other than the one that the American industrial model produces, this is constantly being knocked back and all the pressure from the United States is for unrestricted access to all markets for U.S. films.

Interestingly, in cinema, where the United States is dominant, the Americans talk about free trade, but in other industries where the U.S. is not so dominant they are protectionist—as, for instance, in some sections of the computer industry. They are very protectionist when they want to defend their own domestic industries, but when they think they can dominate someone else's they become very liberal.

BC: *Do you still believe in the possibility of progressive social change, considering this hyper-capitalistic mode of production in which we find ourselves?*

KL: I think the choice is going to be thrust upon us quite soon because obviously we're destroying the planet at a pretty fast rate. And I don't think this mode of production can accommodate the changes that have to be made to stop the using of the world's resources so fast. The big corporations have to show a profit, they have to find cheap raw materials, they've got to find ever-growing markets, they've got to expand. That's the dynamic of their method. The earth is finite, and they're rapidly using it up. So the mode of production is on a collision course with the raw materials with which they've got to work. And sooner or later the situation has to change. Now it may not change, it may end in disaster, or they may make minimal changes and then totter on a little bit longer. But sooner or later the conflict has got to be resolved. And the only way I can see its being resolved satisfactorily is with a planned economy, where production is for what people need, not for private profit; we plan how we use the earth's resources and how we deal with it. That's got to be faced, or it may not be, in which case we all blow up. I have no idea. People say we're in a very extreme period of right-wing political hegemony. Well, we are, but we can't go on like that forever.

BC: *I think, nonetheless that you may feel optimistic about the future, because very often in your films there's an element that makes you think things could get better. Is that by chance?*

KL: I mean, when you look at statistics—I think there was a UN report in a recent edition of *The Guardian* that said there were 225 people who own and control the same resources as 2.7 billion people, which is 40% of humanity. And when you look at those figures, it's quite hard to imagine the resulting level of inequality, and the amount of human suffering. But then you look at the ideological debate that's on the news and the radio and the two things don't really mesh or coincide. So I think there's sometimes a disconnect, and I think that's the great challenge. Many, many people create the language of "flexibility" and globalization and modernization, and it's designed to make everyone else give up and be hopeless.

Still, I'm always reminded of those wonderful words of Woody Guthrie, who said, "All a human being is, anyway, is just a hoping machine." I think there are the possibilities now of great progress. Fifteen years ago people who talked about global warming were seen as cranks and idiots. So I don't think anything is impossible or, by contrast, inevitable. I think it depends on our making decisions and organizing; I think we have to be massively creative and look for opportunities and work together. If we lose faith in that notion of collective effort, I think we are sunk. You know, people like Angie [in *It's a Free World*] have lost hope and say, well, nobody gives a shit out there. Our experience of working out there with so many people in different parts of the world is that they do give a shit. And we have to maintain ourselves and encourage ourselves and do what we can within the conditions in which we work.

BC: *Some people do see your films as depressing, I have to say. And I think it's in the interest of people who don't like your films to portray them that way.*

KL: I hope they're not depressing. People always fight back, and that's the thing which gives you hope. I hope I've indicated that from time to time. The most depressing thing is the political slogan "there is no alternative." But there is. History hasn't ended, contrary to what Francis Fukuyama once said. It's always a dynamic situation.

BC: *Over the course of your career, you seem to have found two modes of storytelling. One is a focus on contemporary stories about the struggles of marginal or oppressed people, and they're very personal dramas. The others, like* Land and Freedom, Carla's Song, *and* The Wind That Shakes the Barley, *grapple with historical events. If it's our duty to criticize our leaders and illuminate the present by looking to the past, do you ever feel that you want to make a movie, through such "telescoping," about the war on terror or the Blair-and-Bush era?*

KL: Yes. In a way, they're huge subjects. I think often it's easier to take a story from the past, the immediate past, because the essential elements of the story emerge much more clearly. And that will comment on what Bush and Blair were doing, maybe as forcefully as if you were to do a contemporary story. Staying contemporary is like trying to see the landscape when you're at ground level, and from there you can't see very far. The clutter of detail is very difficult to see beyond. If you're a bit above the landscape, then you see the contours. It's a bit like that when you do a historical subject—you can see the contours of the event more clearly.

I'm sure there are many films that could be made about Iraq or Afghanistan, for example. Maybe when you're working on such a contemporary subject, one way to tackle it is through documentary. The danger is, if you're doing a contemporary subject, you're chasing the headlines. Something might happen next year that, if you're telling the whole story, you'd want to include. And we don't know what the end of this story is yet. But when you do a story about Ireland in the 1920s, you know what the whole story is—and the taste it leaves, and what it left in its wake. And that then determines what is retrospectively important. You see what I mean? It's easier to get a handle on the whole thing.

BC: *You tend to cast a lot of nonprofessional and unknown actors alongside better-known actors in your films. Why?*

KL: Well, you just try to find the best person for the part and whom the audience will believe. If somebody is a hugely well-known face, and you put that person in a film where you want the audience to think they're watching something as it's happening, when the well-known face pops in, it's disorienting. It can introduce new developments. On the other hand, you just want to find the best person for the part, whoever that person may finally be.

BC: *How do you direct non-professional actors?*

KL: The same as anybody else.

BC: *Tell me about that, if you would.*

KL: Well, I don't direct people in the sense of telling them how to do things. You just put them in a situation with the dialogue and make certain that everything around the scene propels the actors onto a certain path. I would never say to them, "I want you to say it like this." We might talk about it a little bit, but the direction should be self-evident without analyzing it. Directing should be completely hidden, as I see it.

BC: *In order to direct that way, you must have to spend hours and hours getting to know your actors.*

KL: Not really. The audition process takes care of that. You usually see people six or seven times before you cast them, so by the end of that time you know them quite well. But talking about directing and acting in a self-conscious way is very destructive, I think.

BC: *What do you take into consideration when casting a nonprofessional such as David Bradley, the young boy in Kes, or Crissy Rock in Ladybird, Ladybird, who had worked as a stand-up comedian but not as an actress?*

KL: First, as I suggested a little while ago, you don't want to treat them any differently than professionals. In casting, it's best to try little things out, do little improvisations, see who you think is going to touch an audience. A kind of natural eloquence is quite important. Some people will speak and the words don't take off—they've become very pedestrian. Again, it's a class thing. Working-class men and women will often speak with a remarkable eloquence and rhythm and Crissy absolutely has that. She can just turn a phrase brilliantly, and in a way that she's totally unaware of.

BC: *You always cast from the locale where your film is set. For the sake of argument, what would be wrong about hiring a really excellent RADA [Royal Academy of Dramatic Art] actor who did a great Mancunian accent?*

KL: Some actors who have been to RADA are good and have retained their identity, but I think the reason to get someone who really is from, in this case, Manchester—or Glasgow, where I've done a lot of work—is that they don't have to think about how they speak; it is actually part of them, since you learn the rhythm of language where you grew up. It isn't just a question of phonetics, of the sound of words. It's how the language is used, the rhythm of the language and the way of thinking that the language dictates. Speaking is much more than imitating the sound. The language is part of the culture of the place and so, being from there, and knowing that, and not having to consider how you're speaking—all those are much better than having to self-consciously try to make the right sound.

BC: *So you don't iron out regional accents, which tend to be obliterated in mainstream British and American films. Riff-Raff was even subtitled in the United States.*

KL: Yes, that's right. If you ask people to speak differently, you lose more than the voice. Everything about them changes. If I asked you not to speak with an American accent, your whole personality would change. That's how you are. My hunch is that it's better to use subtitles than not, even if that limits the films to an art-house circuit.

BC: *When people talk about "the craft of acting," then, and spending many years studying the Method, do you just think, "What a bunch of nonsense"?*

KL: No, not at all. This is film acting of a particular kind I'm talking about. If you want to work in the theater, then you do need some training and you need to discover how an actor works, because in the theater you need to work out with everyone else the line of the performance and the triggers to the different emotional moments and the changes of mood of the character. You've got to work that out in rehearsal with the text, so that you can play the whole thing from beginning to end in one evening and then do it again the same the next night and the night after that. In film you don't have to do that. It's certainly not the way we work. You just have to make one moment absolutely credible and believe in it totally, and you don't need the theater technique to do that.

BC: *But what about the kind of technique that Robert De Niro or someone like that would use?*

KL: Well I think there's a germ of truth in it, but it's often caricatured and turned into something else.

BC: *Related to this, all of your films have an improvisational quality. How much dialogue is scripted and how much is improvised?*

KL: We work around the script, but the script is always the key. The lines give the actors the tools they need, but then you've got to make it spontaneous. If you look at the script before we've finished the film, and then afterwards, you'll find that we stick pretty close to the original dialogue.

BC: *I know you withhold scripts and play tricks on actors, as it were, to generate a certain sort of immediate or spontaneous response. I wonder how actors generally respond to this kind of improvisation.*

KL: Well, by the time we've cast them, they know that's how we're going to do it, and if they didn't want to respond in that way, we wouldn't cast them. And—touch wood—I haven't yet had a bad experience. I do think it's important that people play things for the moment, or in the moment; you should play a scene so that you don't anticipate what's going to happen. I quite like the actors just to get though the *experience* of the film. So you perhaps give them the script in sections, just what they need to know at that particular time.

BC: *They don't ever feel tricked in any way?*

KL: No, no. Because that's just built into the process and we've talked about that before we do it, as I said. You've got to find people who will enjoy that. I mean most people do. I can't remember the last time somebody ducked out on us. They might have done so thirty years ago, a kind of older actor might not have responded to it, but now everybody just enjoys it really. At least, they are kind enough to say they do. After all, one of the whole points of acting is listening, isn't it? It's reacting. If you've rehearsed it all beforehand, and the people in the scene know what's going to be said, in the end it's very difficult to listen after a bit, because you know what's coming. So part of the trick is to make it so that you have to listen because what will be said to you will be framed differently, and you've got to reframe it so it actually has to go through your mind all the time. And that's really important. I mean it doesn't always work, but the situation is akin to that of a painter when he's painting a house or painting a wall. You always have an open edge and the paint is always wet for your next brush stroke, and I think acting has to be like that. There has to be an openness about it, kind of an uncertainty, a sense of danger, because once it's sealed off and everybody knows what he is doing, when he is going to flick the ash off the cigarette, things die really. And what's crucial here is the cameraman who can catch all that. That again is where other collaborations and other partnerships come in.

BC: *Did you withhold the script from the actors on* Cathy Come Home, *for example?*

KL: I think we did, yes. We certainly did on *Kes*. The kestrel is killed in this film and we smuggled a dead kestrel into the scene where David Bradley, who played Billy, would find it and he didn't know it was going to be there. I think surprise is the hardest thing to act—something like the police raid in *Looking for Eric*, which the actors didn't know was going to take place.

BC: *Could you tell me a bit more about how you work with actors on the set?*

KL: The key thing is finding the right people. Finding people who will just go straight of their own volition. I mean the key thing is to tell the story in sequence so that it unfolds with them and they go through it so that the work they do today is the rehearsal for the work they are going to do tomorrow. When I started, we would do things like read-throughs—you go to a television show and you would do a read-through on the first day—and usually that was the best performance we got. It was often downhill from then on, because the director—which was me in that case—would come in and start asking daft questions, would give the moves, the actors would rehearse it for two weeks, and by the time they got to the end of the second week, they were bored to tears; they had lost that intuition, that impulse, they had lost their sense of instinct about how to say a line. You know we would even, God help us, talk about vocal inflection, which is death—the moment you start talking about that, you should pack your bags and go. The important thing from my point of view is to keep the performer in touch with his or her instinct, because that's really precious; you live off that for the two or three hours that it takes to do a scene. So good directing is just protecting the actors' instinct, I think.

BC: *How has your process developed over the years?*

KL: It's just learning by mistakes. You look at what you're recording and then say, "Well, that isn't as good as it could have been. What would make it better?"

BC: *Do you feel an affinity for any filmmakers working now who, like you, have a bit of a political inflection to their work, like John Sayles?*

KL: Yes, John Sayles has done some very good films. I think we probably work in different ways, but I believe his *Matewan* was a good film. I very much approve of his general view of the world, and I always look forward to his films.

BC: *Are there any other filmmakers working at the moment with whom you feel a connection? Or just admire?*

KL: I like the Dardenne brothers' films. I think there are a few others, but I'm not good at remembering names. I am friends with quite a lot of filmmakers—Mike Leigh, for example. But we do very different work.

BC: *Do you argue about film technique with Mike Leigh?*

KL: No, no, no. You might gossip, but you would never challenge each other. Because everybody's got his own process, his own way, and things that interest him and things he wants to express, and that's how it should be, really.

BC: *Are you committed to the realist mode of storytelling?*

KL: I think it's more interesting than fantasy. It's more exciting. That style of performance is more interesting to me. You might cut stuff together in a nonlinear way—there are all kinds of ways of breaking the storyline up—but I think advances in most art forms come when people just try to get close to the bone of what is really going on in life, the core of our experience. I think art gets decadent when it becomes obsessed with form and style and all the rest. Just to give a crude example, when the Impressionists started painting light instead of objects, they were actually just trying to get closer to the process of looking at something. In a rather more humble way, that's what I am trying to do.

BC: *How do you feel when you're called a realist director? Do you feel comfortable with that term?*

KL: I don't know. I don't think about it, really, and it doesn't enter into my process of working. You just start by trying to find a good story and figuring out how you're going to tell it. I suppose I'm not a non-realistic director or an anti-realist, but, as for the rest, I couldn't care less.

BC: *Were you impressed by the Italian neorealist films when you first saw them?*

KL: Oh, yes. They were very important for me. Not so much at the time, but thinking back, I realize that they made quite an impression on me—films like De Sica's *Bicycle Thieves* and Rossellini's *Open City*, certainly.

There were also other important influences. When I was at the BBC and we started to do 16mm, handheld stuff in the streets, what we had in mind were documentaries. There was also a very famous theater director in Britain, not so well known now I guess, called Joan Littlewood. She had a whole tradition of working-class theater and her work was a big influence. Not directly, because it's not cinema, but the idea that drama didn't have to be about middle-class people suffering among each other. Littlewood had the idea that drama could stem from the lives of ordinary working people. There's also a venerable literary tradition along that line, including Dickens and Zola—you could even go back to Shakespeare for some of this inspiration.

BC: *How important is Barry Ackroyd's contribution to your work?*

KL: Barry's a great cameraman. We've worked together a long time. His great attribute is that he will be able to capture the essence of a scene, judging the moment exactly when to pan from one person to another or when to catch a movement on the wing. To me, he lights well, but his greatest attribute is his operating of the camera.

BC: *Can we look at your beginnings for a moment? Your father was an electrician who went on to be a foreman at a machine-tool factory. How did you get into film?*

KL: Well, I don't know. It was through luck, really. It was a familiar pattern: those who remember the fifties will remember the secondary moderns and the grammar schools, and if you were lucky, you got to the grammar school. And the town I'm from was a town of some 75,000 people, and only sixty boys a year, from the age of eleven, had the possibility of going on to further education and moving on. For 90% of the kids born in that town, at the age of eleven, that was it: they were going to be manual laborers, clerical workers, or whatever. So, I mean, I was lucky. I did what many people did: got the scholarship, did national service, and then I went to university. I was fortunate enough to be part of the first generation that could be awarded a grant to study at university. That was a huge breakthrough for us; it was like being a kid in a sweetshop, just wonderful. It was very beguiling, like walking into paradise, going from being a kid in an industrial town to being at Oxford. A number of us there had done our national service first, so we were around twenty or twenty-one and had gotten over the idea of being in school. We just wanted to have a great time. Work was the last thing you thought about. I had secretly harbored the idea of being an actor, so that's how I got started doing theater. I spent too much time doing acting, nearly got thrown out of university, hung on, got a job in the theater, and from there got a job at the BBC—which I thought was stepping down a bit, really, because the theater was really where the art was and television was selling your soul. But television at that time was very much theater photographed electronically, so that there would be stage sets around the studio and three cameras poking in and it was a very theatrical affair. And what we tried to do in a reaction against that was to get 16mm cameras and make fiction in the streets and, in a way, my career just moved on from there.

BC: *When, in your lifetime, were you first struck by social injustice? Where did your political ideology find its beginnings?*

KL: I got involved in the 1960s, I suppose, when I was working with writers who were looking at the important issues of the day. When I worked at the BBC in the mid-'60s, there was a whole group of us who became political together through the process of our work. We did a series called *The Wednesday Play*, which was on right after the news. The point of the series was to do contemporary fiction. But, again, we wanted to switch from shooting things on a set indoors, which was more theatrical, to shooting with 16mm handheld cameras on the street. And that was the whole politicizing process, really, because that's when the "new left" was really born, a child much more of Trotsky than the Communist Party was. A lot of the writers we worked with were older and I learned a lot from them. Those were very heady days for me and others like me.

It was a very political time: we had a Labour government after a long period of Conservative rule. We helped deliver leaflets for Harold Wilson. And there was a sense that things would change, but of course they didn't. And that process of seeing things not changing and realizing what the Labour Party was and what social democratic politics were was very instructive for us. It was a time when the working class's organizations were stronger and there was a discussion of politics in the air in a way that there isn't now. So I just began to read books about what we were seeing around us. It very quickly became apparent that if you wanted to see change, then you had to push the Labour Party to one side and say, well, there's another analysis. And of course once you are hooked you are hooked. It would be great not to carry that burden around, but what choice do you have when confronted by someone like Margaret Thatcher, whose way of rescuing the economy was to make the working class pay.

BC: *Are you a cinema buff?*

KL: No, I don't go very often. I think when you've been doing it a long time, it's the films you saw when you were young that stay with you. It's the same with everything—music, everything. It's the music you heard when you were a kid that stays with you. For me it was the music of the '60s. Aside from the Italian neorealist cinema, the Czech films of the 1960s were what I really found most exciting: the Czech films of the Prague Spring, films that are just very humanistic, that just enjoy people, that respect them, and where you feel some kind of warmth. I don't see it in the cinema now, which is sad.

BC: *Do you ever go to see big, glossy Hollywood films?*

KL: No! I just get irritated by them. Maybe that's my loss, but I don't go to see them or much of anything else. If you win at football, if your team wins, that does keep you going to the next game; it really does. And I can't remember the last time I had that feeling in a cinema. I remember enjoying films, but not feeling that sense of exhilaration.

BC: *What about the escapist aspect of popular cinema that lets you get away from your everyday life? Any virtue there?*

KL: Yes, well I guess that works. But I think, personally, I get that from music more. I think cinema can do it; I just don't think it does do it very often in a satisfying way. It doesn't for me.

BC: *Especially now, during a recession, it seems relevant to ask whether the role of cinema in bad times is to give an escape to people.*

KL: I think that such a role trivializes the cinema. Of course, that depends if you take cinema seriously. If you take it seriously like a novel, poetry, or the visual arts, the point of cinema, or one of the points of cinema, can be to reflect on why things are bad. They are not acts of God. You want to be able to understand why things are bad because then you go out strengthened, with some sense of an understanding. Understanding gives you strength. If you're just bemused by why things are bad, all that the cinema does is distract your attention, and then it's a pretty useless medium. You might as well have a lobotomy, really. What's the difference? I think that cinema should, that cinema can, give you an insight into why things are bad. What you do with that insight or understanding is another matter.

BC: *One of the things that people compliment you on is your consistency, the fact that you're still making films about the same sorts of people and subjects after all these years. I wonder if you consider it an achievement that you never decamped to Hollywood. Did you ever even feel any temptation to do so?*

KL: I think Hollywood is boring, really; the little I know of the American industry makes it sound like the last place where I'd want to go and work. I just don't find it attractive. I don't find the work they do interesting; I find it predictable. If you're interested in food, by analogy, you wouldn't go to a hamburger chain. I just find mainstream Hollywood production uninteresting. And nobody's waved a lot of money in my face, anyway! I did shoot *Bread and Roses* in Los Angeles—which was surrealist enough!—but that is hardly a Hollywood film and did not have American money behind it.

BC: *How would you describe the popular perception of Ken Loach films, particularly the perception of people who haven't seen any of your movies?*

KL: I don't know. I'm not sure there is a perception, actually. I have no idea. I think the trouble is that sometimes reviewers and film critics overuse certain words. I mean, I'll be truly pleased never to read the word "gritty" again as it is applied to my work. Such an adjective doesn't help perception. You want an audience to come in without preconceptions and just enjoy what's there, without being prejudiced by a stereotypical image.

BC: *Does it worry you that because you're seen as a left-wing film director, all the people who go to see your films will agree with you and you'll end up preaching to the converted?*

KL: Well, I mean if they all do, then we'd probably be doing rather better politically than we are doing, wouldn't we? The thing is that the people who tend to go see independent films or non-mainstream Hollywood films like mine will tend to be more radical anyway, so it's almost a self-selecting group.

BC: *Are you interested in getting your stuff on TV and to a wider audience for that reason?*

KL: Yes. I began in television and all films are seen on television anyway at some point; even if it's through DVD, you see the films on the set. It's all one industry, in the end.

BC: *One of the things I always get from your films is the idea that apparently insignificant lives are important enough and interesting enough to be on screen, just as much as any other ones.*

KL: It pleases me very much to hear you say that. If that is true, then to some extent I have succeeded, artistically as well as politically.

BC: *In several of your films from the 1990s, such as* Raining Stones *and* Riff-Raff, *you moved into comedy, which is still on display in your latest picture,* Looking for Eric. *What prompted this shift?*

KL: I've always done bits of comedy; it's very false to remove it. You can't be in this particular hotel and not have a sense of comedy. You might as well put your head in a gas oven otherwise. Comedy is everywhere. I feel it's always been there in my work, although sometimes you work with writers who have a stronger sense of comedy than others. The guy who wrote *Riff-Raff*, Bill Jesse, was a very funny man—as is Barry Hines, who wrote that film we did ages ago, *Kes*.

BC: *Nonetheless,* Kes *seems quite sober in comparison with* Riff-Raff. *There seem to be links between the early films, though they are not necessarily comic ones—in* Kes, *for instance, the boy's fate is completely determined by the school and family, while a film like* Family Life *doubtless presents the family as an entirely malevolent force.*

KL: Different families, of course. In *Kes*, there was also an older brother with his own problems, whereas in *Family Life* there's this whole oppressive set of familial relationships. The parents have such a clear idea of what the daughter is going to be, such that, in the final analysis, she doesn't have a chance.

BC: *Why are families so important in your films?*

David Bradley as Billy in Loach's *Kes*.

KL: Because the family is where most drama happens in our lives, isn't it? That's where we learn everything. All of the tension, drama, and comedy contained in those familial relationships are incredible. A lot of classic dramas center on the family; it's the raw material for drama quite often. Even though families are the springboard for everything we do—or maybe I should say *because* families are such a springboard—we could say that families are at the same time political entities. Of course, they're not precise mirrors of the world outside, but they do launch you into the world and form you, so you can't imagine a character without a family. Before I start making a film, I and my actors work out a little family plan for everybody, because then you know what's projected you into a particular situation or onto a particular path.

In *Raining Stones*, for example, to make the family function we did little improvisations. The family of actors went to church together or they went on an outing to a McDonald's restaurant together. They just got to relate to each other and it was better than a performer's going cold into the first day of filming, thinking, "Christ, you're supposed to be my wife. How do I talk to you?" That sort of thing should be in place before you start on the first day.

BC: *Like* Raining Stones, *many of your films take place in the north of England—a region that can be considered somewhat marginalized, the periphery as opposed to the center.*

KL: Yes. I myself am from the Midlands, which is closer to the north than it is to the metropolis. When I was young, we always used to go to seaside places in the north and we were familiar with the northern comic sensibility. There's a humor there, but there's also a humor in working-class London. I think it's a class thing, not a regional thing. But it's particularly strong in the north, where there's a whole tradition of stand-up comedy there that I enjoy very much.

BC: *Beneath the surface, it's possible to notice a very consistent set of concerns in your work. Just as alcoholism is not really the subject of* My Name Is Joe, *domestic violence is not really the subject of* Ladybird, Ladybird. *It's merely part of the female protagonist's background, the symptom under which lies a much larger cause.*

KL: Yes. That's really a film about grief and how it can leave a person very damaged, and about someone who was damaged as a child. When do you start blaming people for their actions? When they're young, clearly they have our pity and understanding. Suddenly, they become the villain, but what made some people the villain should engender our ambivalence toward them.

BC: *In* Ladybird, Ladybird *you're ambivalent toward both the protagonist and the social services bureaucracy.*

KL: Yes, it's a very difficult situation. That was a great film to work on, not least because the actress, Crissy Rock, would just take your breath away during the filming.

BC: *Through her character, you don't necessarily portray the working class as heroic; above all, you seem interested in exploring the complexity of its dilemmas.*

KL: There's a kind of fun about working-class characters, you know, and their stories work on a very primal level. Working-class experience is where drama, the raw material of drama, exists. But there's also a political reason to focus on the working class in art: if change is to come, that's the progressive element which will provide it. That's where the engine for change will originate. It won't be brought to us as a gift from above, but through the work of people from below.

BC: *The rapport with your screenwriters—themselves all from the working class—seems crucial, whether it's with Jim Allen on* The Big Flame, *Barry Hines on* Kes, *or Bill Jesse on* Riff-Raff.

KL: It's really central, yes. Good films begin with their scripts.

BC: *Do you have any advice for first-time directors?*

KL: Don't take advice. You have to make up your own mind as to what to do from the very beginning. Don't follow the industry ritual; the industry practice, I think, is very damaging, very sterile. Follow your own voice and get on with it.

Ken Loach Filmography

Television Films
   Diary of a Young Man (1964)
   Coming Out Party (1965)
   The End of Arthur's Marriage (1965)
   Three Clear Sundays (1965)
   Up the Junction (1965)
   Cathy Come Home (1966)

In Two Minds (1967)
The Golden Vision (1968)
The Big Flame (1969)
After a Lifetime (1971)
The Rank and the File (1971)
A Misfortune (1973)
The Price of Coal (1977)
Auditions (1980)
A Question of Leadership (1981)
Questions of Leadership (1983)
The View From the Woodpile (1989)

Feature Films
Poor Cow (1967)
Kes (1969)
Family Life (1971)
The Save the Children Fund Film (1971)
Black Jack (1979)
The Gamekeeper (1980)
Looks and Smiles (1981)
Which Side Are You On? (1984)
Fatherland (1986)
Hidden Agenda (1990)
Riff-Raff (1990)
Raining Stones (1993)
Ladybird, Ladybird (1994)
A Contemporary Case for Common Ownership (1995)
Land and Freedom (1995)
Carla's Song (1996)
The Flickering Flame (1997)
My Name Is Joe (1998)
Bread and Roses (2000)
The Navigators (2001)
11-09-01: September 11 (segment "United Kingdom," 2002)
Sweet Sixteen (2002)
Ae Fond Kiss . . . (2004)
Tickets (2005), along with Ermanno Olmi and Abbas Kiarostami
The Wind That Shakes the Barley (2006)
It's a Free World . . . (2007)
Looking for Eric (2009)

Bibliography

Fuller, Graham, ed. *Loach on Loach*. London: Faber and Faber, 1998.

Hayward, Anthony. *Which Side Are You On?: Ken Loach and His Films*. London: Bloomsbury, 2004.

Leigh, Jacob. *The Cinema of Ken Loach: Art in the Service of the People*. London: Wallflower, 2002.

McKnight, George, ed. *Agent of Challenge and Defiance: The Films of Ken Loach*. Westport, Conn.: Greenwood, 1997.

Index

~

About the Author

Educated at Tulane and Yale, **Bert Cardullo** is now professor of media and communication at the Izmir University of Economics in Izmir, Turkey, where he teaches courses in film history, theory, and criticism. His essays and reviews have appeared in such journals as the *Yale Review, Cambridge Quarterly, Film Quarterly, Cinema Journal*, and the *Quarterly Review of Film and Video*, and he is the author, editor, or translator of many books, including *Screen Writings, Bazin at Work, The Films of Robert Bresson, Vittorio De Sica*, and *Playing to the Camera: Film Actors Discuss Their Craft*.

Breinigsville, PA USA
25 January 2011
254097BV00002B/2/P